GIRLS

CAN KISS

NOW

GIRLS

CAN KISS

NOW

essays

JILL GUTOWITZ

ATRIA BOOKS

New York   London   Toronto   Sydney   New Delhi

ATRIA
BOOKS

An Imprint of Simon & Schuster, Inc.
1230 Avenue of the Americas
New York, NY 10020

Some names and identifying details have been changed
and some events have been compressed or combined.

First Atria Paperback edition March 2022

ATRIA BOOKS and colophon are trademarks of Simon & Schuster, Inc.

For information about special discounts for bulk purchases,
please contact Simon & Schuster Special Sales at 1-866-506-1949
or business@simonandschuster.com.

The Simon & Schuster Speakers Bureau can bring authors to your live event. For
more information or to book an event, contact the Simon & Schuster Speakers
Bureau at 1-866-248-3049 or visit our website at www.simonspeakers.com.

Interior design by Kathryn A. Kenney-Peterson

Manufactured in the United States of America

1   3   5   7   9   10   8   6   4   2

Library of Congress Cataloging-in-Publication Data

Names: Gutowitz, Jill, author.
Title: Girls can kiss now : essays / Jill Gutowitz.
Identifiers: LCCN 2021037696 (print) | LCCN 2021037697 (ebook) | ISBN
9781982158507 (paperback) | ISBN 9781982158514 (ebook)
Subjects: LCSH: Gutowitz, Jill. | Popular culture--Humor. |
Lesbians--United States--Biography. | BISAC: HUMOR / Form / Essays |
HUMOR / Topic / Celebrity & Popular Culture | LCGFT: Essays.
Classification: LCC PS3607.U846 G57 2022 (print) | LCC PS3607.U846
(ebook) | DDC 813/.4 [B]--dc23
LC record available at https://lccn.loc.gov/2021037696
LC ebook record available at https://lccn.loc.gov/2021037697

ISBN 978-1-9821-5850-7
ISBN 978-1-9821-5851-4 (ebook)

For Emma, with kisses

CONTENTS

GIRLS

CAN KISS

NOW

INTRODUCTION:
THE FIVE ERAS OF CELESBIANISM

WHAT MAKES SOMEONE a "pop culture junkie"? I've been called many things in my lifetime—"dyke," "too much," mostly "dyke"—but the badge of "pop culture junkie" has always felt off. Yes, since childhood, I've voraciously consumed pop culture nuggets and talked people's ears off about arcane celebrities who have zero cultural relevance. (Remember Jessica Szohr? I miss her. Wait, you don't? Okay, that was a test.) But the word "junkie" implies that I'm *addicted* to pop culture, and I'm not sure that's true. Some days I wish I could throw my phone and all its dumb little apps into the sea, follow it briskly into the waves, and free myself from the chains of being Severely Online. Caring about famous people is a full-time job with no days off. So, yeah, I *have* historically overindulged in entertainment. I *do* always come back for more, even when my eyes and deadening soul are begging me to stop. But I wouldn't call it an "affliction" so much as a fascination—a justified one.

Taking interest in current trends and entertainment isn't a waste of time, or some vapid pastime—we should care about other people's stories. Despite this, being a "pop culture junkie" has been painted as vacuous or meaningless. It's not. I've made a career out of dissecting and examining pop culture, cultural figures, and entertainment trends and phenomena. Nothing has ever been more spellbinding to me than A) celebrities and how they handle attention, B) the general population—the "gen pop," if you will—and who we choose to give our attention to, and C) the relationship between A and B, one that has always existed and will continue to flourish as long as humankind remains (which is like, about five more years before the inevitable nuclear winter. Ten if we make it to the climate apocalypse). I've always cared—probably too much—about pop culture because I've always been transfixed by the ways other people's stories affect our own, my own. Pop culture influences the way we dress, the way we talk, the words we use, the conversations we have, our politics, even how we define love. It molds us, and in return, we mold it. We are a direct reflection of the people we choose to glorify and the narratives we venerate. Pop culture ebbs and flows as society changes, and society changes as pop culture ebbs and flows. And right now, we're in such a cultural sweet spot; as a dyke and a pop culture "junkie," I'm totally biased, but what's transpired in entertainment recently has left me absolutely gobsmacked—because it's just so fucking gay.

When I was a teen, the word "lesbian" sent fear rattling through my flesh tomb. As a teenage closet-case, I actively participated in homophobia; I was scared of homosexuality because I was uneducated about it, wholly un-exposed to LGBTQ people, both in the small, conservative, Catholic bub-ble of a hometown I was raised in and in the media I was consuming. I was born in 1991, a time when LGBTQ people were being reduced to stereo-types, pigeonholed into outdated narratives, shamed for fucking and loving and wearing oversize Umbro shorts—none of which we should apologize for. If I had any exposure to queerness in the '90s and early aughts, it was via one-dimensional depictions of gay men—a gay best friend on *Sex and the City*, a tragic victim of the AIDS crisis—but as far as queer female fig-ureheads and stories go, the media landscape in my youth felt nearly barren.

In middle school, the only famous lesbian I was aware of was Ellen DeGeneres—she was a trailblazer, just visible enough, gay enough, and brave enough to stand out. But as a result of such narrow exposure, I figured all lesbians were like Ellen, an adult woman who looked and acted nothing like me—me, an Alex Mack–looking tween who psychotically filled sketchbooks with pencil drawings of Baby Spice; me, more of a Mary-Kate than an Ashley; me, who wanted to be Xena, Warrior Princess, or maybe be Gabrielle so I could be held by Xena, Warrior Princess. And to support that bulletproof hypothesis, the only lesbian I ever remember meeting as a kid was a friend of my father's, a butch-leaning woman who was named— you guys—she was fucking named Ellen. Both Ellens sounded cool (except one's BFFs with a war criminal), but I never even remotely identified with either Ellen—after all, my name was Jill, I wasn't necessarily masculine-pre-senting, and I didn't know people were just *allowed* to be gay. I found out at twenty-three, the age I was when I realized that I was a lesbian, that ANY-ONE can be gay—not just people named Ellen.

These days, when I hear the word "lesbian," I see more powerful im-agery than the supercut of my own life that I'll watch moments before dying in the climate apocalypse: I see Rachel Weisz grabbing Olivia Colman by the throat and slamming her against a bedpost in *The Favourite*; I see Lena Waithe winning an Emmy; I see a paparazzi photo of Cara Delevingne and Ashley Benson lugging a sex bench into their home; I see Janelle Monáe birthing Tessa Thompson through her "Pynk" vagina pants; I see Cate Blanchett telling Rooney Mara "What a strange girl you are"; I see Piper and Alex on *Orange Is the New Black*, Santana and Brittany on *Glee*; I see JoJo Siwa coming out on TikTok.

The past few years of pop culture have been studded with lesbian icons and stories that have been widely elevated and celebrated, rather than shunned or shamed, something that's brand-new in our hell-world. It took WAY too long, like embarrassingly long, but nevertheless, lesbianism and celebrity have finally merged—much later than male gayness and celebrity did, mind you. But just because the mainstreaming of queer women in pop culture is painfully recent doesn't mean that famous women haven't always been fingering each other. They have; we've just ignored them. Until the 2010s, we habitually turned a blind eye to queer female narratives. But no more, say I.

Speaking of "I"—I'm a culture writer. Over the past few years, I've written predominantly about queer women in film, TV, and music. I wrote about how *Orange Is the New Black* made me—and TV—gay, for *Time*. I dissected queer clues and Easter eggs on Taylor Swift's albums *Lover*, *folklore*, and *evermore* for *Vulture*. I also wrote a very cutting-edge and urgent piece of investigative journalism for *Elle*, in which I researched what *exactly* heterosexuality is, and why it leads women to thirst after Adam Driver.

Online, I've accrued a following on Twitter for my cultural commentary on queer media—specifically, Cate Blanchett's bottomless closet of suits, Taylor Swift's rumored romantic relationship with former BFF Karlie Kloss, and a viral fake Coachella lineup meme, which ultimately led to random celebrities like Selma Blair following me on Instagram—like, I'm not sure why you're here, but I'm happy you are. Now I identify as the Overlord of Lesbian Twitter—a title I'm told is too aggressive to give oneself—and I traffic in memes about lesbian movies and middle-aged actresses with a dogged persistence and untethered horniness. Out in the real world, I live in Los Angeles and traverse through lesbian Hollywood with bulging eyes and an off-putting eagerness to tell queer stories. As a result, I've lodged myself in the heart of gay media, both online and IRL.

What I'm trying to say is: As an observer and participant in lesbian culture, I've spent the last few years chronicling the merging of celebrity and lesbianism—celesbianism—throughout the past few decades. I'm a millennial, which means I'm old enough to remember what it felt like to be discriminated against for being gay, to be repressed, to hide myself, to change myself, to feel different and othered and scared and alone. But I'm also young enough, and lucky enough, to have witnessed the world change.

Still, unfortunately, the damage had already been done. Pop culture—in all its spectacular, mind-bending beauty and its numbing, tragic scarring—molded me. These days, we hear bellows for "representation," but what does that actually mean? Pop culture is currently studded with out queer figureheads like Sarah Paulson, Tessa Thompson, Kate McKinnon, and the Golden Gate Bridge (do not bother disputing this—she is a large, hulking lesbian), but I'm starkly aware that older generations weren't so fortunate. Things are better, yes, but they're not "fixed." Many of us are still grappling with the trauma of growing up steeped in narratives far more sinister than "every lesbian is named Ellen." Many queer women's stories, even those of quite famous queer women, have been swept under the rug or altogether scrubbed from history.

The way I see it, there are five distinct chapters of celesbianism. First, an era I'll nickname "The Scrubbing," which starts at, uh, I don't know, the beginning of recorded time, and ends with the 1980s. I know what you're thinking: How do you group Lucy, the most famous early human ancestor and undeniable queer icon, with the evolved culture of 1970s America? Um, because we weren't that fucking evolved. And also because I'm not an LGBTQ or feminist scholar—I'm just an obnoxious white person who went to college for "music industry." I'm not an expert, nor a historian, nor am I certified by any institution to record lesbian media for posterity. No, I'm simply a thousand-year-old gay witch trapped in a human body, waiting for the curse to be lifted, spending my days blending in by writing about Lindsay Lohan. So just take this with a grain of salt, okay? The Scrubbing.

This period is sprawling, yes, but it's also an expanse of time in which female queerness was erased from history—just scrubbed entirely from our texts and accounts, a homophobic outlook that didn't really begin to morph until the 1980s. Basically, it was humanity's flop era. The Scrubbing was an epoch of revisionist history in which we pretended women weren't fucking each other, even though a plethora of extremely notable women were finger-blasting the ever-loving shit out of their "gal pals." Like Queen Anne, who was banging her best friend in a chilly-ass stone castle in eighteenth-century England (goals). Or Anne Lister, a gender-bending property owner who was collecting rent checks and the moans of women in nineteenth-century Halifax. Or Virginia Woolf, the embattled author who wrote intense love letters to wealthy white women in twentieth-century England. Queen Anne, Anne Lister, Virginia Woolf: we know these names, but we barely remembered them for being queer—that is, until the late 2010s, when all three of their stories were dusted off and turned into major motion pictures or HBO dramas (*The Favourite, Gentleman Jack,* and *Vita & Virginia,* respectively).

Other notable figures in The Scrubbing include Eleanor Roosevelt—yes, fucking first lady Eleanor Roosevelt—who was blackmailed by the FBI for having a relationship with a female AP reporter. And Sally Ride, the first American woman in space, who we all remember as a feminist hero, but whose queer history often gets skipped over: Sally had relationships with women throughout her life, one of which lasted two decades and ended with Sally's untimely death. I have to ask the same question: Why don't we remember Roosevelt as being queer? Or Ride? Or Billie Holiday, Katharine Hepburn, Emily Dickinson, all of whose queer narratives *were* actually recorded? Their queerness was purposefully eschewed and scratched from our memories like I scratched heterosexuality out of my life in 2015. (Though, like with *Gentleman Jack,* Dickinson's gay life was adapted for the small-screen in 2019.) I can't help but mourn for these women: If the fucking Queen of England wasn't allowed to be out and queer, what was it like for queer women who weren't the actual queen? How were they affected by a landscape completely devoid of visible queerness? How much would their quality of life have improved if Queen Anne were out as a giant dyke, had *she* even been afforded that opportunity?

After The Scrubbing came the 1980s, a decade I'll call The Leaking, when lesbianism was actually starting to be spoken about in media—though not in a positive light. This is when the gatekeepers of heterosexuality failed to keep our stories buried any longer, and female queerness began leaking through the cracks. However, just because queer stories were being published in the '80s doesn't mean that queerness was accepted. "Leaking" doesn't just mean that lesbianism seeped out of the gay sewers we were relegated to; it also means that our stories were *leaked*—as in, people were outed. Public-facing queer narratives were painted as salacious, secret affairs, too lewd to be welcomed or normalized.

There was Billie Jean King, the tennis superstar who was outed in a palimony lawsuit brought about by her ex-girlfriend that hindered King's career. Or Whitney Houston, one of the most famous pop stars of the decade, who had a relationship with her friend Robyn Crawford that was maliciously speculated about, and Robyn, more visibly queer than Whitney, was unfairly labeled a "bad influence." None of these celebrities were able to come out on their own terms—and some of them tragically died before being afforded that opportunity. Again, why don't we remember Whitney Houston as being queer? And what message did those "salacious" stories about her send to queer teens in the 1980s? Call Whitney Houston bisexual, you cowards!!!

Then came the 1990s, an era that I can speak to personally. I'll call this The Outcasting—after queer women were scrubbed and leaked, we finally began recognizing lesbians as people, rather than cryptozoological, *X-Files*-like myths. Queer visibility rose, but society still tried to silence women, shame them for being out, position them as outcasts and weirdos simply for living their lives. In the '90s, the patriarchy's vise grip on media clung to the outdated notion that being out had life-altering repercussions, like it did for Billie Jean King or Eleanor Roosevelt. This period was the patriarchal, heteronormative media's last-ditch effort to stain lesbian stories before the floodgates of visibility and normalization opened.

The '90s engendered a swell of queerness in media: TV was gayed with characters like Willow and Tara on *Buffy the Vampire Slayer*. Music was gayed: k.d. lang and Melissa Etheridge popped the fuck off on strummy songs about women. Lang covered a 1993 issue of *Vanity Fair*, intertwined with a scantily clad Cindy Crawford. (Fuck, that photo shoot is so hot. Please google it immediately. It's an emergency.) Movies were gayed: We got *Bound* from the Wachowski sisters, which broke boundaries for portrayals of lesbian sex, and *But I'm a Cheerleader*, which pioneered the queer teen sex comedy, and was also the first of multiple *important* Natasha Lyonne lesbian roles. Everything was gayed in the '90s: Sporty Spice, who wasn't actually queer, popularized gay fashion with her athletic lewks (Umbro shorts—I'm telling you, teens, please bring these back). Politics were gayed: Angela Eagle became the first openly lesbian British member of Parliament. Shit, in the '90s, even murder was gayed: Aileen Wuornos, the serial killer who slaughtered seven men in Florida, was a lesbian, and Charlize Theron won an Oscar for portraying her in 2004. Not a great look for the community . . . but okay!

With all the rising visibility queer women had in the '90s, they were still treated to a collective side-eye from the public. That harmful worldview shaped the first twenty-three years of my life. I often wonder how much I could've experienced in love and life had the pop culture I was consuming just told me that being gay was okay. Why did I have to wait until 2008, when Hilary Duff ended homophobia by partnering with GLSEN for a PSA asking teenagers to stop using "gay" as a pejorative? I want to talk about what it was like to grow up in this era, to exhume it from my bitter core and examine the message we were sending to '90s girls—girls like me, who dressed like Sporty Spice and wanted Harriet the Spy to spy on *me* but was just too young to know about k.d. lang or Willow from *Buffy* or to watch teen sex comedies. (And I will talk about it; keep reading.)

At the turn of the millennium, things began to change—like, really change. Lesbianism went from being functionally erased, to being leaked, to being outcast, to being exploited during The Spilling, or the aughts. Yes, exploiting female queerness for the male gaze was yet another harmful media practice, but nonetheless, in the 2000s, lesbianism came spilling into pop culture via TV, film, and blogs.

When I look back on 2000s lesbianism, I of course reminisce about the loose ties, bandannas, and inexplicably tiny vests of *The L Word* fashion (using the word "fashion" VERY loosely here). But, having been sheltered and too young to watch explicit Showtime shows, what I really remember about the 2000s is the portrayals of queerness that shaped my understanding of women who love women, like the "lesbians" in *American Pie 2*, who Steve Stifler asks to kiss and rub on each other while he and his shitty friends watch. Seriously, between his role as Jim Levenstein in the *American Pie* movies and his role as Larry Bloom in *Orange Is the New Black*, what has Jason Biggs done for lesbians? Nothing. Although he does follow me on Twitter—maybe he's trying to repent.

The 2000s were brimming with coded queerness, like the sexualized relationship between Demi Moore's and Cameron Diaz's characters in *Charlie's Angels: Full Throttle*. Or the *Rolling Stone* cover shoot that depicted *Gossip Girl* costars Blake Lively and Leighton Meester sucking each other's thumbs, and ice cream cones, and, in turn, every drop of heterosexuality from my teenage body. Also, let the record show that both *Charlie's Angels* and the *Gossip Girl Rolling Stone* cover slap—they're just male-gazey as hell.

Celesbianism was commodified and monetized in the aughts—which, in itself, was progress at the time, just not the right kind. Public-facing queer couples like Lindsay Lohan and Samantha Ronson, or Ruby Rose and the Veronicas' Jess Origliasso, were being papped and exploited and splayed across every gossip blog, like the Brangelinas and Bennifers and Zanessas of the world had (although the Bennifers of the world weren't being shamed for queerness or written off as "crazy" or "wild" for straight-dating). In the 2000s, we weren't quite *there* yet morally—sure, we were treated to brief queer story lines on *The O.C.*, *House*, and *Grey's Anatomy*, but stars like Lindsay Lohan were still being sexualized or dubbed unstable for daring to date women publicly. Yes, Lindsay Lohan was battling addiction at the time, but I absolutely remember thinking that her bisexuality was a direct result of her plummeting mental health. Oh, what marvelous things the media taught me, and generations of people, about same-sex attraction! (More on this specific relationship later—way more. Like, an exegesis on this later. *forces self to refocus after thinking about Lindsay Lohan and Samantha Ronson*)

Finally, we arrive at the fifth and ongoing chapter of lesbian history: the 2010s through today, The Mainstreaming of lesbianism. Around the time *Orange Is the New Black* hit in 2013, the dam broke, and lesbian shit came deluging out of our screens, magazines, and headphones. In this decade, our televisions were flooded with queer female stories, like *Glee*, *Faking It*, *Lost Girl*, *Killing Eve*, *Gentleman Jack*, *Schitt's Creek*, and Naomi Watts's absolutely batshit erotic thriller series *Gypsy*, forgotten already by everyone but me. The 2010s gifted us with iconic lesbian movies like *Blue Is the Warmest Colour* and *Carol*. We even got major-studio teen sex comedies like *Booksmart* and *Blockers* (as opposed to indie ones like *But I'm a Cheerleader* in the '90s).

After 2013, celebrities followed suit: Elliot Page came out as gay during a livestreamed event (and later came out as trans in 2020). In 2014, it was still monumental for an A-list actor to come out on a world stage—because we simultaneously had come so far and yet hadn't made any progress at all. After Page's 2014 announcement, there was also this boom of a new generation of celesbians: Model Cara Delevingne and Fast & Furious actress Michelle Rodriguez were papped drunkenly kissing courtside at a Knicks game. Kristen Stewart mowed through Hollywood like a fucking gay ATV, sparking Sapphic rumors about her costar in *The Runaways*, Dakota Fanning; then with St. Vincent; then with Stella Maxwell, a former flame of

Miley Cyrus's. Then Cara Delevingne dated St. Vincent. Celesbianism in the 2010s was so rich and entertaining that it's hard not to blur the timeline.

During The Mainstreaming, there was this mass coming out, and not just amongst celebrities. Especially on the internet—suddenly, YouTubers and social media stars were coming out left and right in viral videos that replayed endlessly on the *Today* show, leaving the "Love Is Love" Facebook-mom crowd to weep into their morning bran. You might remember the Rhodes twins, those two crystal-eyed, blond-haired boys who came out to their father on speakerphone and filmed it. Or Ingrid Nilsen, a beauty influencer who also bawled into her point-and-shoot and posted her coming-out story on YouTube. Queer female influencers started crafting what online lesbianism looked like—from the GIFs we trafficked on Lesbian Tumblr, to the gay fashions we double-tapped on Instagram, to the way we expressed queer thirst on Twitter. (Example: I want Cate Blanchett to hurl a grand piano off a skyscraper, aimed directly at my body. More on the violent expression of queer desire, the "step on me" trend, later.)

Additionally, music stars like Lady Gaga, Miley Cyrus, Demi Lovato, Cardi B, and Kesha came out as queer. Mainstream pop was studded with out queer pop stars, like Janelle Monáe, Hayley Kiyoko, Kehlani, and Rina Sawayama. And, of course, once the bubble of homophobia popped and splooged onto the face of every Republican in America, *Obergefell v. Hodges* happened. Although the timeline is very "chicken or the egg," as in: Was the vindication of marriage equality in 2015 a response to the queering of pop culture, and transitively, culture? Or was the gen pop just ready for a holistic normalization of queerness, which transpired in a queering both politically and culturally? It's hard to say, and it's also difficult to measure the effects all of this had on the gen pop and the way we viewed homosexuality, as it's all deeply personal, which means it's complex and human.

I'm still battling the internalized homophobia I retained as collateral damage from consuming patriarchal, homophobic media for twenty years.

Every day, I find myself recovering from two decades of repression, a span of time I spent crafting a personality that fit the mold of acceptability in the '90s and 2000s, rather than living my life as the *Harriet the Spy* lesbian I was dying to be. Repression severely delayed me from experiencing love, sex, and dating like many heterosexual teenagers had the luxury of doing. And that's just *me*, a person who was born in 1991; older generations of queer women have endured immeasurable trauma growing up alongside media landscapes that told them to feel ashamed, or threatened them to fit in or get outed.

I think there's this collective assumption that Gen Z—a bullheaded, progressive, flamboyant generation—is so past all of this, that they're as free and open and devoid of shame as their depictions in movies like *Booksmart* or *Blockers*, that they're all fine, that our work is done, queerness has been normalized. That's not true. How can it be when our country is so divided, most of us wading in the tides of change, the rest drowning in Hades's pool of souls? Narratives that eschew the real and present pains of the current queer experience aren't pushing the narrative forward—they're still erasing our stories, just in new, nuanced ways.

Can we really even unravel or reverse the harm that was done to women via these insidious media narratives? Reverse—certainly not. Unravel—I'm not sure. In order to move forward, we all must examine our past. I'm tired of lugging around the big bag of little traumas I've collected from pop culture. I want to look at what was done right, what wasn't, what changed me, and what I have the power to change now. Each essay in this book is an attempt to revisit and exhume my pain through a pop culture lens. Though the essays differ in material, decades, and discoveries of self, they're all, thematically, some version of *this*, some piece of entertainment that changed my mind or broke me open, which I'm still grappling with, letting go of, suffering from, or grateful for. I wrote these essays, selfishly, as a stab at healing my own wounds, but I also wrote them for you: for every LGBTQ person who has felt weird about their queerness, for every woman who's struggled with self-worth, for every person who has felt othered, ashamed, ghastly. I hope you'll find something here that tugs at you, or that makes you laugh, or at least that makes you say, "Wow, I feel bad for her."

If any of that sounds good to you, join me: It's time to listen to that Ashlee Simpson song and see what it brings up for us. It's time to go over those paparazzi photos of Cara Delevingne and Michelle Rodriguez at a Knicks game with a fine-tooth comb, pressing our sweaty foreheads to a magnifying glass and dragging it down the page like a detective whose boss keeps telling them "You're getting emotional." We must press on as horny, dykey, pop culture "junkies," and we must do it with bountiful pride and joy. Now peel yourself away from that *Gossip Girl* × *Rolling Stone* cover photo I know you're still looking at and read my book.

MEMEING WITH THE FBI

AMONG THE FUNNIEST things that've ever been said to me is: "We're with the Federal Bureau of Investigation. Do you have any intent to kill a U.S. senator?" It should at once come as *no* surprise to you and yet be absolutely shocking that the reason I was interrogated by the FBI is . . . because of something I tweeted. How does the actual FBI show up on the doorstep of some flop from the internet, asking if she's a threat to the lives of American senators? Well, I've always been Severely Online, and this wasn't the first time it had gotten me in trouble. Here's my entire Internet History, uncleared.

1997

I'm six years old. Bill Clinton is president. The Spice Girls are famous. And I am . . . LIVING. Lisa Frank stickers freckle my Lisa Frank folders. My hair is middle-parted, but not in a chic way, and is looped through an oversize scrunchie. My teeth wiggle in their sockets. I'm so hyperactive that, at times, my body vibrates off the floor and zooms through every room in my house like a vengeful spirit that transcends space-time. I'm obsessed with Nickelodeon, walkie-talkies from RadioShack, and my dad, a techno-nerd who says things like "Macintosh" and "massage chair." It's after dark, and earlier today, my dad alerted my mom that he'd be home late because he has to run an errand, and when he returns, he will have in his possession something sure to light any kid's body with unmoored electricity: "a surprise."

The weather was sticky, beads of sweat collecting on my twiggy arms, left uncovered by the yellow tank top I insisted on wearing because I thought it made me look like Sporty Spice. Mosquitoes nipped at the humid air; fireflies twinkled across our grassy yard. My mom, my two-year-old sister, and I waited anxiously in the living room, pinging off the walls while my dad set up this mysterious "surprise." What could call for such an elaborate setup, such secrecy and drama? Was it a new toy just for me?? A new composition notebook à la *Harriet the Spy*? A book of spells and incantations to read from that would finally unlock my secret witch powers in my seventh year of life? My dad, bustling about the kitchen, turned the lights off in there, then in the hallway, then in the living room. The house was nearly dark, save for an eerie green glow emanating through the kitchen's doorframe. He was ready. He called us in.

I approached slowly, my eyes never wavering from the glow: it was pale green, alien, as inviting and hypnotizing and mysterious as a UFO probe. I turned the corner, my pink, dirty feet sticking to the hardwood floors, and stood in the kitchen doorway, wonderstruck: sitting on the kitchen table, flanked by darkness and the blinks of outdoor fireflies, sat a brand-new PowerBook G3, one of Apple's very first mass-market portable computers, or as we know it today, a laptop. I waded toward the greenish-blue glow of the screen like Carol Anne in *Poltergeist*, marveling at this spectacular machine. What was she? Who was she? What did she do? I inspected the machine, touching the raised, luminescent apple on its slate-black back.

"It's a computer," my dad explained, "like the one in the basement, but portable." I couldn't imagine what the machine was capable of. I just knew she was utterly breathtaking: The pageantry of it all. Her radiance. Her drama. She was now my North Star, and I would follow her into the dark.

2002

I'm eleven years old, 9/11 has left the entire tristate area feeling like an old-money mansion with a live-in demon, and honey? I am LIVING. My dad is rich now and I live in a new, big-ass house with a pool. My bedroom walls are painted turquoise, a Britney Spears poster has been erected, and I'm an absolute slut for electronics. I own a periwinkle boombox, a handful of Hit-Clips (those miniature MP3 players that preceded actual MP3 players, which played only like, forty-five seconds of each song) including two *NSYNC singles and "He Loves U Not" by Dream, and a Tiger Electronics Poo-Chi robot dog, and I've exchanged my kelly-green Game Boy Color for a purple GameCube and orange Nintendo controller. Oh yeah, and my dad owns a first-generation iPod, the one with the spinny wheel, and while he refuses to sync my Britney collection to it, he lets me borrow it and listen to the Foo Fighters. Basically, I am that bitch, and being a kid in the 2000s fucking slaps. Every night, I lie awake in bed, comforters pulled to my chin, hands trembling, staring out my bedroom window, living with the constant fear of being bombed. I ask my teachers how many people survived Hiroshima. I can't look the kids in my class whose parents died in 9/11 in the eyes. I grapple with my own mortality. I press a bunch of little buttons on a bunch of little electronics and say, "Bleep bloop, life rocks, I feel fine. Bloop bloop, bitch!"

One day, my aunt Marcia—my mom's eccentric, funky sister—comes over, probably to see all my cool new shit, and brings my cousins, Lee and Rosie, who are probably desperate to see all my cool new shit too. Though not out yet, Lee and I are the only two queer people in the family. Lee will later come out as a trans man, and I, a lesbionné—but at the time, we were just weird kids with no boundaries who both identified as a *Super Smash Bros.* Link. While our parents sit in my expansive new living room, which had—not to brag—wallpaper—and ate—not to brag again—Brie cheese, Lee asks me a question that blows my eyebrows clear off my face: "Do you know what porn is?" We head upstairs to the computer room, leaving our parents to say things like, "We need another Clinton in the White House. That will fix EVERYTHING!" *matrix glitches*

Lee shows me how to type words like "penis" and "boob" into Google. Until now, I didn't know computers could be used for such important work. Lee is a master at his craft: First he shows me how to google sex. Then he shows me how to slither into the night like Uma Thurman in a jumpsuit: after googling sex, one must *always* "clear history." Lee and I are trailblazers, pioneers on the very frontier of Being Horny Online. We are resourceful. We are brave. We are going where no boomer has gone before: traumatizing ourselves with bottomless, gruesome depictions of sex before our brains or bodies are ready to receive them.

Soon after, the "computer room" (my dad's home office) becomes my domain, his rolly chair on a plastic mat my throne. I swipe all my dad's jewel CD cases, work tapes, and loose hard drives off the desk to clear space for the pressing and urgent work that needs to be done: googling "boob." Here I am, an innovator at Mission Control, staring at the warm welcome of the blue-green light: the internet, an untapped wasteland of information.

I go to work: I determine which sites are free, which links lead to pop-up ads and viruses, what keywords churn out the most efficient results. I tear through Porn Internet like a California wildfire. I find a website with a bright purple background (like my GameCube!) and pretty pink links (I love pink!) and a cornucopia of boob videos. The videos are much different from anything I learned about reproductive organs in Ms. Kenny's science class. One day, in fifth grade, Ms. Kenny separated the boys and girls into different rooms for one single hour, and we girls learned about periods, and the boys learned about . . . I don't know! Maybe they just talked about dogs or played tag. It's still a mystery. But did you know that people put their bodies inside each other's bodies? I did not! And there are so many ways to do it!

I develop rituals. Each day after school, I come home, fumble upstairs to the computer room while my mom's busy with my little sister and my dad's still at work, lock the door for as long as I can, sometimes hours at a time, and watch thousands of clips of porn, my eyes glazing over, my heart blackening, my thus-far-unborn relationship to sex withering. And when I'm done, I click "clear history," and slither back into the night to feel disgusting. After all, this is my *dirty* little secret—I'm not allowed to talk about sex, or think about it, or know about it. But for some reason, I still do those things!

Eventually, I become familiar with how sex works and who can have it (really anyone: grandmas, twins, babysitters). I need to level up: I need to interact with other Hornies. I get heavy into chat rooms. Love chat rooms. Big chat rooms guy. A room full of strangers where everyone talks openly about Being Horny? Frick yeah. A couple of years back, my dad helped make me a screenname and email address—Pokegutz—a portmanteau of "Pokémon" (I love Bulbasaur!) and my last name. My email address and screenname are registered under my dad's parent account on AOL—but that's okay! The internet is vast and dangerous and I still sleep with about thirteen Care Bears.

In the chat rooms, I learn the lay of the land, the language of the Hornies. I log online, burst into a chat room like the Kool-Aid man through a cement wall (I love Kool-Aid but my mom never lets me have it), and ask a random person to "cyber." We start a private Instant Message conversation, exchange our A/S/L (age, sex, location: I usually say I'm sixteen to eighteen; sometimes I'm a girl, sometimes I pretend to be a boy; and New Jersey), and we get into it. Mostly I pick a new person to cyber with every day after school, but sometimes I have recurring conversations, forming the bud of a relationship with a total stranger.

I get bored again. The words I'm exchanging with my new internet friends who are either three decades older than me or also my age and pretending to be three decades older than me turn meaningless. I need the real thing—well, not the *real* thing—but like, a *real* picture of *real* body parts. So I decide to exchange pictures with an old guy I meet in a sex chat room. Normal! The deal is, I can see a photo of his penis if I send a picture first. Of course, I can't send a picture of myself, so I google "naked girl" and copy-paste the first image available. He doesn't like that. I don't know what it is he doesn't like: the watermark across the girl's face, maybe the way she's professionally lit in a photo studio with a backdrop, or maybe that it was the first image available when you google "naked girl." Either way, he reports me. It's like, you think you know people . . .

The next day, after school, I resume my routine, except my dad is home, which is weird, but I don't ask questions because I legitimately *only* care about the picture of a real-life penis that may or may not be waiting for me behind that beloved message: "You've got mail." I eat Cheez Doodles with my parents, then very calmly and coolly attempt to bolt upstairs to the computer room, but my dad stops me. He says he needs to talk to me about something serious, and I'm like, oh my god, bin Laden is back. But no, it's so much worse: My dad says he's been on the phone all day with AOL. My account was reported for unimaginably dirty and sick emails, including images of naked girls, and since our accounts are attached, my dad was notified. Do I know anything about this? He has evidence, even: He shows me printed-out screenshots of the infamous "naked girl," of my own leaked Pokegutz emails that say really personal stuff, like, "I crave balls." He and my mom look at me like they're afraid of me, and I don't want them to be—I'm not a monster! I'm just a kid! I'm just their sweet, naive daughter!

I lie. I cry and cry and say I've been hacked. My dad says AOL maintained that it's basically impossible for a "hack" to look like this, unless someone else had my password and repeatedly logged on to use my account, and I'm like, "Yes, THAT, it's THAT!" I cry for my mommy and they finally exhale and hug me, and say that the world is big and scary and twisted, and that bad people are out there on the internet, and I'm like, "Totally agree!" And then it's over.

Well, parts of it. I mean, the message is clear: thinking about sex, seeking it out, learning about it, and talking about it is absolutely revolting, foul, depraved. No one should do it. So I don't. I stop searching for porn and cybering and talking about sex cold turkey. My parents and I never speak of it again. I never get my screenname Pokegutz back. No one else even knows what happened, not even my cousin Lee, because it's too embarrassing. I don't want anyone to know how perverted and debased I am. I keep this secret close to my heart, that I'm a depraved sexual monster who has questions about her body that adults outright refuse to answer! Shame on me, ROFLMAO, pwned.

2005

I'm a freshman in high school. I have a hot pink flip phone, a tonal version of "Big Pimpin'" plays when I get a phone call, neon rubber bands flank my braces, and I. Am. Living? I'm the worst possible age a girl can be, my soul has evaporated inside my body, and I am a shell. I still haven't gotten my period, which my friends make me feel super weird about, and they can already smell the reek of lesbianism seeping out of my skin. I've yet to recover from Pokegutzgate and likely never will, I feel shame every moment I breathe, and I smile the kind of smile where the top half of my head never moves. George W. Bush is still president, the world feels increasingly bad, and I no longer use the internet to actually acquire information or learn. What am I gonna read about, weapons of mass destruction? Grow up! No, I use the internet for social networking—not sure if you've heard of it, it's pretty new.

Me and my friends do this cool thing where we rank each other, not based on any sort of system of merit, but MySpace encourages us to place our coolest friends in our Top 8, so we do. I'm in no one's Top 8, but I move popular girls in and out of my Top 8 all the time, seeing if anyone who's been fingered (Chloe), anyone who's drunk beer (Julia), anyone whose brother has weed or who's texting with a junior guy from another school (Kelsey) might add me back. They don't!

Every day after school, I come home and jog upstairs to my room (still turquoise, still slathered in Britney Spears propaganda). I open my crisp new

MacBook—my very first computer of my own—and I log onto AIM. I bounce around the interwebs: I check MySpace to see if I have any new comments or friends (never); I tend to my page, make sure it's running smoothly and my GIFs aren't coded wrong or crashing my page (I have a black-and-pink emo girl background, a sarcastic GIF that reads BLING BLING, and "Amber" by 311 plays—a multitudinous vibe is being curated). I listen to the sounds of doors opening and slamming as my friends log on and off AIM, I Instant Message with my best friends about whether or not Chloe actually got fingered or lied about it for attention, and I throw up away messages with Fall Out Boy lyrics that are like, "And I'd bleed the blood I bleed to bleed for your blood. Hit the cell." Sometimes I do upkeep on my Xanga blog when away messages just aren't enough Expression for the day, and tell my three followers that actually Chiodos sucks and Hayley Williams is better.

I do this for hours until my mom asks me to come downstairs for dinner. Sometimes, when I actually get a comment or a message (truly never), something in my brain oozes and tingles and drips down my spine, like a Snickers ice cream bar melting on a sandy beach. I've never felt anything like it before. It's validating, knowing that every piece of communication done via the internet is so intentional, that someone might go out of their way to talk to me while I'm home, even though they could just wait till we're in school tomorrow to tell me they liked my double-layered camisole combo today. And every time it's from a popular girl, even if she's kind of being mean to me and I'm pretending like I don't know because I really am just happy to be receiving a comment from Chloe or Julia or Kelsey at all, my brain pings around like a pinball in a pinball machine. The internet is so cool. It makes me feel so good. I'm so happy I grew up with it. I love it here!!!!! *eye twitches*

2010

I'm nineteen, I'm in college, I eat pot brownies and fall asleep watching old episodes of *Cosmos* or *iCarly* alone in my dorm, and I think it's totally cool and normal that every white person in this school has a poster of Bob Marley. Every bit of community or safety or identity that the internet afforded me was ripped away in my youth and replaced with feelings of guilt, disgust, and a bottomless need to connect . . . I . . . am . . . technically alive. This movie called *The Social Network* just came out about the guy who created Facebook, Mark Zuckerberg, and it's awesome. I love Facebook. I spend pretty much every hour I'm not in class on this fun website, commenting on my friends' pictures, writing funny jokes on their walls, looking at photos of people my age partying and enjoying themselves. Things are so much better these days. I actually get tons of comments on Facebook; I'm in constant communication with my friends via the internet, which makes me feel like a person worthy of occupying flesh; and I no longer have the fear of nuclear war looming over my head. Oh, also? America is fixed. Two years ago, Barack Obama was elected president, and everything's better now. Anyways, Facebook rocks, Mark Zuckerberg seems super cool and smart and not at all misogynistic for creating a website that compares pictures of girls at his school, and not at all like he might become a megalomaniac with dark political aspirations. Things are good!

2016

Things are not good. I'm twenty-four. I came out as gay last year. I'm obsessively tweeting about my sexuality as if I'm either making up for lost time, trying to re-create a community that was ripped from my fingertips in my youth, or stuck in a shame loop that compulsively asks me to own up to whatever I'm feeling and doing in regard to my body and sex so I don't feel like I'm hiding anything anymore . . . or all of the above. Also, Donald Trump has been elected president, America's being sucked into a vortex of its own collapsing systems, and turns out Mark Zuckerberg is a bad guy. But it's okay, because my own personal freedom of speech, American politics, and my internet-identity complex likely won't intersect at any point in the near future.

I'm twenty-six. I've made a career out of compulsively oversharing musings on my identity, sexuality, pop culture, and politics. In turn, I've developed a following on Twitter, which feeds the voracious, grinding beast in my belly that booms, "Bring me attention, connection, validation!" and at a softer volume, "and people to tell me I'm worthy of love, sex, inhabiting a body!"

It's a sunny October morning in Studio City, around 11:15 a.m., and I'm annotating Sally Ride's biography at my kitchen table. (Why? Well, why not?) I hear a knock on my apartment door. I trudge the eight steps between my chair and the door, I don't look through the eyehole (the last time I'll be making that mistake), and I open the door. "Jill Gutowitz?" a man inquires. It's FedEx. I take the package, bored by the insipidity of my mortal coil. He walks down the stairwell outside my apartment, and two men in black suits jog up the stairs to catch me before the door closes. One repeats, "Wait, Jill Gutowitz?" Thinking they're Jehovah's Witnesses, I begin to close the door in their faces and say, "No, thank you." The urgency with which they approach makes me distinctly aware of how vulnerable I am in this open doorway to my apartment, where I'm alone. My roommate and neighbors are at work, pretty much no one is around, and now there are two large men dressed like Party City detectives jogging up the narrow stairwell that ends at my apartment door.

One of them, who has a fuzzy blond buzz cut and a JCPenney-looking blazer, says, "Hi, we're with the Federal Bureau of Investigation." I laugh and say, "Seriously?" The other one, who looks like Paul Ryan dressed in *Men in Black* cosplay with cop sunglasses on his forehead, says sternly, "Seriously." The blond continues, "We're with a department that investigates threats of violent crime," and my mind races. *Someone in my family was murdered*, I think. *No, someone stole my identity and they turned out to be an unrealistically hot and extremely dangerous assassin*, I think. *This is like in* Law & Order *when detectives show up to some pedestrian's house and they're like, "Can we do this later? I've got dinner on the stove," which, given that my heart just dropped through my asshole, seems like a pretty laughable thing to say,* I think. *I wonder if me and the hot assassin will end up falling in love . . .* Then he says, "Do you have any intent to kill a U.S. senator?"

I don't have a *giant* social media following, but because I'm a silly little woman who has silly little thoughts and writes those silly little musings on the internet, I've been trolled. I was targeted by Nazis after I wrote an article for *Teen Vogue* about Logan Paul's white privilege, which riled them because they claimed Paul was, like me, a Jew, *"not* white." A *Daily Stormer* hit piece was once written about me, and among their list of complaints was that I was probably mean to my mom as a kid. (They're not wrong and I feel really fucking bad about it, but like . . . get a job?). Also, America is about to burst into flames. The Senate just voted Brett Kavanaugh, a sexual abuser, onto the Supreme Court. In doing so, Senate Republicans sent women, people of color, and LGBTQ people, all of whose lives are endangered by a conservative-leaning Supreme Court, this message: *We are coming for your bodies, your rights, and your comfort, and this country values your abusers more than we value you.* So, in this moment, I'm quite worried that, amid the rising national anger in America, I've been doxed. After all, doxing—when someone's personal information or address is published with malicious intent—has become common practice. I figure, two Republican trolls have found my address and are about to shove me into my apartment and beat the pulp out of me in broad daylight. I'm sure of it, because the alternative just seems too impossible, too alien, like a story I would've made up in middle school about the feds showing up to my house in order to scare my cousin who smokes cigarettes out of wearing leather jackets. But still, my mind and my gut swirl, searching hastily and hopelessly for an answer as to why I could possibly be faced with a visit from the FBI, and somewhere in a pocket in the back of my mind, I wonder . . . this couldn't possibly be about . . . *that thing* . . . right?

In what feels like slow motion, the blond agent hands me two sheets of paper, printed in black and white, and as I shake in my Adidas slides and begin seeing spots, I glimpse my stupid Twitter avatar in the top left corner of the page. These two men, these two federal agents, are handing me printed screengrabs of *that thing* I thought this *couldn't* be about: my viral tweet about Brett Kavanaugh.

Here is the tweet:

Jill Gutowitz ●
@jillboard

[Arya Stark voice]
McConnell.
Manchin.
Collins.
Flake.
Grassley.
Hatch.
Graham.
Rubio.
Cornyn.
Cruz.
Capito.
Corker.
Heller.
Kennedy.
Rounds.
Sasse.
Young.
Wicker.
Toomey.
Shelby.
Thune.
Tillis.
Sullivan.
Roberts.
Perdue.
Portman.
Shelby.
Scott.
Risch.
Paul.
Moran.
Lee.
Johnson.

4:34 PM · Oct 6, 2018 · Twitter for iPhone

7.7K Retweets   **415** Quote Tweets   **29.4K** Likes

The day that Brett Kavanaugh was confirmed by the Senate, emotions were running high, especially for survivors of sexual abuse. As a person who's had her own clashes with sex trauma, and also as a fan of *Game of Thrones*, I tweeted an "Arya Stark list" meme. If you watch the show, you know that the second-youngest Stark, Arya, keeps a list of those who've wronged her. (Joffrey Baratheon, Walder Frey, Meryn Trant, Tywin Lannister, etc.) It's a revenge list, a kill list. She recites the names every night before she sleeps, keeping vengeance at the top of her mind. So, I tweeted in "Arya Stark voice" a list of the senators who voted to confirm Brett Kavanaugh. As a joke. Obviously.

The men in black hand me two pages, one of my tweet, another of a response to my tweet in which another *GoT* fan edited the list of senators' names onto a photo of Arya. Trying to get a grip on my current reality, I grab hold of one of the millions of thoughts flitting through my skull: *Do the thing you always see in cop movies and TV shows, the thing that Facebook moms send in chain mail about knowing your rights. Ask for their ID.* I say, through my numb face, "I don't know if this is a thing that people actually do, but can I . . . see your IDs?"

They pause, as if taken aback, like people don't actually ask them to do this in real life, and I immediately feel stupid, or like this is the moment where the jig is up and I get murdered. But no, they flip open their movie-prop-looking leather-wallet FBI IDs, and I realize, I'm just a dumb bitch entertainment writer! I don't know what a real FBI ID looks like! In actuality, this is a completely useless exercise in safety! *Sure, looks good to me, a noted expert in government identification*, I think. I shrug at the IDs, not even offering the illusion that I understand what they're showing me.

They ask if I have any guns in the apartment, or if I own any weapons. I cower, my body folding in on itself, and vehemently insist, "I'm very anti-gun! I'm even anti-weapon!" They gaze over my shoulder, into my apartment, where a series of Taylor Swift magazines are splayed across my coffee table and a painting I made of a Jamie Lee Curtis meme (the one of her wagging her finger in fury) hangs on a wall. It's clear that I'm not a "threat," but rather a stuttering, trembling clump of flesh whose soul escaped through its pores a decade ago. They grow more candid.

They ask me to explain the tweet, and it dawns on me that, right now, in this moment, I am going to explain a *Game of Thrones* meme to the literal FBI. And it's not a joke. It's not funny. The air is being sucked out of my lungs. But here I go. I motion stupidly toward my TV and ask them if they watch *Game of Thrones*, to which they say, "No," and I think, *Great.* I say, "Well, Arya Stark, the second youngest child of Ned Stark—" and already I realize they don't need this information. I point to the black-and-white photo of Arya Stark that I'm holding, and say, "Arya has a list of people who've wronged her, which she recites every night before bed, and—okay, I see how this sounds, but—a kill list. But it's actually more of a revenge thing than a murder—" They stare at me. Why did I say "murder"? I add, "I was pretty heated after the Kavanaugh hearings, like many people were, so I tweeted an 'Arya Stark list' of the senators who confirmed him." They stare at me. "I do . . . I do see how this sounds, but it's a very popular meme and it's actually not even very original, I wasn't the first one to tweet an 'Arya Stark list.' It's like, a thing. I don't want revenge. I'm not seeking revenge. It was just a joke." My cheeks are on fire, and every childhood feeling of getting in trouble or going to the principal's office or being found out swells in my throat as I try not to cry. Am I in trouble? Am I about to be sitting in a cold, dark, damp room in an undisclosed location, swearing my allegiance to Donald Trump? I have no feeling below my neck. In fact, my feet seem to be floating in the doorway. I am hollow. I am a ghost.

They loosen up.

They tell me that they do this all the time, that doing *this* all day is *their* mortal coil. All day, they visit the homes and musty apartments of Flops and Nobodies, interrogate them about some vaguely threatening meme they posted online, and then they cross them off a very long list. They tell me not to worry, assuring me that this ends here and they're not going to sit outside of my apartment in an unmarked vehicle or anything, which actually doesn't make me feel like they're not going to sit outside of my apartment in an unmarked vehicle.

I say, "Can I ask how this happened? How you came across, uh, me?" And I'm proud of myself for having my wits about me enough to ask any questions at all. I tell them that, after my tweet went viral (why am I standing here talking about my viral tweets with the FBI, what the fuck), a bunch of people with "MAGA" in their Twitter handles started to tag the FBI and Secret Service's official accounts, as if to snitch on me. I ask, "The FBI isn't sitting around all day checking their mentions . . . right?" And they say no. They say, "A few people—Republicans" they add frankly, with a smirk, "filed real reports with the FBI about you, or this incident." They tell me that, after the Parkland massacre, in which the FBI had received reports of the shooter's threats prior to the incident and didn't act, giving the public the ability to say "the FBI knew and did nothing," there are new protocols. Now they must "investigate," AKA send feds to Flops' and Nobodies' homes, all threats of "violence" that are reported to the FBI. They say, "Freedom of speech is obviously great, but we just have to check these things out," which actually makes me feel like freedom of speech is not "obviously great." And then the conversation falls flat and they say "Thank you for your time," and I say "Thank you for your service" like a goddamn bootlicker, black spots flash in my eyes, and I close the door.

What?

I hover to my bedroom window, which has a view of my street, and watch them put their cop-ass Oakley sunglasses on, debrief for a moment, then get into separate cars—one of which is an old, tan Ford, like an FBI car that tails you in a '90s movie—and drive away. I call my friend Sam. I call my parents. I call my friend Debby. She puts me on speaker and I tell her fiancé. I call the girl I just started seeing. I spend the entire day talking about this thing that happened that sounds made-up as fuck. I try to calm my nervous system, to see clearly out of my eyes, to process what just happened, to discern whether or not I should feel blood-curdling terror or like a fucking rock star, or both. I think about how abnormal this is, how I've never heard of this happening to anyone, ever—not even a reporter, or a celebrity, or a contentious news pundit. I'm officially the only person I know who has been interrogated by the FBI. I'm the only person I know who has had to explain a pop culture meme to federal agents. And I'll tell you: there was certainly no part of me that thought, *Let me just regroup and ask them to come back at a better time*—"Sorry, dinner's on the stove." In what world, *Law & Order* writers?

Later that day, I continue to shake. I embark on what I'm sure will be a lifetime of living in putrid fear. I walk to 7-Eleven for some caffeine or sugar to return feeling to my body. I see a black car turn down my street, and I think I'm being followed. I look over my shoulder the whole walk back. I glance inside the windows of every car outside of my building before reentering. When I reach my apartment door, I look down the stairwell, ensuring I'm alone, wondering if that FedEx guy heard them say they were FBI agents investigating "threats of violent crime" and thought, *Holy shit, I just delivered a package to a serial killer.* I lock my doors. I continue to text my friends, part joking, part petrified, that the FBI is watching this space, and write, "FBI IF YOU'RE READING THIS I'M JOKING ABOUT EVERYTHING I'VE EVER SAID." I remember that the last meme Sam had sent me, which I saved to my camera roll, was an edit of Taylor Swift standing next to a car with curly, glittery text that reads, *When I see a Republican, I floor it.* I delete it and then delete it from my Deleted folder.

Then I start panicking again: What if that wasn't the FBI, but they actually *were* trolls who found my address? Like I said, I don't have a clue what an FBI ID looks like. I google "how to call the FBI." I dial the Los Angeles bureau, explain what just happened and that I'm seeking confirmation that these were federal agents and not two threatening men who found my address. The man on the phone makes me feel like a moron for even asking. I'm baffled, I can't understand why. I say, desperately, I can offer my address, my social, anything to confirm my identity. He asks, condescendingly, "Do you understand why I can't confirm any of that over the phone?" And I think, silent on the line, and say, "You can't confirm my address because I may not be who I say I am?" And he says, "Yes, have a nice day." I say I can come in and bring my ID, my passport, birth certificate. He says the FBI doesn't just take in-person appointments. He hangs up. I hold the phone to my face, stunned.

I call back. I talk to a woman and ask if there's any way I can work around this—I need to be able to confirm, for my own safety, that these were real cops. She says I'd need to give her the names of the agents. I say I can't remember their names because I was in a blackout panic when I glanced at their IDs. She says she can't help me. She hangs up.

I call Sam again. Sam, who works at a news magazine, connects with his politics reporter in D.C. who has worked with the FBI on stories. He's stunned; he's never heard of anything like this. I google everything I can possibly learn about contacting the FBI, fully aware that my search history now looks fucking bananas. I reach out to former FBI agents on Twitter, asking them to follow me so I can DM them. They do, and I explain the situation, and they don't answer. They quickly unfollow me. I talk to another mutual friend, an editor at the *Washington Post*, and his advice to me is to drop it, that they're the FBI and it's not worth stirring the pot any more than I already have. I say I want to write about it. He says he doesn't think it's a good idea.

I talk to a third reporter, Ken Klippenstein at *The Intercept*, who walks me through filing a FOIA request. The Freedom of Information Act states, essentially, that Americans can request previously unreleased government documents, and while the government isn't required to provide them, they *are* required to respond to the FOIA request. Ken says that I should be able to get my hands on, at the absolute least, the FBI reports that were filed against me. A person should, in theory, be able to gain access to a copy of their own records with the federal government, right? I fill out the form online. Weeks later, I receive a letter in the mail stating that a "search of the Central Records System" was conducted, and they were "unable to identify any main file records responsive to [my] request," and thus, my request is being "administratively closed." The letter goes on to state that "this response neither confirms nor denies the existence of your subject's name on any watch lists." Basically, I get Glomar'd. A Glomar response, in the United States, is a governmental response that will "neither confirm nor deny" the existence of information in a FOIA request. The term originated in the '70s when a journalist requested information from the CIA confirming the existence and use of the *Glomar Explorer,* a submarine that was used for a Soviet intelligence operation, to which the CIA said they could neither "confirm nor deny" its existence.

I try another FOIA request, this time including as much information as I possibly can. I get Glomar'd again. I try to write about my experience for *Elle,* then for the *Washington Post,* neither of which feels comfortable publishing the piece without explicit proof from the FBI that this actually happened. I feel gaslit. I feel muzzled. I feel insane. And where's my hot assassin wife???

I go back to tweeting lesbian conspiracy theories about Taylor Swift and emotionally divest from politics. I don't want to be targeted by any group that's angry enough to sic a federal agency on me in my home. I don't want to get doxed, or swatted. I decide that my activism can be loud but not too loud, never too "threatening" or contentious. I see other people—comedians I know, activists I'm friends with—tweet careless stuff about wishing the president would drop dead, and I shudder. I wonder if I should reach out to them and warn them, or if that makes me sound like a narc, or like a paranoid recluse. I wonder if I will fade slowly into obscurity, becoming some old nut with tangled gray hair who owns many birds and lives in a cabin in the woods and can never get past her one "alleged" rap from the FBI. Will I rattle off conspiracy theories about being watched by the government, and how the government sees all, and how you can't even tweet anymore without federal agents showing up on your doorstep? But it's real, it happened. I should've kept the papers they handed me, then took back. I should've taken a picture of their IDs. I guess the only thing I held on to was the trauma of enduring it.

Mere days after the incident, something terrifying happened: Cesar Sayoc, AKA the MAGA bomber, mailed sixteen packages of explosives to prominent Trump critics, like Hillary Clinton, Barack Obama, and Joe Biden. On October 26, 2018, nine days after the FBI showed up at my door, the FBI arrested Sayoc. Apparently fingerprints from a past run-in, DNA, and social media posts helped them make that arrest. Sayoc had been tweeting vitriolic, misspelled, violent threats to his targets, telling Joe Biden to "Hug your loved son,Niece,wife, family real close everytime U walk out your home." The FBI missed all those posts. Nobody reported him. And the same week that bombs began arriving on politicians' doorsteps, two agents interrogated me about *Game of Thrones*. Sayoc was later sentenced to twenty years in federal prison. I can barely begin to wrap my mind around the absurdity and closeness of these two incidents. My parents once told me that there are bad people out there on the internet, and that's always been true—Sayoc being extremely one of them.

For me, the internet is like when you figure out how to masturbate and you do it so much that you basically break your sex organs and you're like, *Fuck, fuck, fuck, rash, what do I do?* I loved the internet so much that I ruined it for myself. I think about my six-year-old self, this dykey little Carol Anne floating toward the blue-green light of a computer, this mesmerized, virtuous girl on the shores of discovery. I wonder how much of the hypnosis was physical, natural, my animal body moving toward an attractive light like a moth flitting near a lamp, a plant leaning toward sun. I think, *Oh gosh, this poor little girl. Walk back into darkness!*

I entered my relationship with the internet pure of heart. I gave her everything. And she crushed me, time and time again. Now the threat of getting hurt again, of being left so raw and exposed and naive, lingers over me like the thundercloud of heartbreak. Yet, much like real heartbreak, it's never been enough to repel me. I keep falling in love, taking a leap of faith, unmasking myself in the name of a sweet Top 8, a poignant away message, a bunch of retweets. But I live in fear, wondering each time I express myself or reach out in search of connection or community whether AOL will out me as a pervert, if the FBI will interrogate me about my latest meme. Maybe if somebody had just put me in their stupid Top 8 I wouldn't have built an entire life around desperately needing to feel noticed.

I'll never float toward any blue light as doe-eyed as I did in 1997, but I have to cut myself some slack, to forgive both my internet history and all my younger, unadulterated selves. Carol Anne was literally swallowed by a haunted wall, and no one blamed her for walking toward the light.

I'M A FAMOUS ACTRESS, MOM!

"SOMEDAY I'LL BE big enough so you can't hit me" is one of the many Taylor Swift lyrics that has stuck with me throughout my expansive and enduring years as a Swiftie, a period of standom that began in the mid-2000s. The aughts were such a dogshit period of time to come of age—it has to be the least romantic era of pop culture, or just culture, in modern history. When we look back on being young in the '60s, we think, "Psychedelics! Hendrix! Joplin! Revolution! Gloria Steinem!" Or like, the '70s, we think about the coming-of-age movie *Dazed and Confused*, where the beer flowed like wine, bell-bottoms reigned, the Runaways blared, and getting high was a rite of passage. The '80s? Come on. How many movies about denim-clad, rock-and-roll, hair-metal, fast-life-chasing teens with blowouts do we need to see?

You know what a coming-of-age tale looks like in the 2000s? Tinted sunglasses. Spaghetti-strapped camisoles. Denim skirts. Juicy jumpsuits. Tiger-stripe highlights. Camcorder sex tapes. Growing up, I thought MTV's *Spring Break* was peak culture—the absolute pinnacle of young adulthood. I figured if I wasn't packed like a sticky sardine on a beach in Mexico, getting watered-down tequila sodas poured on my titties while Sisqó and Carmen Electra writhed onstage behind me, then I had failed at being young. And you know what I was listening to? Ashlee Simpson. Paris Hilton. Hilary Duff. The Pussycat Dolls. To me, *these* were rock gods. I thought Avril Lavigne was the king of rock and roll. These were not romantic times (though to be clear,

Avril was and is the king of rock and roll). The 2000s were the dark ages of pop culture—and that goes for the messaging too. "Someday I'll be big enough so you can't hit me" is not from the aughts, but rather the 2010 song "Mean." But its ideology, much like my own adolescent creed, was an idea that was incubated at the turn of the millennium: Get famous, and *nothing* else will matter.

In the year 2000, my parents moved my younger sister and me to the sole contemporary house in one of those wealthy, Republican, Catholic, CEOs-who-commute-from-suburbia-to–Wall Street, white people towns. Outside of our anomalous house, Mountain Lakes, New Jersey, was brimming with Craftsman mansions that were built to look mostly the same, varying only slightly in size, shade of mauve, and psychotically manicured landscapes masterminded by evil white women.

The town is named for its eight lakes, most of which are just ponds, and its central attraction, the eponymous Mountain Lake, which was a mucky, barely swimmable sinkhole that was large enough for sailboat lessons and kayaking but small enough that you could swim across it (and ice-skate across in the winter). This dewy, forest-studded hole in northern Jersey was tiny, both physically and in its lack of imagination: it was only two square miles and had two restaurants, one lunch market, and a gas station. If you needed groceries or coffee, to go to the movies or get Taco Bell, you went to a neighboring town. Many people who didn't live in town, like teachers and guidance counselors who were familiar with the storied, Stepford-esque place, often referred to Mountain Lakes simply as "the bubble."

We moved from a middle-class town called West Caldwell, a twenty-minute drive away but a world apart. Our West Caldwell house was perfectly quaint: painted dark red with a green front door and a garage that matched; a fenced-in yard with a swing set; lawn lined with lilac bushes, yellow honeysuckle, and a big tuft of hydrangea. It was basically lesbian cottagecore heaven: a haven of scraped knees, creaky hardwood floors, Pokémon cards, and giggles. When we moved to Mountain Lakes, everything changed for us. To me, a wide-eyed nine-year-old, our new house contradicted the size of the town: it felt *sweeping*. Perched on a corner of two very steep hills, our dream house stood angular and white, with a royal-blue garage, turquoise doors, a red chimney (my parents are very eccentric). They bought it from an architect who designed it himself and lived there with his daughter for many years. He was a unique fellow: In the kitchen sat an emerald diner booth surrounded by pink-and-purple-tiled walls; my bedroom had a carved-out hole in the floor for a bed (which my parents filled in—to my dismay); and, well . . . this architect also cemented numerous metal animal sculptures into the ground (my parents left them there, since they were, um, cemented into the ground). So our front lawn had a human-size, immovable, rusted metal donkey sculpture. Our foyer had a unicorn (same size and highly visible through the windows). And the pool was surrounded by little rusty birds. When people in town would ask what house we moved into (yes, townies were familiar with each *house*), and we'd describe it ("the corner of North Glen and Laurel Hill," or "the contemporary house"), they'd say, "Oh, the donkey house." Our dream house had quite the reputation. And as a hyperactive, flamboyant kid, I felt special there. It was clear to my little sister and me, even at the young ages of nine and five, that we had upgraded. We were now "come swim in my pool" people.

My parents were (and are) artsy types. My mom, Susie, was a visual arts major at Syracuse University and then worked in fashion photography. She was fascinated with the aesthetics of television sets—she collected old TVs and displayed them in our home, painting scenes of them, little TVs personified as lurid butterflies. My dad, Mike, had a hoop earring—need I say more? He studied photography at RIT and then began working in production (editing commercials, broadly). Early in his career, before I was born, he struggled to put food on the table, but eventually, after years of working his way up, he launched his own post house and hit it big: he rented a prime office space in Times Square, next to the Viacom building, which was home to those infamous *TRL* concerts. My dad worked with MTV often, so he was very tuned in to when "cool" concerts were coming. It's safe to say my parents' proximity to TV and entertainment, as a business and as a hobby, incubated my early interest in the medium (I mean, my dad had a vanity license plate throughout my entire youth that read TV HEAD).

My parents' decision to move us to Mountain Lakes both made sense and didn't. With my dad's new six-figure salary, he wanted to upgrade everything: our cars, our house, my and my sister's education—at the time, Mountain Lakes High School was one of the highest-ranking public high schools in the state. My parents wanted the best possible life for us. On the other hand, my parents stuck out like a pair of sore thumbs. Outside of Susie and Mike, Mountain Lakes was made up of country-club-looking, tennis-skirt-wearing, "what sport does your kid play" types of people. There were no purple-haired teens. No synagogues. No Al Gore stickers on the back of anyone's G-Wagen. So when the financial crisis hit seven years later and took everything away from us, it was both holistically gutting and a blessed return to normalcy. When disaster struck, I was old enough to know I needed to help, but way too naive and sheltered to develop a real plan. This next part is what we, in the queer community, like to call "an evil plan."

It was 2007, and I was wearing aqua Soffe shorts—rolled once to reveal that *stylish* elastic band—and a heinous magenta tank top from Free People. It was spring in New Jersey, or maybe it was fall—regardless, it was sixty degrees and that was "shorts weather."

I sat on my bed, which was covered in a pink, purple, orange, yellow, and green polka-dotted comforter. One corner of my bed was reserved for the stuffed animals: a big Care Bear, a little Care Bear, a Paul Frank monkey-head pillow, plus all of the fuzzy neon creatures I had acquired over the years from playing fair games on the Jersey Shore boardwalk. I had squishy royal-blue carpet, screaming turquoise walls, a hot-pink studded pleather mirror with corners of photos of me and my friends lodged in its creases, and a sprawling poster of Britney Spears sitting on a truck. I was "a lot," as they say.

My tabby cat, Rocket, rubbed his head against my shins as my mom joined me on the edge of my bed. My plucked eyebrows gathered in the center of my forehead; my curt lips stuck together like magnets. I asked my mom if we could chat about something that had been weighing on me. Something I'd thought very long and hard about. Something I needed to talk to her, my most trusted confidante, about in private—too embarrassed to even tell my friends yet. "Mom," I started. She looked into my big hazel eyes with that weighty maternal concern, knowing that she would be there for me no matter what came out next. I opened my mouth again to speak, but hesitated. "Mom," I said. "I think that I'm . . ."

She held her breath.

". . . An actress," I said.

She stared at me.

Rewinding a bit: 2008 was when the financial crisis hit, but my dad's business caved a bit earlier. Once the recession began, corporate spending dwindled, and many people—despite not working in finance—became collateral damage, including my dad. His biggest and most lucrative clients began to choose cheaper, younger laborers instead of his full-service post house, and eventually it collapsed. He didn't handle money perfectly: Like, a few years earlier, he splurged on a Porsche without consulting my mom. Later on, our Suburban got repossessed in the middle of the night, an avoidable consequence. But he also took care of his employees until it bled him dry. And finally, he went bankrupt, and our dream house was to be foreclosed. When his donkey house of cards came tumbling down, I was sixteen years old and repressing a big part of my personality (that I was an actress). But now I wasn't hiding anymore. Now I could fix this.

"I want to be an actress," I told my mom, "like Amanda Bynes or Miranda Cosgrove." She continued to stare at me, as any human who breathes air would.

"Is that something you really want to pursue? You've never, um . . . acted before."

"Yeah, but I can start now. Look at the Jonas Brothers. Look at Miley Cyrus. They're my age and they're out there doing it." More staring.

"Well, most of these people have been acting and performing since they were four years old, Jill." My heart sank. I knew that admitting you want anything out loud was completely humiliating. She was right, I was too late. "But if that's what you really want, we should look into it. Maybe you can take an acting class."

"No," I said, privileged and white and unfamiliar with the concept of an obstacle. "That's embarrassing." But then it dawned on me, a lightbulb appearing over my hollow skull. "Wait. You know Elizabeth McMahon? In the grade below me? She has an agent in New York. She auditioned for a commercial in eighth grade. Also she got on *OceanUp* once because she allegedly made out with one of the teen actors on *Hannah Montana*." Elongated stare.

" . . . Right. Well, you need to show an agent that you can act, or that you're working on acting, to be able to get an agent, I think." I blinked at her, totally blindsided by my inability to access instant success. "You can definitely do this. I know you can. You're the funniest person I know." (I'm paraphrasing here.) "But you should know how tough a career like that is. You have to really want it, and work really, really hard at doing it. And you can't give up. If you really want to be an actress—"

"I want to be on *iCarly*, yes."

"Then you have to pour your heart and soul into this. Is that something you can do?"

"Doy."

She put her soft hand on my shoulder. "Then let's find a way."

This may come as a surprise to you, but that bizarre conversation went absolutely nowhere. I did *not* become a Famous Actress on *iCarly*, nor did I take an acting class or meet with an agent (though I did cold-call one once; she looked like Liza Minnelli on her website, and she was extremely confused by my utter lack of experience or dedication to My Craft). The only thing I can even remember doing to push me in the direction of Becoming a Famous Actress was . . . Oh god, this is so chilling that I've never admitted it to anyone . . . There were these recurring ads, casting calls of sorts, that used to play on Z100, which claimed to have broken out stars like Miley Cyrus and the Jonas Brothers, and YOU could be NEXT! These "casting directors" claimed they were searching for fresh young talent for roles on Disney Channel shows like *Hannah Montana* and *Wizards of Waverly Place*. My mom actually agreed to let my fame-horny ass and my little sister go. We straightened our hair, groomed ourselves into our final forms— AKA North Face–looking motherfuckers—got in the car, and drove to, like, an event space at a Ramada Inn lined with metal folding chairs. And then, apparently, we were "seen" by these scammers. I say "apparently" because, hand to a God I don't believe in, I don't remember a single thing inside the Ramada Inn. That's how you know the experience must have been scarring, because my noggin is truly empty—and that feels like the kind of uniquely grotesque journey you'd remember. Nothing came of it, obviously.

Here's the thing: I didn't actually *want* to be an Amanda Bynes–type "Actress." What I really wanted, what I *knew* I really wanted deep, deep down, buried in the same repression hole where I was keeping my sexuality, but was too smothered in shame to ever admit, was fame. I wanted to be extraordinarily famous.

The mid-2000s is the cursed era that bore what is known today as clout-chasing (also see: social climbers, clout demons, fame monsters, fame whores—side note, *love* that we used to call people who wanted to be famous literal "whores"). Try to imagine a time before Lesbian TikTok. Now go even further back, before Vine. Keep going. Before YouTubers came out to their parents on *Ellen*, or whatever. Before Twitter. Before "Leave Britney Alone." There. I know, it can be hard to recall such a period of time *existed*. This was the Before Times, when we didn't have uninterrupted access to every celebrity in the palm of our hands; when people who made really good coffee or plated their meals in an aesthetically pleasing way were just "hipsters," not aspirational fake-Famouses who could monetize their relatable lifestyle; back when there was actually a distinction between a "celebrity" and, well, any old person. There's a reason that Elizabeth McMahon was a living legend in our high school simply for appearing on *OceanUp*, a teen celebrity gossip blog that trafficked in leaked photos of Disney stars, because she *allegedly* kissed an obscure teen actor from *Hannah Montana*. We didn't have the same access to fame or followers in those Before Times. People like me, who felt personally invested in the lives of celebrities, were relegated to the barbaric prison of reading gossip magazines and blogs. In the mid-aughts, there was still a clear distinction between celebrity-folk (those in the magazines and blogs) and people (those reading the magazines and blogs). Just like we've come to understand the concepts of gender and sexuality as such, fame is now a spectrum. There used to be Famouses and Normals. Now the concept of fame itself has been cremated and sprinkled over the gen pop. We are all living in a sliding scale of visibility: some people are just more *visible* than others, as in, have more followers. For the purpose of continuity and ease, I will keep saying Famouses and Normals, mostly because I like doing it, but just know that I don't believe anyone is truly a Famous or a Normal anymore. Think about the feeling of seeing someone at the grocery store and wondering, *How do I know you? Did you go to my high school? Do I follow you on Instagram? Were you on TV once? Are you my cousin?* Consider the access you have to your ex's new girlfriend, or your ex's exes. We're all so visible to the world these days that it doesn't really matter who's "famous" and who's not. We are all being seen and familiarized with each other, within our own communities and outside of our little bubbles, constantly, tirelessly. Of course, this is only partly true, as recent global events like the pandemic have illuminated; the revealing of the growing class divide started patching up the portal between Famouses and Normals once again as we all collectively began to realize that the stars were *not* "just like us," and actually had unmitigated access to, you know, food, health care, concierge coronavirus tests.

It was around the time I was sitting in a metal folding chair at a Ramada Inn and repressing a memory I may never access again that this change began to take place. A movement was swelling; Disney Channel was burgeoning, churning out the kind of mega–teen idols that even Olds knew about and became personally invested in, thanks to their kids' all-consuming obsessions. Miley Cyrus, Selena Gomez, Demi Lovato, the Jonas Brothers, Taylor Swift. At first, they were just the new Disney Channel class of teen stars, but what these kids had that their predecessors (Hilary Duff, Raven-Symoné, Christy Carlson Romano—the greats) didn't was YouTube and social media, which transformed them into a whole different beast of celebrity.

Miley Cyrus made YouTube videos with her best friend and backup dancer, Mandy. The two of them would just sit in Miley's bedroom, make funny sketches, gossip—just *be* teenage girls. Similarly, the Jonas Brothers made short, silly videos of the trio being goofy teen boys, which they posted on MySpace. We'd seen inside celebrities' homes before, sure. But we'd seen them photographed professionally, staged, printed in glossy magazine pages. In these Before Times, when we saw inside a celebrity's life, it was on someone else's terms: a journalist's, a photographer's, a magazine's, a gossip rag's. But with tools like YouTube and MySpace at the fingertips of a generation who knew how to utilize them—suddenly, celebrities could project images of themselves on their own terms. Miley Cyrus and the Jonas Brothers invited us, the teenage audience watching from the other side of the blue screen, into their lives. Because the production of such a connection and tuning in was a mutually agreed-upon choice, we began to feel a different kind of bond with these strangers who, until that moment, had seemed bound to TV screens and magazine pages. To Normals, Famouses were suddenly reachable. To Famouses, Normals were accessible in such a newly intimate way. We felt like we knew them, because they wanted us to know them. It was like the notorious scene in *Fleabag* when Hot Priest looks us in the eye for the first time, shockingly breaking the fourth wall; or in *The Chronicles of Narnia* when Lucy crosses through a portal to another world: the barrier just dissolved.

Soon after—or concurrently; timeline-wise, there's some overlap— Justin Bieber happened. Bieber is widely regarded as the original internet superstar. Someone like Miley Cyrus was already extremely famous because of her successful TV show and music career. But Bieber's rise to fame began on the internet, and continues to thrive in the physical realm. Bieber is the type of public figure we now regard as an influencer; he formed an organic, grassroots connection between himself and his fans. He's the type of star that fans feel ownership over because they played a part in his creation and elevation. Justin Bieber, who famously went from a Canadian kid busking on the streets of his hometown, to a YouTube star whose cover-song videos went viral, to an international icon, was *not* a celebrity first. He was just like us. We *made* him into a celebrity. We gave him the "gift" of fame. The reason we still pay attention to what people like Justin Bieber or Miley Cyrus are doing today is that we felt personally invested in and connected to their lives, and like a childhood friend you can't stop stalking on social media ("Oh shit, Kelsey's pregnant AGAIN? Why are racists so fertile??"), they hold a grip on our youthful selves that we can't wriggle out of.

I was a teenager, in my most vulnerable and malleable state, and I was offered a peephole into the lives of kids my age who were extremely rich, famous, and, above all, universally adored. Behind my dirty-blond head, which had tunnel vision for the bluish glow of my MacBook laptop, was chaos. My dad's business shuttered. Our cars repossessed. My parents on the brink of total emotional collapse. I got a job working as a snack bar attendant at the local country club and began serving all of my friends and their tennis-whites-wearing parents. I was beginning to understand social class and the death grip that money has on most of our throats. I saw my dad cry, so hard, and for so long. I sat through an absolutely heart-wrenching conversation he had with us in which he tried to explain how the bank would foreclose on our dream home we'd created together, and how unsure he was about everything that came next. It wasn't even about the money. I could see that in my dad's puffy, red, crestfallen face: In his eyes, he had failed us. His sense of self and worth was tied tightly to his ability to be our father, our caretaker, our provider, and in his eyes, that meant being able to provide *things*, material things, a grand life filled with *stuff*, just like the people of Mountain Lakes had. This financial nightmare had shattered my dad, and so, for the next decade—or probably for the rest of my life—I would come to associate my own self-worth with financial success. Given the scope of our world today, I'm aware of how "world's tiniest violin" this "upper-middle-class kid gets a job" anecdote sounds. Looking back, I'm grateful to have endured it, so I didn't grow up to become like most of the people I was raised with in Mountain Lakes (posting Blue Lives Matter memes on Facebook, etc.). The world I knew, "the bubble," collapsed around me, and as a teenager, I wasn't equipped with the emotional or intellectual tools I needed to actually reckon with my familial trauma, financial stress, or the repression I was still refusing to acknowledge.

Instead of dealing with any of this at the time, I entered a Disney Channel fugue state. When my parents fought, or when I watched my dad sob, a hole was scooped out of my chest. And each time a hole was scooped out, I filled it with a Jonas Brothers song. It's called escapism, look it up, sweetie. The Jonas Brothers were from a nearby town in New Jersey, and if you were my age and from New Jersey during their meteoric rise to fame, then you knew multiple people—even if one of them was your aunt's coworker's son's best friend's classmate—who "knew" the Jonas Brothers. MySpace aside, the Jonases just felt so tangible to me. Here were three kids my age, from similar circumstances, in a nearby neighborhood, who escaped the trauma of financial instability and familial wounds and *made it*. The story of a from-nothing star who "made it" is timeless. But in the mid-2000s, this specific tale represented a generation of kids who *needed* a beacon of hope.

My generation endured a national tragedy and the political and economic instability that followed it way before we were old enough to begin grappling with it. And when we were old enough to begin understanding and wrestling with terror, disaster, political strife, and a vehement post-9/11 xenophobic uptick in hate speech, we were hit with another major blow—boom, the financial crisis. When Obama was elected in 2008, there was this wave of mixed political and personal messaging that we, or at least I, internalized: it was like, "Follow your dreams! Be yourself! YOU could be president one day—Barack Obama is proof!" But for women, especially women of color, queer people, fat people, disabled people—anyone who strayed from the white, Christian straight (literally) and narrow (also literally), the message got refracted. Obama's clarion call for change and hope and the general implication of "embracing" what makes you "unique" was often confusingly negated by tabloid media, which was hideous (see: Britney Spears being a "crazy slut," or Amy Winehouse being a "despicable train wreck"). The message that was being transmitted through Disney Channel, which was, at the time, a booming machine proliferating megastars, was: Be yourself, as long as "yourself" looks like these thin, non-disabled white people with Christian values. But no no no, embrace YOU!!!!

This was a moment of time that was trapped between future and past, between progress and regression; we were finally beginning to talk publicly and widely about certain identities, but weren't yet ready to celebrate them. So whether you were a kid who was affected by the financial crisis, queer, bullied, othered, if your identity wasn't previously accepted, or even tolerated, or even *recognized*, the Jonas Brothers and other "one of us" internet-fueled celebrities offered an escape to a sprawling group of us in the mid-2000s who had turbulent lives and were looking for a chance to dissociate. With the political, social, and economic circumstances growing so dire, I thought becoming extraordinarily famous was my escape plan, my one chance at survival.

So that became the objective: Get famous. Get so fucking famous that I could be yanked out of my own misery and trauma, and eschew the nightmare that is . . . feeling. I had to get fuck-you famous. Reading it now, it's almost funny, or at least misguided, but I wasn't misguided—I was just guided.

Off the top of my head, there are a series of songs from around that period of time, or just after, that propagate this message: "Popular Song" by Ariana Grande and MIKA (2013), a forgotten song about a mean popular girl who bullies Ariana, but the joke's on the bully—now she's in the front row of Ariana's concert, because Ariana's song is "popular." "Sk8er Boi" by Avril Lavigne (2002), about a girl who dumps a boy because her friends said he was emo and weird, and now he's a rock star and all she has is a stupid baby that cries. "Mean" by Taylor Swift (2010), same shit, different song—bullies, the tables have turned because I'm super, ultra, mega rich and famous now, and what the fuck do you have?

In "Sk8er Boi," we can now see how this woman with a child is obviously an idiot who lives a life devoid of meaning, because she used to date a person who's on TV now. Ah, yes, motherhood—that thing which is notoriously meaningless and unfulfilling. Take a look at the bridge of "Mean" by Taylor Swift: "Someday I'll be big enough so you can't hit me" says it all. Becoming something so supermassive that you transcend your *self*, your human form, and metamorphose into a larger being: a billboard, an icon, a *thing* that's representative of a groupthink, a collection of a generation's conscious thoughts—that's the goal, right? One can harm a person, but one cannot harm an *idea*. By this theory, which is pervasive in pop culture, you can become so gigantic that it's actually invisible; if you achieve a Taylor Swift level of fame, you are no longer a singular human person; you are invisible energy. You've grazed every corner of the planet reachable to a human person, vibrated through the bones of more masses currently alive than anyone has. You have transcended. And when you have become so much more than a person, just a little old person who drinks beer and has a family and no other greater meaning ascribed to their fleshy meat that will one day turn to dust while your legacy lives on, then those meaty flesh things can't touch you physically, financially, or emotionally. You are dark matter; words cannot hurt you. Except that's not true.

I said earlier that we gave Justin Bieber the "gift" of fame; at the time, we thought it was a blessing. Now we've come to understand fame as more of a beast or a curse, thanks to the numerous public-facing "downfalls" we've witnessed. The portal into the other side has skewed our view of what it means to be a celebrity. I think if you asked Taylor Swift, or Miley Cyrus, or Justin Bieber, or the Jonas Brothers if fame soothed any of their wounds, they'd say emphatically no. Quite the opposite; fame aggravated those wounds, high-lighted their most cavernous insecurities, and twisted the knife.

Similarly, burying myself in an endless scroll of gossip blogs or day-dreaming about being a Famous Actress on *iCarly* didn't actually alleviate any of my pain, it just delayed my dealing with it. When the facade of teen stardom melted away along with my desire to be one of them, what was left was the rot: I was scared and alone. I wanted to be universally adored, freed from financial burdens, extricated from everything I tried desperately not to feel. Dissociating didn't work. It didn't make my parents not bankrupt. It didn't fix what was wrong with my family, or my new deep-seated belief that having *stuff* was what made you successful and happy. It didn't make me fit in with other kids in Mountain Lakes. It didn't make me like myself. It didn't make me any less *me*. That's what I was really looking for: an escape from who I was, a trapdoor I could crawl through to leave my own body, my own self—anything that could make me not *me*, not *this* thing I didn't want to be. I've spent more than a decade examining why I feel this insatiable need for attention and external gratification, to make people laugh, to feel seen and noticed and understood; trying to make sense of why nothing I ever do or say or create feels good enough without a financial reward or widespread appreciation, things I've tied to my own self-worth, which I can't seem to untether. But how can I? Once you tie *anything* to survival, espe-cially in those adolescent years, untangling that knot is tough stuff.

If I could go back in time, alter the course of my own life, and offer advice to my sixteen-year-old self—this wilted person who felt different and othered and helpless, who tried desperately to ascribe meaning to *why* she felt that way, or how she could escape *being* different—I might not want to go to the Ramada Inn at all. Or to get fuck-you famous, despite what every element of ego-escapism culture had been selling me. I wasn't secretly a famous actress. I would've ripped off the Band-Aid. I would've said, "You're not special. You're just gay."

ONE DAY, YOU'LL ALL BE GAY

AS I MENTIONED once before, the word "gay" was actually used as a pejorative until Hilary Duff definitively stopped homophobia in 2008 with a
"Think Before You Speak" PSA. So much has changed since then—fashion,
music, Donald Trump has passed away (just putting this energy out into
the world—maybe by the time this book comes out, it'll be true). Also, pop
culture has done a near-180 with its view of queerness. The tables have
turned; while being associated with queerness used to be scary, now it's
chic as shit. Gay isn't just "okay." Gay is everywhere: We have LGBTQ
elected officials in Congress. We have bisexual pop stars and movie stars,
lauded by journalists, writers, and fans for being out and proud. Even the
largest corporations have special "pride" lines of clothing, merchandise, and
mouthwash, all in the name of (predatorily profiting off a group of people
in a massive reversal of their previously held views now that queerness is
widely regarded as cool) . . . pride! What I'm saying is, you can walk down
the street in any major city and hear a straight woman at brunch, spilling
her strawberry mimosa, shouting, "I wish I was a lesbian—it'd make everything so much EASIER" at anyone who'll hear her. Which like, okay,
lots to unpack there—you know anyone can be gay, right? Like, if you want
to date women, you just . . . can? Also, being gay isn't "easier"—have you
heard of homophobia? But what the brunching straight woman is trying to
signal, above all, is that she knows—like Listerine knows—that being queer,

or even liking queer people, is cool now. Also, ingratiating yourself with a community that's consistently on the forefront of fashion, music, and cultural trendsetting makes you cool too. But obviously this notion that your product or preferences being gayer could actually *add* value to your brand or personality is *very*, very new. And it took a lot of activism, overthrowing of cultural supervillains, and emotional gymnastics to get here.

The 2000s were hell for women and queer people. When I heard about queerness in TV or film, or in music, or in the news, it was mostly centered around the idea of queer speculation: cruel jokes about girls being "dykes" because they played sports (or something), malicious headlines about who was secretly dating who, exploitative girl-on-girl allusions created for gross men to jack off to, bottomless, unenduring quips about women BFFs being "too" intimate together, and their responses ("I'm not a lesbian!"). Unless a woman's queerness was being exploited for male pleasure, which was considered a digestible display of lesbianism, queer people were being speculated about. Being closeted and young in the 2000s felt like a constant tickling of whispers at the back of my neck; the more it compounded, the more it felt like the whispers were wrapping their long, spindly fingers around my throat. If a person was outed, the cloak of normalcy and acceptance that heterosexuality provided would fall. Back then, I saw queerness through this jumbled, mind-fuck, cracked lens. I didn't want anyone to speculate about *me*, and I certainly didn't want them to be right. Because if they were, my cloak would fall, and I'd have to forfeit the acceptance I clung to for a much, much more difficult life.

I tried super fucking hard to think of the one truly gutting, life-altering experience I've had that would "prove" how awful this era was for me. One specific bully or how one TV moment ruined my life forever. But honestly, the 2000s come to mind as a supercut of mini traumas, a slow and painful whittling away of my self-worth, which, in my teenage and college years, was tied to maintaining a facade of this aforementioned normalcy, AKA heterosexuality. I think about being nineteen and a virgin, walking home from class with this girl I was friends with and listening to her talk about a twenty-year-old virgin she'd encountered: "I mean, if she hasn't lost her virginity by now, she *has* to be a lesbian." I'm reminded of a friend from college lambasting me for wearing Steve Madden combat boots—which I'd previously loved, then subsequently despised after they told me: "You look like a lesbian." I think of Perez Hilton drawing a cumshot on Clay Aiken's face, of Bradley Cooper yelling "paging Dr. Faggot" in *The Hangover.* It was all so negative. And then there was Courtney on the Rancho Carne Toros cheerleading squad in *Bring It On,* who calls Missy—in retrospect the only objectively fucking cool Rancho Carne cheerleader—an "uber dyke," like that's anything short of the greatest compliment a girl in a choker necklace can receive. That one hurt.

The *Bring It On* incident—along with the probably forty thousand other "lesbian suspicion" jeers from 2000s movies and TV shows—made quite an impact. Missy, played by aughts-heartthrob Eliza Dushku, is a middle-finger-raising, choker-necklace-wearing, all-black-sporting, literal wallet-chain-donning transfer student and gymnast. She's introduced in a way that's confusing to the average preteen viewer. Because she's presented as the quintessential alt/goth-skewing bad gal, one who both frightens you with her confidence and sexuality and—no, that's it, she frightens you because she's hot. And when Missy shows up late and auditions for the Toros, she blows everyone away with her gymnastics routine (which I think we *all* remember: front handspring step out, round off back handspring step out, round off back handspring, full twisting layout). So Missy is frighteningly hot and extremely good at what she does, but when all is said and done, Courtney, the mean girl, lobbies for her best friend's sister to fill the spot instead, insisting that the team already voted for the aforementioned sister. Then she adds, "Besides, Missy looks like an uber dyke." Hurt by the "mean" comment, Missy grabs her wallet chain and storms out (*clink clank clink clank scratch clunk*). Torrance (Kirsten Dunst), the cheer captain, gives Courtney what-for, but not about calling Missy a dyke. Rather, she only reinforces how good Missy is at tumbling ("Missy's the poo, so take a big whiff"), because throwing around a word like "dyke" was nothing to lose sleep over in the 2000s.

Intent is important here—and bear with me while I psychotically overanalyze a single word from a (near-perfect) 2000s movie. One could argue that the intent behind the "dyke" comment was to illustrate how evil Courtney is, as one of the movie's villains. It accomplished that. But the fact that the word bears no further commentary from the other cheerleaders in the film actually highlights the POV of the movie, rather than that of the characters. The movie's outlook is: *Courtney is evil because she says mean burns like "dyke,"* when it *should've* been *Courtney is evil because being homophobic is wrong*—but Torrance wasn't mad that Courtney was homophobic. She was mad that Courtney would associate someone Torrance liked with something Torrance *knew* was bad: lesbianism. *Bring It On* really captures the casual homophobia of its era: Being a mean girl was worthy of reprimand, but being homophobic was assumed. The movie was released in the year 2000, but I didn't watch it until a few years later, when I was thirteen, at which point I lacked the skills necessary to navigate "portrayals of queerness in media." All my thirteen-year-old doo-doo brain heard was "Don't be gay. Gay bad." When you're a thirteen-year-old girl, is there anything scarier than hearing that everything you find to be relatable or aspirational will lead to being outcast?

That's when the deprogramming began. What was most damaging to my lil' psyche was that the comment forced me to actually distrust my own instincts. My initial instinct aligned with what I *thought* was being spoon-fed to me by the movie's POV, that Missy was *cool*, like actually "too cool for school." So my gut reaction was, "Whoa, that girl fucking rocks. I want to look like that girl and act like that girl. I want to be as cool and confident and hot as Missy is." But then, almost immediately following her introduction and her bomb-ass gymnastics routine, comes the "uber dyke" comment, which tore the rug out from under me and made me think, "Oh, Missy looks *gay* . . . And gay is not just bad, but gay forfeits any sense of normalcy, acceptance, inclusion, and community in the current social climate!!!" I was tricked. So if my instincts told me to *like* Missy's look, but Missy's look was gay, and gay was bad, then what had to change was my instincts, what I found to be cool, what I interpreted to be either relatable or aspirational. I never wanted to give anyone the excuse to humiliate me in front of a cheer squad by calling me gay and sending me running through the door with my wallet chain (*clunk clunk clack click*). I couldn't let anyone *ever* suspect *me* of being gay. What I deduced pretty early on was that a worst-case scenario would be someone scanning me and saying, "Lesbian detected." Because that's how we talked about gay people in the 2000s, like they were straight people's tethers, and any "normal" heterosexual could have a shadow gay self they had to snuff out.

So much of the 2000s were like this, smaller stuff that adds up. There was so much visible lesbianism that appealed to me—more trickery—which subsequently led me to self-correct. And honestly—if Eliza Dushku with a choker necklace and chain wallet isn't *for* lesbians—who was it for??? Well, that's the thing. Visible queerness was okay if it wasn't *for* queer women. One thing that became pretty clear to me was that lesbianism was for men. That's right, lesbians are *for* men. It would be weird for a girl to enjoy lesbianism, that thing that happens between two girls, because if a girl liked the lesbian thing happening in front of her, then one could speculate that she too was a lesbian. But if a man saw a lesbian thing happening in front of him and liked it, that would just mean that he's a big, manly straight guy. (This is not to be confused with: if a man saw a lesbian thing happening in front of him and *didn't* like it, then he himself was gay. Please keep up.)

Earlier I mentioned a lesbian scene from *American Pie 2*, which I both remember vividly and don't remember at all because each time it came on, I would stare so hard at the floor that the floorboards would splinter from the sheer weight of my shame. The four protagonists, all dudes, watch as two women pretend to be lesbians to mess with them. The women undress each other, furtively laughing to each other at how *hilarious* it is that they're pretending to be gay (because being a hot girl who does gay stuff is unbelievable!), while the men stare and sprout boners. It's a truly disgusting scene moralistically—but to me, a young and questioning teen who wanted to know more about what would happen if two hot girls touched each other without laughing—it was, um, triggering. I mean, you have to be truly starved for meaningful queer content to think something like that is anything other than foul—but reader, I was. I was fucking famished.

There's other stuff from the aughts that I'm embarrassed to admit that I was *highly* intrigued by, because it wasn't *for* me. It was for men. I remember when Britney Spears and Madonna kissed at the 2003 VMAs and I basically flatlined. There was the 2000 film *Charlie's Angels* and sequel *Charlie's Angels: Full Throttle*, both of which feature three highly sexed women touching each other gratuitously, only one of which features Cameron Diaz and Demi Moore flirting in bikinis for no clear reason. Katy Perry released "I Kissed a Girl" in 2008, a number one hit about being attracted to girls, which was fucking mind-boggling back then—but it also reduces girl-on-girl attraction to something to do while your boyfriend is away (men, always the main event). There was one, ahem, particularly hot aforementioned *Rolling Stone* cover shoot featuring Blake Lively and Leighton Meester of *Gossip Girl* sucking on each other's fingers, tonguing the same ice cream cone, and doing other stuff that made me shame-stare at the floor. All of these things, which were created for male pleasure or meant to evoke a sense of shock, unintentionally hooked me. In the aughts, I was collateral damage of the scourge of the male gaze. But what choice did I have? For a questioning young girl at this point in time, there wasn't much crossover between digestible queerness (hot, femme, It Girl–looking shit) and the kind of queerness that evokes a public lashing from the in crowd (like Eliza Dushku in a choker with a chain wallet??? Apparently??? Seriously, what the fuck was wrong with all of us, were we INSANE???). Which brings me to not only the most ambitious gay–It Girl crossover event in history but also my supervillain origin story. Of course, I'm talking about Lindsay Lohan. Who the fuck else?

The Cut has a column called I Think About This a Lot, in which different writers reveal a nugget of pop culture that they, well . . . think about a lot. Most times, the topics are obscure, usually inconsequential (example: "I Think About This a Lot: Keri Russell Walking in Stilettos After a Blizzard.") I've only submitted an idea for consideration once, and it was "Paparazzi Photos of Lindsay Lohan and Samantha Ronson Arguing." The editor said no. Upon facing rejection, I ruminated endlessly about this. How could they possibly turn me down? Isn't *everyone* CONSTANTLY thinking about paparazzi photos of Lindsay Lohan and Samantha Ronson, sifting through Google Images and saving them to a meme folder, editing them on photo apps and juxtaposing text over pictures to send out as invites for birthday parties or game nights? I was under the impression that thinking bottomlessly, tirelessly about Lindsay Lohan and Samantha Ronson's late-aughts relationship, memeing them, texting their photos to friends and saying "us," was a shared, universal experience. I was gobsmacked to find out: it is not (but it should be and I stand by this).

In 2008, I was obsessed with Lindsay and Samantha. I was a senior in high school. I was pretending to be sexually attracted to Joe Jonas (or maybe I really was into him—he's pretty lesbian-adjacent). Everyone in my high school called each other "fags" and "dykes" for fun (yes, how "fun").

Lindsay Lohan was THE It Girl. Everyone my age was obsessed with her in that old-school "girls want to be her and guys want to fuck her" type of way. Except that I—and I cannot stress this part enough—wanted to stare at her from across a river and long desperately for her touch.

I had grown up watching Lindsay eat peanut butter and Oreos in *The Parent Trap*, so I ate peanut butter and Oreos. I watched Tyra Banks brush Lindsay's hair in *Life-Size*, so I wanted to brush Lindsay's hair. I saw Lindsay absolutely fuckin' shred with the greatest rock band in history, Pink Slip, in the 2003 reboot of *Freaky Friday*, so I wanted to shred with Pink Slip at Wango Tango. And yes, I saw Lindsay wear army pants and flip-flops in *Mean Girls*, so I bought army pants and flip-flops. I thought Lindsay Lohan was the most talented actor and singer to ever live (Meryl Streep retire bitch). I wanted to be like her, dress like her, and act like her. She was the epitome of cool, largely because she had already been, for a long time, widely lionized as such. Around the 2004 mark, Lindsay was one of those young Hollywood "stars" that was just everywhere—her music frequented *TRL* and MTV, her debut album *Speak* was legitimately successful, she had two popular movies come out in one year (*Confessions of a Teenage Drama Queen* and *Mean Girls*), she won numerous MTV awards—she occupied every space that a teen megastar possibly could in the mid-aughts. And a huge part of her ubiquity was that she was ravenously exploited by tabloid media. A few years later, between 2007 and 2009, while witnessing and nearly rooting for the demise of Britney Spears, the photographers and bloggers also became obsessed with Lindsay, as if she were some second coming of the innocent Disney-star-turned-disaster. By now, of course, we know that both women should've just been afforded empathy and help.

But in the midst of all this chaos, rumors (lol, "Rumors," great song) were drummed up about Lindsay, the apple of my teenage eye, forming a Sapphic bond with some DJ in Los Angeles. My reality tore at the seams like low-rise jeans ill equipped to house a normal human body. It was the first time I can remember seeing queer women on a world platform—and not just queer women but ones who were young and cool and famous in that Hollywood, tabloid-darling, teen-star-adjacent way that I, personally, cared about. It was earth-shattering and mind-bending and hot. I genuinely remember thinking: *Girls can kiss . . . each other?!?!?! For their OWN PLEA-SURE?!?!?* Lindsay Lohan was the official Trojan horse of female queerness. We loved her so much and for so long, and then, when no one was looking, BAM, she hit us with That Gay Shit.

As I look back on everything Lindsay and Samantha, I realize there's so much that I've either purposefully or subconsciously redacted from my memory. I remember living for their paparazzi photos, but I don't remember most of what actually transpired between the couple, or the extent to which they were terrorized by the media. In fact, as much as I know they were mistreated by gossip bloggers, my inner narrative about Lindsay and Samantha is actually quite revisionist. So I did some digging. Here's what I found.

Because of my tunnel vision for Lindsay, and my newfound obsession/ spiral/realization that queer women could also be femme, I never took time to look into Samantha, or what that whole media tornado was like for her. I mostly just remember the speculation surrounding Lindsay's sexuality, and how that affected my relationship to my own. But it was so much worse than I remembered, and the speculation around Lindsay transpired in truly horrific, homophobic lashes that really came crashing down on Samantha— the one who was visibly queer in a way that wasn't considered digestible at the time.

Here's the gist: Samantha Ronson is Mark Ronson's younger sister. Before Ronson was a DJ, she released a few songs as an artist. You know that song from *Mean Girls* that everyone slow-dances to at prom? ("And I wonder, if I'm just . . . *built this way*.") That song, "Built This Way," is the cornerstone of the movie's soundtrack, and is also written and performed by . . . Samantha Ronson! Okay, these are just fun facts. On to the real stuff.

In 2007, Lindsay Lohan crashed her car into some shrubbery in Beverly Hills. Pop culture fans may remember this as being the most notable of Lindsay's incidents during her slurry late-2000s romp with addiction. It was so significant that if you take one of those cheesy TMZ bus tours through Los Angeles, they actually stop on the corner of Sunset Boulevard and Foothill Road and say, "This is where Lindsay Lohan crashed her car in 2007." I know this, because I'm garbage, and have taken that bus tour more than once. (FYI: The TMZ tour can be a very dark two hours—the tour guide is often some actor working out their trauma through a microphone on a bus full of tourists. Don't do it.) Anyway, during the investigation of the crash, where Lohan left her Mercedes abandoned on Sunset, police found cocaine in the car. They assumed it was hers, but didn't have evidence to support that claim.

This was a time when blind items boomed and gossip blogs gnawed on celebrities' flaws like vultures in an arid desert. It was the peak of Perez Hilton's unique reign in Hollywood; A-listers (at the time) like Lady Gaga and Katy Perry befriended Perez, and he subsequently painted them in a positive light on his blog. Other celebrities, mostly B–Z listers, were reduced to harsh nicknames, their images used as templates for Perez to doodle penises and cumshots on. And queer people had targets on the backs of their heads. If we're going to talk about anything gay in the 2000s, we have to talk about Perez Hilton, who got heavily involved in the aftermath of Lohan's Sunset and Foothill crash.

If you're unfamiliar with Perez, here's who he is . . . was . . . is? He's still technically living, but I'm 90 percent sure he's being kept alive by drinking twink blood, like Voldemort stayed half-alive by drinking unicorn blood. Anyway, Perez Hilton's supervillain origin story: His real name is Mario Armando Lavandeira Jr. He's a Miami native who attended NYU on scholarship for acting. After graduating college in 2000, he tried out being an actor, then briefly worked in media relations at GLAAD (the Gay and Lesbian

Alliance Against Defamation, an LGBTQ media organization that monitors representations of queer people in film and TV). He became a freelance writer, then an editor, and then got into blogging—a new fad that was taking the world by shitstorm—where he pushed the exact opposite agenda from GLAAD, pivoting from encouraging positive representations of LGBTQ people in media to purposefully outing gay men and women in Hollywood and exploiting their sexualities. Yes, you read that right: Perez Hilton, a gay man, made it his mission to out famous gay people.

Hilton speculated ad nauseam about celebrities like Lance Bass and Neil Patrick Harris before they came out. A 2006 *Los Angeles Times* article called Hilton "a one-man celebrity outing operation, doing his best to uncloset as many gay celebrities as he can, because, as he sees it, they have forfeited their right to privacy on that point." Perez told the outlet, "In American culture, a lot of people still think that being gay is bad, and that being gay will hurt your career. I generally don't think that." He added *why* he wanted to out famous people: "I am not some safe, cookie cutter, queer-eye-for-the-straight-guy homo. I am dangerous. I am gonna push the envelope. I am gonna be who I am: a loud, gay Latino that has opinions and in my own way, subserviently, I am trying to make the world a better place." That logic, that more representation in Hollywood would engender a normalization of queerness, may have actually tracked for some, but it didn't for me, because outing people before they're ready is dangerous. Outing—essentially revealing someone's identity before they're ready to do so themselves—has been linked to suicide among LGBTQ people. And with homelessness and violence disproportionately affecting LGBTQ youth, outing someone before they're ready isn't just damaging to their own mental health but can endanger them in their own homes or communities.

But the 2000s were, um, unique. In 2006, USC professor Larry Gross told the *L.A. Times* that, in this new age, bloggers actually *wanted* to be first to out a celebrity, as opposed to the '90s, when no media outlet wanted to take credit for such bad-faith news items. "In the previous round of outing in the early '90s, everybody wanted to be first to be second," Gross said. "No one wanted to take the heat for starting it, but the blog phenomenon has changed that by lowering the threshold to the point that other media can't avoid it. What we are now seeing is Outing 2.0."

In that same article, Hilton takes credit for Lance Bass coming out on the cover of *People*, that now-infamous "I'm Gay" cover story released in July 2006. Perez insisted that had he not been writing about Bass's sexuality since 2005, Bass wouldn't have been relevant enough to nail a *People* cover. "I don't want to sound full of myself, but if I had not been talking about Lance Bass as much as I was before he came out, there is no way he would have gotten the cover of *People* magazine," Perez said. "He would have gone about it the traditional way, coming out on the cover of the *Advocate*, which is read by 70,000 people instead of the 3.4 million who read *People* every week. So I offered him this silver platter, you could say." It's sickening to hear how Perez talks about his own speculation about Bass, which seemed to come from this place of malice and anger and revenge, as if it's a point of pride. Like, outing Lance Bass—despite what consequences Bass might face for being outed— is something he's proud of, that inflates his ego. Lance Bass was still a person—a person whose cloak of normalcy would fall once the still-homophobic public knew the truth about him—but Perez used Bass's celebrity as a justification to speculate about his sexuality. As in, he's a public figure, and we, the public, deserve to know his truth. And on top of all of that, Perez uses his own queerness as another justification for such. He's gay, and he wants queerness to be normalized and pervasive, so he's allowed to speculate—right? Again, intent is important here, and while Perez insists that, in his supervillain mind, he was doing this for the greater good, he didn't exactly do it with any grace, respect, or pure intentions. Just in case you thought Perez didn't know *exactly* what he was doing, that his malicious outing mission wasn't totally calculated, there's this: In 2006, Hilton told

Access Hollywood, "I know there is some controversy about outing people, but I also believe the only way we're gonna have change is with visibility, and if I have to drag some people screaming out of the closet, then I will."

Like I said. As I see it, this is a supervillain origin story. Perez was basically like, "If I have to be judged and scoffed at for being gay, then ALL OF YOU DO!" Which, in some fucked-up, radioactive repression blast shame-stare-at-the-floor-for-too-long way, I almost understand and can empathize with. I mean, it's always been my personal villain fantasy to stand on the ledge of a skyscraper in a black latex bodysuit and bellow, "One day, you'll ALL BE GAY" as thunder booms and a zeppelin drops toxic yellow powder over a city, turning everyone gay. Being queer is HARD. Enduring homophobia SUCKS ASS. Perez Hilton is a person who felt the harmful reverberations of homophobic media himself. He appears to have turned his own anger at the world and self-loathing into a profitable website that trafficked in celebrity sexuality; he understood the nature of shock-value media and weaponized it. And for a while, he was rewarded for this behavior, achieving the fame he desired: VH1 picked up a talk show hosted by Perez; *GQ* published a four-page spread on him; he made a slew of TV appearances on *MADtv, TRL*, a weekly guest-hosting gig on *Extra*, and even went on to cameo on kids' and teen shows like Nickelodeon's *Victorious* and *Glee*. This era of ambient homophobia allowed a person like Perez to thrive, because in a way, he was digestibly queer—after all, he was advancing the homophobic agenda: outing people.

Hilton was, eventually, heavily criticized for his schoolyard-bully tactics. In 2010, he appeared on *Ellen* to announce that he'd be changing the tone of his blog, wanting to encourage more positivity, in an attempt to bring awareness to teen suicide and gay bullying. But the "new" Perez didn't last. Shortly after his faux come-to-Jesus moment, he hopped right back on his bullshit and continued gossiping and nicknaming and outing. Even in this day and age, when it's—for the most part—okay to be publicly gay, even common and *cool* to be gay, Perez is still speculating and leaking. As recently as 2016, he outed Fifth Harmony band member Lauren Jauregui by posting private photographs of her kissing a rumored girlfriend in a photo booth. Like Lance Bass and Neil Patrick Harris and all the public-facing queer people who came before her, she came out as queer shortly after—but it wasn't on her terms. However, things are so much different now. Fans of Fifth Harmony and queer writers lambasted Hilton for participating in something as archaic as outing a person, and supported her for being queer. All of this showed how truly out of touch he was and continues to be, and luckily, the LGBTQ community and its allies have no tolerance for such nonsense anymore.

As depraved as the plight of Perez was, it wasn't being outed that scared me about queerness; I didn't necessarily know I was gay in the late aughts, so I wasn't yet afraid of being *outed*, so to speak. What got to me, personally, and probably millions of other kids and teens who grew up in the 2000s, was the harmful language Perez used to discuss queerness, despite being gay himself. He called Lance Bass "Princess Frosty Locks." He called Clay Aiken "Clay Gay-kin" before the *American Idol* star-turned-politician came out. He called Lindsay Lohan "LezLo" once she began dating Samantha Ronson, and he called Ronson "lezbot" and "SaMANtha," criticizing her gender presentation. Perez wasn't *only* mean to queer people—he also called Mischa Barton "Mushy Farton," which, upon writing this, I'm ashamed to say I tittered at—but the damage he did to queer celebs, and all the people who were reading his words, was immense. He nurtured and profited off of a nasty public interest in speculating about queerness, or exploiting it to be consumed by straight men. So, in 2007, when Lindsay Lohan, who was already embroiled in this sexy and tumultuous relationship with Ronson, crashed her car, Perez cracked his knuckles and got to work.

Hilton reported that the cocaine found in Lohan's car was Samantha Ronson's, relying on a "source" cited on another gossip blog, *Celebrity Babylon*. To make matters worse, he cashed in on Lohan's battle with addiction and Ronson's sexuality and began selling T-shirts that read BLAME SAMANTHA. Ronson was painted as a predacious bad influence on the vulnerable Lohan.

Besides the obviously harmful insinuation that Samantha was a "predatory lesbian," a common trope, the conflation of lesbianism with mental illness and addiction was hurtful. Similar to its portrayal in *Bring It On*, there was this insistence that queerness was so "other" that it existed on the outskirts of accepted behaviors, like being an addict or a Mentally Ill (also bad in the 2000s). I remember doing the math in my head: if Lindsay struggles with her mental health and suffers from addiction, and she's dating a woman, that must mean that the crazies and junkies are the people who end up being queer. In a way, this made lesbianism into an illness itself, turning it into something I had to fight and could *beat*, like it was this dark force I was meant to fend off the same way addicts fight urges to use. I remember thinking: *I'm a good student. I come from a great family. I have a bright future ahead of me. I don't use drugs. My mental health is fine. I'm not some weak-minded chump, able to be indoctrinated by lesbianism. I won't fall victim to the evils of Samantha Ronson like Lindsay Lohan did. I can fight this.* That's a terrible way to feel about myself, like there was a part of me I needed to *kill*. But that's what it looked like to me. I didn't want to be jeered at by a room full of hot cheerleaders. I didn't want some widely disseminated nickname meant to evoke shame, like LezJill. I didn't want to crash my car at the corner of Sunset and Foothill because my "evil" lesbian lover made me do it. I didn't want to be speculated about, or to suffer any of the repercussions of actually being gay. And I didn't want people to be right that I was a lesbian, because the ambient homophobia of the 2000s proved to me time and time again that being gay wouldn't go over well. It was easier to kill that part of me and continue to fit in.

And Samantha Ronson suffered real repercussions due to Perez's decision to villainize her, huge financial ones, in addition to, you know, severe emotional trauma and a battered reputation. She sued him for defamation, only to lose and be ordered to pay Hilton's legal fees, $85,000(!!!). So over the course of 2007, Ronson's sexuality was preyed upon and denigrated by bloggers like Perez, then Perez launched a "blame Samantha" campaign against her, and Ronson ended up losing $85,000, all because a blogger stained her image as the "lezbot" responsible for Lindsay Lohan's collapse. I don't believe Perez Hilton's intent was to benefit anyone but himself, and his actions—both the speculative and the overt—caused real-life consequences for Ronson, who seemed to bear the brunt of the homophobia surrounding her and Lindsay's relationship.

When I'm asked the question "What radicalized you?" and jokingly respond "Lindsay Lohan," I'm not *totally* kidding. The whole narrative surrounding Lindsay, Samantha, and Perez was painful both to endure as a teenager and to revisit with an adult eye. There was so much hurtful speculation in media—whether it was "uber dyke" jokes in *Bring It On* or circulated nicknames like LezLo and SaMANtha—that I internalized, which absolutely curdled my sense of self and distorted what I valued in myself and others. What's also challenging to examine is the role that I, a once-vulnerable kid who grew up to write about pop culture, have played and continue to play in the queer speculation space. Those kinds of vulnerable kids, at least in superhero origin story movies, could either turn out to be super . . . or quite evil.

Things are much different today. Because so many celebrities *are* loudly and proudly out, the way we speak about queer celebrities has shifted. Well, again, it's a bit of a chicken-or-the-egg situation—has the conversation around LGBTQ people swung more positive because more celebrities are out, therefore normalizing queerness? Or are more celebrities out because queerness has become more normalized, accepted, or even valued? I'd posit mostly the former, but it's certainly a push-pull between Famouses, Normals, and the pervasiveness of queerness. Regardless—the conversation has shifted. I wouldn't necessarily say there's less of an urge to speculate about who's gay and who's not. But rather, there's been a huge pendulum swing toward *who* is doing the speculating and *why.*

There's a reason Perez Hilton isn't popular anymore. Ultimately, I don't believe he helped or accomplished what he thought he was accomplishing. He put more hurt, more anger, and more vitriol into the conversation. The tides of acceptance didn't change because Perez Hilton pushed a few people out of the closet. Would I have known Lindsay Lohan, my fave at the time, was queer if not for him? Probably at some point. But yeah, he did popularize that narrative. I guess it really always comes down to intent, and *how* conversations like that are handled: had Lindsay Lohan's queerness not been painted as scandalous, shocking, or something a "wild child" or a person who was fucked-up would do, then I also probably wouldn't have been so fucked-up about my own sexuality. The way we talk about sexuality matters. Intent matters, as does the culture a conversation like that exists within. That's why the way that we gossip has changed, because, as a culture, our tolerance for bullying queer people has diminished. In the 2000s, bullying *was* the culture. People were bullied for anything and everything that strayed from the skinny, white, Christian, heterosexual path—all of which was painted as "normal." Being fat, Black, gay, brown, too prude, too slutty, poor—it was all reason to be ostracized, to be othered. So many people suffered an absolutely baffling amount of tolerated cruelty within their own communities and in the media they were consuming. Finally, someone had to say *enough.* And that person was Ellen DeGeneres (I'm kidding omg I'm kidding).

As a teenager, I participated *heavily* in the gossip blog boom, reading sites like *Perez Hilton* and *OceanUp* compulsively, refreshing the pages dozens of times per day. I was a millennial born in the internet generation, and

I wanted real people, young people, to feed me stories about people like me. I didn't necessarily want to watch sex tapes, per se, but I genuinely *craved* the overly personal, the leaked photos of Miley Cyrus ripping bong, the TMZ footage of Lindsay Lohan stumbling home, the blind items about who was dating who. I wanted fan videos submitted to bloggers of celebrities holding hands, kissing, smoking weed, acting like my friends and I did, messing up, being human. The 2000s was when the veil of glamour, of traditional "celebrity" as we knew it, was pulled away. Social media, digital cameras, cell phone cameras, blogs, and forums created this underground-feeling network, a teenage dark web, where teens could trade overheard information about celebrities, and celebrities were no longer confined to the fuzzy screens in our living rooms.

What I'm getting at is, I was the type of person that 2000s media preyed on, someone who wanted—no, *needed*—stories about celebrities' personal lives and was too young to understand that it was wrong to consume or disseminate certain kinds of information. I was vulnerable, thirsty, curious, and closeted; Perez Hilton pulled back his arrow, aimed directly for me, and hit the bull's-eye.

One might think that a person like me, having lived through the predatory blogosphere boom and reaped the traumatic consequences of such, would move *swiftly* away from invasions of privacy, musing about celebrities' sexualities and sex lives. To do so publicly would feel amoral to a person like me, one might surmise. One would be, well, wrong.

From 2019 to 2020, I covered Taylor Swift's album releases, music video releases, and documentary release for *Vulture*. That entailed listening to each song, watching all of her content, and decoding the clues and Easter eggs she left behind for her fans to collect and exchange and hypothesize about. There is a very popular fan theory within the Swiftie fandom—one that's *very* polarizing, causing a stark divide between the stan factions— that Taylor Swift is secretly queer. I could take you through the whole history, but truly, you should just go to Tumblr for the full manifesto—there's way too many screenshots to squeeze into the pages of a book. The whole thing looks like a Carrie Mathison–esque detective wall strung together with red yarn. And also, I'm scared to release my own diatribe on this. Like I said, these are polarizing fan theories—the Swifties who hate that other Swifties speculate have sought vengeance on queer fans by outing them to friends and family. Swifties, in general, are terrifying. When *Pitchfork* reviewed *folklore*, Swift's eighth studio album, and gave it a score of 8.0/10, certain Swifties doxed the writer, disseminating her address and threatening to harm her. I don't want this—I have been through *enough*. Once the FBI shows up at your door and asks if you have any intent to kill a U.S. senator, doing things like writing contentious lesbian pop star theories about a celebrity whose fans crave blood just doesn't feel . . . worth it. I've been trolled on social media by actual Nazis, I've been the target of an organized campaign that landed feds on my doorstep, and trust me when I say: nothing fluffs me more than a Taylor Swift superfan tweeting me "Aren't you like 40? Mind your business."

That said, here's the gist of the "Gaylor" fan theory, and boomers, plug your ears—this is going to sound like gibberish. There's a faction of Swifties called Kaylors—a portmanteau of Taylor and Karlie—who believe that Taylor Swift and her ex-best-friend Karlie Kloss were actually romantically involved. There are other lesbian conspiracy theories about Swift and her former best friends who were secretly her girlfriends, like *Glee* actress Dianna Agron (see: the Swiftgron faction), but the Karlie Kloss theory is the most famous. In my opinion, the smoking gun of the Kaylor fan theory is a 2015 video, taken by a fan, of Swift and Kloss kissing (allegedly) on a balcony at a The 1975 concert. Again, look it up, judge for yourself. All you need to know is that the footage exists, as do dozens of lyrics that fans believe point to Swift's relationship with Kloss.

The other thing you need to know is that I am a Kaylor. And I'm not just a Kaylor. I'm basically a professional Kaylor, paid by *Vulture* to go over Taylor's songs and videos with a fine-tooth comb and cull any evidence that may point to a former romantic relationship with Karlie Kloss. The articles I wrote about Swift's three album releases in 2019 and 2020, *Lover, folklore,* and *evermore,* proved wildly popular, both on *Vulture* and on social media. During the three album releases, I spent days poring over the "evidence" and theories, trading observations with fellow Kaylors, Gaylors, and Swifties, writing about it, then continuing to tweet and share more theories, no matter how ridiculous, not for a paycheck but for my own personal amusement. I did this because I found community. Because I was intrigued. Because it was fun. That all sounds, uh, kinda bad after the past fifteen pages I wrote about Perez Hilton's sinister pursuit of outing Lindsay Lohan.

Maybe it is bad. My fear is that it is. Having lived through the absolute terrors of the 2000s, having witnessed the real, dangerous consequences that can come from speculating about queerness, having felt the emotional repercussions of such myself, I somehow basically became Q of QAnon for Taylor Swift fans ten years later. There I was, in my black latex catsuit, arms akimbo on a skyscraper, leading the charge in disseminating unproven theories about a pop star's sex life, stirring the pot in giant, windmill sloshes. Did I choose being evil over being super? What if I'm the Joker? What if I walked along Perez Hilton's path to becoming a supervillain, becoming radicalized in the same way, making the incisive observations like "We live in a society." I'm joking, of course, to cover the real fear that I've become the villain I never wanted to be. Admittedly, I *have* gained a larger following and been given more work from *Vulture* because of the popularity of my Taylor articles. Am I him? Am I??

Being realistic about the effects of speculation matters. Perez knew that outing Lance Bass or launching his "blame Samantha" campaign would drop these stars into the fiery, mean-spirited pits of the culture wars (which they did). Conversely, if Taylor Swift—or any of the celebrities who are widely speculated about today, like Harry Styles or Shawn Mendes—came out as queer, she'd be praised voraciously by her fans for being out and queer.

And again, intent also matters. The truth is, speculation is still burgeoning as a pastime of many queer fans. I'm not saying it's right. I'm just saying it happens. But as a person who's seen the bitterness this phenomenon used to be steeped in, I've noticed a shift in the reason *why* people speculate. The way I see it, people like Perez felt aggrieved by the lack of visibility queer people had in Hollywood, and set out to out others for their own personal agendas (or in Perez's supervillain mind, for the good of humanity). I—and other obnoxious gay stans—feel excited by the possibility of Swift, arguably the biggest pop star in the world, being *alien voice* *one of us*. I've always been enthralled by these fan theories because I was fucking ecstatic that Taylor Swift, who I'd grown up listening to and stanning despite not being able to *truly* relate to her once deeply heteronormative lyrics, might actually be more relatable to me than in my, dare I say, wildest dreams.

For queer people, there's something special about finding another queer person. And we do—we find each other, don't we? "Gaydar" feels like a term invented by a straight woman for the sole purpose of outing closeted men, but there's an underlying and universal purpose to the concept of gaydar. It's finding your pack; it's survival. Queer people have never, ever—even now, when so much about the world is objectively better than it used to be—been able to live our lives as freely and openly and spectacularly as straight people have. We've always had to find each other, in dark corners of gay bars, in back alleys, in niche Tumblr fandoms, to survive. It's simply human nature to find those who are like you, to gravitate toward them, to stick together and find power in numbers. Sorry to get all deep and emotional about fucking Karlie Kloss—who, let's all remember, is married to Jared Kushner's brother—but I'm being completely sincere when I say this: Lesbian conspiracy theories exist today *not* with the malicious purpose of outing a person for personal gain or profit, or against their will for the "greater good," but because queer women still aren't embraced everywhere! It would still be a huge deal if the biggest pop star in the world said, "I'm gay." It would be so validating to know that, to feel that closeness to my favorite artist—because it feels that way when any queer person comes out to you, another queer person. So, yeah, it'd be *sweet* if Taylor Swift was *alien voice* *one of us*. But it's not on my agenda, like it was on Perez's, to out her, because I know the real harm that causes, and because I have—what's that thing called when you—oh yeah, empathy!

There's so much queer speculation out there about other pop stars. But when it comes from queer people—queer people who don't have any agenda other than to find community—does it matter? Fans who "want" Taylor Swift—or whoever they're stanning—to be gay aren't doing it to cause harm. Or to make any dangerous conflations between queerness and, say, mental illness, drug abuse, coercion, or being a "bad girl." These are fans of their favorite musicians—whether they're public, deranged, verified-on-Twitter magazine writers like me, or closeted fourteen-year-olds hiding behind Taylor Swift avatars so their classmates don't uncover their feverish gay tweets—hoping and praying and manifesting visibility and relatability. These are *not* bullies trying to find out if someone at school is gay so they can tell everyone and ruin their lives. Speculation and outing used to be about *that*, coming from a sour, venomous place. I want Taylor Swift to be gay because I want to be able to give more of myself to her. I do believe that Perez wanted people to be gay so he could slither back into the sea with another chest of doubloons, and that the harm he caused to Lance Bass, Samantha Ronson, and people like me was unforgiveable. But I can also understand that he himself might have felt wounded and afraid as one of the sole out gay public figures at the time. Maybe he too wanted to be less alone in the world, even if achieving that meant creating chaos in innocent bystanders' lives.

I fear I did that thing people are always warning each other about in superhero movies: "You either die a hero, or live long enough to see yourself become the villain." I'm afraid of that, that I've crossed lines I swore I wouldn't cross, caused harm to people I insisted I wasn't negatively affecting, become the villain of my worst nightmares. I hope that's not true; I hope that the energy I hock into the universe is positive and lighthearted and humorous. But it's difficult for me, having suffered through the malicious aughts, having participated in queer speculation anyway, to say definitively what's right, wrong, or just a genuine expression of the human desire to connect, to feel community, to feel close to those I admire so dearly.

So here I am, at my wall of red yarn, praying that Taylor Swift is singing about some new hot girlfriend that *isn't* married into the worst First Family in modern history, insisting that writing music in the woods, crying near lakes, dressing in thick cardigans and plaid coats is just so, so Sapphic. Saying you're too much but also not enough? Gushing over Lorde and writing pretty intense fanfic about Haim?? Queer women are Taylor's true energetic matches—and I say that from a place of utmost respect, not with any kind of secret agenda. It's okay to be gay. And if she's not, that's okay too. Because one day—*lightning cracks*—you'll ALL BE GAY!!!

THE TEN MOST IMPORTANT SAPPHIC PAPARAZZI PHOTOS IN MODERN HISTORY

AS A TEENAGER I didn't know shit about relationships. I was young and repressed, and in my real life I had nothing to latch on to emotionally or sexually. But I didn't need to. Luckily, everything I needed to quench my thirst was in the checkout line at CVS. Stacks and stacks of glossy photos of celebs doing everything I could ever hope or dream of doing. All I had to do was tell my grandma I loved doing the crosswords in the back of *People* magazine, and voilà, a subscription was delivered to my doorstep. I was rich—rich with photos of couples dining al fresco, exiting nightclubs, spilling in and out of black cars. This is where I learned everything I needed to know about dating and romance. As I understood it, there were a few things that every legitimate couple did together:

A) "Cozy up in Miami." Couples are always cozying up in Miami. When I was fourteen, I felt called to South Beach, spiritually. I just knew that, though I was young, I would soon need to make the great migration to Miami, where every couple inevitably trekked in order to "get hot and heavy." But "canoodling" wasn't the *only* thing to do in Miami as a couple. One could also smoke cigarettes behind a DJ booth; wear a fedora and vest while Lindsay Lohan danced on you; argue near a dumpster. But still, cozying up in Miami was an absolute *must* for happy couples.

B) "Leave LAX." The most successful couples in the world were always photographed "leaving LAX" together. Just off a tiring flight, their faces obstructed by bulky sunglasses, chins buried in scarves, bundled up in expensive sweatpants, celebrities loved spending quality time by leaving LAX. I always hoped that one day, I would grow up, find someone to join a "rumored couple" with, and leave LAX hand in hand.

C) "Kiss courtside." There are some romantic experiences that are absolutely essential in reaching romantic nirvana. At the very top of the pyramid is kissing courtside at a Lakers game. Show me one happy couple who hasn't kissed courtside—you can't. If you and your partner hope to canoodle much longer, then you'd better get your asses to Staples Center and kiss.

But in all my experience as a consumer of true romance, I never really saw *me* in the checkout line at CVS, you know? I mean, cozying up in Miami, leaving LAX, and kissing courtside were all on my love bucket list, but they were somewhat unreachable to me, as a lesbian consumer of gossip magazines. I was raised on paparazzi photos, and came to love all the classics: Jennifer Lopez giving Ben Affleck a lap dance on a yacht. Zac Efron motorboating Vanessa Hudgens in Turks and Caicos. Justin Bieber straddling Selena Gomez on a Jet Ski. Even the celebrities going through tough times were represented: Nicole Kidman jumping for joy leaving divorce court. Kirsten Dunst eating salad while Jake Gyllenhaal glares at her. Lindsay Lohan, Britney Spears, and Paris Hilton driving a car in West Hollywood (this one isn't romantic per se, but . . . in the art sense . . . isn't it?).

Still, I craved something more. I mean, let's face it: paparazzi photos are essential queer viewing, because when you're repressed, isolated, and a frequent customer at CVS, all you have is living vicariously through others' sex-filled lives. But lucky for us, within the past decade or two, some pioneering queer women have dared to go where no LGBTQ had gone before. Cozying up in Miami, leaving LAX, and kissing courtside were suddenly no longer experiences exclusive to heterosexuality. What's better: these women redefined what it means to be in love and to have it all papped.

Someone has to do the brave and essential work of recording these images for posterity. Please stop begging (no one is begging), I'll do it. Stop clapping (no one is clapping), I'm not a hero. Sit down (no one has stood up), someone has to do the work. These are the most important Sapphic paparazzi photos in modern history.

CARA DELEVINGNE AND
MICHELLE RODRIGUEZ VAPING

If there's one thing I've learned, it's that straight couples sit courtside at Lakers games; lesbian couples sit courtside at Knicks games. In 2014, model Cara Delevingne and Fast & Furious actress Michelle Rodriguez shut down *TMZ* with a photo set of the duo at Madison Square Garden kissing, drinking, yelling, and vaping. In their tenure as a celesbian couple, these women performed all kinds of romantic feats for the paparazzi: making out topless in the ocean in Cancún, entering and exiting airports, and, of course, sloppily making out at a basketball game. When I saw this photo set in 2014, I realized that queer female couples don't have to behave like their heterosexual predecessors who were photographed courtside did. Many people don't know this, but each time a lesbian or bisexual woman blows hoops or wisps of vape smoke into the air, a space is queered. What this couple and this paparazzi photo did for queer women who vape . . . cannot be understated. Marla Grayson in *I Care a Lot* has these two to thank for the freedom she enjoys to vape while being a lesbian.

MILEY CYRUS SPOTTED KISSING
KAITLYNN CARTER ON A YACHT IN ITALY

I had no idea the summer of 2019 would be a summer we'd *never* forget. In August, Miley Cyrus vacationed in Lake Como with Kaitlynn Carter, who media outlets referred to as "Brody Jenner's ex," but is also a person. The tanned duo was photographed getting "hot and heavy" (kissing beneath the shade of well-placed sun hats) on a yacht. They didn't last long—which was surprising, given that kissing beneath sun hats on a yacht in Lake Como is something that *every* happy and successful lesbian couple does. Cyrus and Carter broke up soon after, but not before doing some cute coupley things, like posting together on Instagram, making out at West Hollywood's Soho House (according to Page Six), and holding hands backstage at the VMAs.

QUEEN LATIFAH LIES ON GROUND
TO CAPTURE CONTENT FOR HER GIRLFRIEND

Straight people who love Barack Obama know that there's no higher honor than being an "Instagram Husband" or, rather, performing the sacred duty of capturing content for your significant other. In 2015, on a trip to Brazil with her longtime partner, Eboni Nichols, Queen Latifah fulfilled her role in simping for her girlfriend and lay down on the ground to take cute pics of Eboni with the Christ the Redeemer statue. In queer culture, there are numerous kinds of relationship dynamics that couples might adhere to: tops and bottoms, subs and doms, blondes and brunettes (according to white lesbian period pieces). Here, Queen Latifah shows that there are other, more nuanced ways to have a sexy-couple dynamic. My question for straight people is this: If you're part of a couple, then which one of you poses for hot content, and which one of you lies on the ground to capture the hot content?

GILLIAN ANDERSON AND MEGAN FOX WALKING

Gillian Anderson isn't necessarily known for publicly dating women, though she has spoken openly about being bisexual. Most importantly, the *X-Files* "starlet" has been known to walk near other noted bisexuals, like Megan Fox. In 2007, Gillian Anderson and Megan Fox were photographed holding hands on the set of the movie *How to Lose Friends & Alienate People*. Anderson was wearing a busty blue dress, Fox, a low-cut lavender one. Not much else is known about these photos other than some fanfic I found on social media. Still, to hold hands and be photographed with Gillian Anderson or Megan Fox is everything any queer woman with dreams of being in a "rumored couple" could hope for.

GILLIAN ANDERSON WALKING WITH
ELLEN DEGENERES AND ALEXANDRA HEDISON

Gillian Anderson loves a stroll. The *Sex Education* seductress was once photographed walking with Ellen DeGeneres and Alexandra Hedison. If you don't know who Alexandra Hedison is, she was basically the St. Vincent of the aughts, in that she dated numerous famous women like DeGeneres and Jodie Foster, who she's now married to. Just a quick social studies lesson for you (I'm kind of a history buff). Anyway, on this fated night in the '90s, Gillian, Ellen, and Alexandra all wore jackets: Anderson is pictured wearing a shaggy, striped blue jacket, car keys in hand, absolutely beaming. DeGeneres sports a leather varsity-style jacket, Hedison, a brown denim one. The origins of this photo remain somewhat unclear. But what's become quite clear to me is that being photographed walking near Gillian Anderson is something that every queer woman does at some point or another. Gillian Anderson walking and wearing jackets with Ellen DeGeneres and Alexandra Hedison is a cultural touchstone of modern lesbian history. Upon gazing at the photograph, we are forced to put ourselves in their shoes and ask. What's the move tonight? Where's my car? Which one of us will marry Jodie Foster?

CARA DELEVINGNE AND ST. VINCENT
SQUIRT PAPARAZZI WITH WATER GUNS

While straight couples were stuck in South Beach or Cancún, Cara Delevingne and rock star St. Vincent were busy queering the phrase "wet and wild." In 2015, while leaving the *Love* Christmas party in London, the since-split couple squirted photographers waiting outside with Super Soakers. In her tenure as a bisexual dykecon, Delevingne has transformed what it means to be public-facing and horny. Sorry for saying "Cara Delevingne," "St. Vincent," "squirted," and "Super Soakers" in such close succession.

LINDSAY LOHAN AND SAMANTHA RONSON POSE FOR A PHOTO AT FASHION WEEK

Sometimes, just taking up space in a historically heterosexual narrative is bold and landmark. Especially in 2008. When Lindsay Lohan and DJ and producer Samantha Ronson began dating in the late 2000s, they transformed the landscape of gossip media simply by existing as straight couples do. The couple was photographed performing all of the classics: arguing in an alley outside a nightclub, turning up the heat in Mexico, stealing a smooch in Miami. But of all the truly artful paparazzi snaps this duo nabbed together, my favorite was an image taken of them posing for a photo at Ronson's sister's New York Fashion Week event. It was a major "public outing" for the two women, who were once just a "rumored couple," but now a bona fide "item." This photo is an image of glamour in 2008: the camera's view partially obstructed by other cameras clamoring for attention, Lohan's searing red-carpet gaze, Ronson's harrowing oversize leather vest. Nothing is sexier, gayer, or more 2008 than this single paparazzi photo. Standing lesbian ovation.

JANELLE MONÁE AND LUPITA NYONG'O GRINDING AT MET GALA AFTER-PARTY

Not since Cara Delevingne's tear through young Hollywood has celesbianism seen such immaculate inner-circle drama. This is the only photo on my list that isn't *technically* a paparazzi photograph, but the duo was still, in the broader sense of the word, "papped" by someone. In 2019, after the Met Gala, Janelle Monáe was photographed grinding with and getting "rather chummy" with Lupita Nyong'o. Some things you should know (and full disclaimer that none of the women involved have ever commented on this, so it's all speculation—though it's been adopted by Lesbian Twitter as a fan-fave "dyke drama" moment): Between 2015 and 2019, Janelle Monáe allegedly dated Tessa Thompson, who starred in Monae's *Dirty Computer* music videos in 2018. Tessa Thompson is out as bisexual, and Monáe is out as pansexual. Lupita Nyong'o kissed *Black Panther*'s Danai Gurira in a "funny" video posted to social media in January of 2019. By the time the Met Gala rolled around in May of 2019, a seemingly single Janelle Monáe and a highly flirtatious Lupita Nyong'o were photographed canoodling next to Danai Gurira, who is walking away from the steamy moment like, "Not this shit again." Remember, this is all speculation, but in lesbian folklore, this moment was a cultural reset.

KRISTEN STEWART HANGS OUT OF MOVING CAR
TO TAKE HOT PHOTO OF STELLA MAXWELL

Again, in queer couples, there are some women who capture hot content, and there are some who pose for hot content. In New Orleans in 2017, Kristen Stewart, with her bleached, buzzed gay head, leaned out of one side of a moving car to take hot pics of her girlfriend, Stella Maxwell, who hung out the window on the other side of the moving vehicle. Show me a single straight couple who could outperform Kristen Stewart or Queen Latifah in simping for their hot girlfriends. You can't. It doesn't exist.

CARA DELEVINGNE AND ASHLEY BENSON
CARRY A SEX BENCH INTO THEIR HOME

Finally, the most legendary and most lesbian paparazzi photo taken in modern history was this: In West Hollywood in late spring of 2019, Cara Delevingne (a-fucking-gain) and Ashley Benson were photographed carrying a large, hulking, brand-new, still-in-box (lol, box) sex bench into their home. Thanks to *Jezebel*'s investigative reporting, we now know that sex bench was either the Master Series Faux Leather Sex Bench with Adjustable Restraints, which cost $384, or the upgrade, the Dicktator Extreme Sex Machine, which cost $438. As a spawn of the aughts who was raised on paparazzi photos, I finally know what I want out of a relationship, love, and romance, and that's carrying a $384 sex bench into my home with my rumored girlfriend.

A SUPERCUT OF LESBIAN YEARNING

YOU'RE TWELVE YEARS old. You've never been kissed. The closest you've come to having a romantic relationship is imagining yourself violently brushing your teeth next to a hot person, like in *Bring It On*. You're horny as fuck, but you're not just horny to be kissed, you're horny to *feel*: You want to be lodged in a love triangle with a vampire and a werewolf. You want to be flown first-class to a European country by a rich man who turns out to be a criminal and ultimately leaves through the window during the night and abandons you on the Italian coast. You want to tell people that your boyfriend, who doesn't go here—but definitely goes to another school—just died tragically in a car accident (your brain is kinda fucked-up 'cause you're only twelve, so you romanticize death; and yes, it was a drunk driver, your boyfriend was drag racing with his cousin). You're just stupid, and twelve, and sitting in the back seat of your parents' Ford Explorer, and they're driving you to your grandparents' house, which suxxxxxxx, so now you're moping, head leaning against the cool glass of the window, thinking of the thousand lives you could live, the tongue kisses in the rain you could receive, the tragic deaths of teen boyfriends you could endure, if only your parents weren't so lame and basically tyrants. And then . . . it happens. It begins to rain. Suddenly, you feel like you're in a music video, probably an Avril Lavigne one. All of the wistfulness of staring out of a car window, that yearning for something, *anything*, to whisk you away from your sad, dull life with zero dead boyfriends and into your exciting future. All of that. Everything I just described. THAT'S lesbianism.

I know the adolescent phenomenon of staring wistfully out of a rainy car window and pretending you're in an Avril Lavigne music video doesn't belong exclusively to lesbians, but I'm talking about the collective *energy* of this experience. Lesbians are the *energy* of staring wistfully out of a rainy car window and pretending you're in an Avril Lavigne music video, personified. And that's because yearning is an inherent part of the queer female experience. And I'm not talking about, like, the 2018 awards cycle, when Bradley Cooper and Lady Gaga essentially performed yearning to sell their movie. I'm also not talking about Sally Rooney's *Normal People*, which is about a heterosexual couple who, for reasons unbeknownst, cannot be together because one plays football and the other one . . . reads books? Straight people, someone needs to tell you this once and for all: You are allowed to be together. You have always been allowed to be together. *Romeo and Juliet* is essentially hetero fanfic about what it's like to be gay. Your parents hate each other—who cares! For people who experience same-sex attraction, sometimes yearning is all we have. For me, yearning used to be *everything*—so much so that it damaged the relationships in my adult life. But before I had yearning, I existed in the Thirst Vacuum—a space that was so dark, so desolate, I couldn't yearn for anyone at all.

Before I came into my thirst, I lived an insipid life, like how the *Harry Potter* centaur Firenze describes drinking unicorn blood as a means of revival: It'll keep you alive, but it'll be "a half-life, a cursed life." (I know I've already mentioned the unicorn blood, I just really like this part of *Harry Potter.*) I dated men until I was twenty-three. That's ten long years of dating people I didn't actually want to date. Okay, six years of dating, and like, four of having horny AIM conversations. I dated my first real boyfriend, Jason, when I was seventeen. It's funny, the things you remember about a person after you date them. Especially with less significant relationships, or ones that happened long ago; you end up boiling down millions of moments together into just a few sentences or bullet points, a need-to-know Spark-Notes version of the relationship. For example: Jason was a junior and I was a senior. He played hockey. He chewed orange Trident gum, the smell of which still makes me *cringe in teenager.* Jason had fluffy blond hair and skinny sprinter legs, and always wore a navy-blue hooded sports sweatshirt. He made me cry after prom because I didn't want to lose my virginity to him. Other than that, I don't remember much about him. He was bland, vanilla, a "Live Laugh Love" sign dangling over a kitchen sink.

After Jason, I dated many men like Jason. I embarked on a series of microrelationships with white men who looked so similar, one might surmise that I was headed toward becoming a serial killer. I won't use names because who cares? You don't want to get lost in a maze of Zacks, Matts, and Chrises. Most times, when we're talking to friends, we don't even use full sentences to describe our more trifling relationships. We just say, "Hey, you remember Banana Peel Guy?" and our friends know what the fuck is up. Anyway, my pre-lesbian dating history, AKA my pre-yearning love life, was brimming with "Banana Peel Guys."

There was Hereditary, a guy who lived down the hall from me my sophomore year of college. He loved Rage Against the Machine (which is a band). We dated for three months. It ended after I came stumbling into his dorm one night, tore my clothes off, and declared that I wanted to have sex for the first time. He panicked and told me that his dad had erectile dysfunction and he might have it too, because it's "hereditary." I'm going to put my clothes back on now.

There was Sex Offender, who I made out with in an improv theater in college, only to discover that he was two-timing—no, three-timing—me with two other girls in my improv group (this whole sentence is one long shiver down the spine). After college, I found out Sex Offender slept with a high school student, and, you guessed it, was convicted of statutory rape. So that's . . . someone who touched my body.

There was Lena Dunham Guy, who I went to high school with. Though we did not Talk in High School, we did Kiss a Couple Times in College. Lena Dunham Guy was jacked. He lived down the block from me. I decided to lose my virginity to him the summer before my senior year of college. When I told him I was a virgin, he said, "Whoa, this is just like that episode of *Girls* where the girl is a virgin" (yes, I actually lost my virginity in the referential time of Lena Dunham's *Girls*). Though he was very nice, he did break it off with me via text message, and his dog also swallowed my underwear whole, both of which feel very Lenavellian.

In the Thirst Vacuum, everyone I dated was just Some Guy: They all looked like their moms cut their hair using a mixing bowl. They all had farmer's tans on their arms and sock tans on their calves. They were all "into Akon." Basically, I dated "Live Laugh Love" sign after "Live Laugh Love" sign until my heart and brain were smooth, and I had come to believe, like so many others, that sexual desire, romance, and love were just concepts propagated by Hollywood. By the time I was twenty, I thought that neither love nor sex was actually exciting; Hollywood just wanted us to think they were so we'd keep leaving our "Live Laugh Love" boyfriends home and going to the movies just to feel something.

In the Thirst Vacuum, I did what I felt I was "supposed to" be doing: dating men. And I especially dated ones I felt like I "should" be dating, ones that my friends would date—athletes, future Wall Street douchebags, guys who were physically close in proximity (down the street, down the hall). I dated guys who were familiar, who seemed "normal," achievable, par for the course as the dull, suburban white woman I thought I was fated to become (I probably am still headed in that direction, to be fair). Still, the men I dated were a fractured, fun-house-mirror reflection of my peers' desires, but not my own. And the hardest pill to swallow, looking back on it all, is that I didn't even think much about what I *did* want. I didn't fantasize. The people I dated didn't matter to me. I was so wholly unperturbed by love and sex that

I didn't even wonder what might feel *better*, what I might crave, what I might yearn for. I just floated through my "love" life dead-eyed, unaffected, numb. I felt nothing at all. I remember when I started yearning, though.

I graduated from a small college in New Jersey when I was twenty-one, and having spent my second-to-last semester in Los Angeles enrolled in a film and TV program, I knew I wanted to move back to L.A. The summer of 2013, I saved up money from babysitting the kids who lived across the street and moved to Los Angeles with just under $1,000 in the bank. I worked as a production assistant three days a week on a Nickelodeon show, and two days a week at E! on a rotating roster of shows that got canceled.

I moved into a two-bedroom townhouse apartment with five (that's FIVE) people, and my rent was $575—a number so low it currently makes me want to be dead. One bedroom slept me and my friend Kera—a super bubbly, actual forest sprite I met in college. In the other bedroom, there was Sarah, a Catholic Kera interned with who openly expressed her repulsion toward lesbians, which made for a very fun and safe environment to realize I was gay in. The bunk bed above Sarah slept her hometown friend Allison, who got involved in a pyramid scheme and made us all sit through a recruitment presentation in our living room with her supervisor, in which I pointed to his graph and said, "That's shaped like a pyramid," and he said, "No it's not." Also in Sarah's room was her younger sister Chelsea, a sixteen-year-old actress who was staying with us for the summer to audition for Disney Channel shows. And finally, in our basement/boiler room slept Anthony, another friend of Sarah's, who was a musician and a sweetheart. It was a madhouse. While I lived in this nightmare-plex, I met someone who changed everything for me. Darcy.

My first real yearn happened at a cult. Okay, not a *cult* cult, but—religions are cults. Sorry, they are. It was one of those cool, windy nights in L.A. when the cloudless blue skies turned to a deep, resonant black. I was at my cult, "Dinner Crew." Hosted by a family of actors who lived in the Valley, Dinner Crew was a weekly Sunday-evening gathering that I'd been invited to by one of my new L.A. friends, Ian, a standup comedian who had recently started attending. Ian promised it wouldn't be a religious thing. Cut to: a group of teenagers and early twentysomethings holding hands in a circle under the stars while the patriarch of the house praised god—sorry, "God." The first time I went, I was mortally uncomfortable being there—it was like being a kid and going to a friend's house for dinner, only to realize their parents are gonna make you drink this glass of milk before you leave the table. As a nonpracticing Jew, I had zero experience with Being Christian, and this was extremely not my shit.

To make matters worse, or just weirder, the kids there were all teen actors, ranging from age fifteen to twenty-three. Today, most of them helm their own shows on Netflix, Amazon, and the CW. But at the time, they spanned from auditioning for years and years to no avail, to having nabbed a recurring role on an MTV show, to being the biggest stars of a kids' show at a major cable network. Here's how it would go: Each week, the afore-mentioned patriarch, Billy, asked everyone to circle up and say one thing they were proud of themselves for doing this week, then the previous week's holder of the "Giving Key" would choose a new person to take the Giving Key, making it that person's job to bring a plate of food from Dinner Crew to an unhoused person the following day. Then, we would drop our heads, pray, and eat dinner together. I realize that the concept of the Giving Key is objectively positive, but reader, I've never been to church. I've been to temple like eight times, and I was very young. This was not only the most religious thing I had *accidentally* done, but it was also the closest I've come to joining a cult. Dinner Crew was an abrupt and jarring foray into L.A. culture.

How does a person like me—a twenty-two-year-old production assis-tant who was *not* a teen star—end up in a (literal) circle like this? When I moved to L.A., Ian was one of the only people I knew in the city, as we were friends from New Jersey and had moved there around the same time. He, because he booked a recurring role on a cable show. Me, because I was co-incidentally working on a different show at the same network. Ian had been going to Dinner Crew every Sunday for weeks now. He was dating Darcy, an actress, and even though Darcy resented organized religion as much as I did, she also got sucked into the vortex of Disney Christians. And through a chain of indoctrination, the three of us all got duped into joining the Teen Actor Cult.

Darcy and I had met once or twice before this chilly L.A. night. Ian had invited me to dinner with a big group at a Mediterranean restaurant, where he introduced me to Darcy. Though that was the first time we'd met, I had known about her. Leading up to the summer I moved to L.A., I was still babysitting for cash to save money. The tween girls I babysat obsessively watched Disney Channel. Before I left New Jersey, my days were filled with blaring scenes of WACKY kids with ZANY voices, seemingly saying, "WoOooOOoOaaaAAhhH!!!" over and over again, daring my forehead to split open. One of those older actors was Darcy. So I had seen Darcy's face about forty thousand times before I found out that my friend Ian was dating her. And when I met her, I was somewhat wonderstruck. I thought she'd be as intolerably "wOoOoOoOaaHHH" as she was on TV. Instead, she had these big, blue eyes, a gritty New York accent, and a cigarette constantly locked between her fingers. She was a tired trope of a cool girl, and because I'm a tired trope of a thirsty lesbian, I thought she was SO cool. And zany "woOoOOOahs" aside, there was a naive part of me, being recently plucked from a fame-barren forest in New Jersey, that was dazzled by Darcy.

At the Mediterranean restaurant, I made her laugh, and we exchanged numbers, both still relatively new and friendless in L.A. Afterward, we hung out in group settings a couple of times, and I texted her to hang out without the baggage of our mutual friends one night, but she couldn't make it.

Darcy's guaranteed presence at Dinner Crew was the *sole* reason I returned to the Teen Actor Cult. And to all the religious zealots out there who think a strong belief in Christianity is the way *out* of homosexuality, know this: homosexuality is the sole reason I got *into* Christianity. So, I went back for my second Dinner Crew.

I walked over to the snack table, feeling totally out of place, already having exhausted my ability to small-talk with rich, white, sixteen-year-old Christians with god complexes who said things like, "This week, I'm proud of myself for talking to a homeless person," or "I'm proud of myself for auditioning for an MTV show—it's a *really* mature role." I saw Darcy and Ian enter, making their rounds, but I didn't want to seem as needy and desperate as I was to barnacle myself to the only people I knew at this twenty-person-ish gathering. So I grabbed a corn chip and swiped an enormous lump of guacamole into my mouth, hoping they, or rather she, would feel my forlorn energy and approach me before we had to get in a circle and make each other feel like we were good people. I saw her walking toward me, and I thought, *Don't react, don't even blink, don't let her know that you know that she's approaching.* And when she did, and my shoulders were turned toward the guacamole, my hand heading for chip number fourteen, I almost didn't hear her when she said, "Hey, I missed you."

I turned around and said stupidly through a glob of avocado, "Me?" There was no one else around us. I couldn't fathom why, or rather how, this person who seemed so magical, exotic, and magnetic could see my humped shoulders, Jewish nose, and evaporated sense of self and think, "Wow, I really missed *that.*" Yes, she was a "she" and I was a "that."

Darcy laughed at me and said, "Yeah, you!"

"I missed you too," I offered, wondering if I even meant it, because I barely knew her—yet I was fucking dying to have just one more interaction with her. A spark of a yearn had ignited before I'd even known. I think that's what it feels like to have a crush on someone: Even when you're with them, staring at them, laughing with them, offering them a chip with a wad of guac, you think, *God, I would fucking kill to do this one more time.*

Darcy and I became fast friends. I barely remember what happened between "I missed you, yeah you," and the following summer, when I offered to stay at her apartment for two months and cat-sit while she filmed a TV show in Vancouver. She met my family, I met hers. We were in touch constantly, to the minute. We texted each other when we woke up and went to sleep. Everyone on the set of the show she worked on knew me, and everyone on the set of the show I worked on knew her. She was my plus-one to everything, and vice versa. When a friend or coworker would invite me somewhere, they'd assume Darcy would join, like she was my husband of forty years. She adopted a little orange cat. I took care of the cat while she was on set for long nights. In a way, we had built a family together, despite living in separate apartments. When she and Ian broke up and she asked if I'd like to house-sit for her that summer, I swiftly moved out of my nightmare-plex in Studio City and moved into Darcy's.

While she was away, I loved every second of being in her apartment: melting into her couch, which felt like our couch; bingeing her Netflix queue, which was really our Netflix queue; and squeezing her fluffy orange cat, which was really our fluffy orange cat. But "absence makes the heart grow fonder" is a platitude that truly cannot be understated in the world of lesbianism. At the time, I had never wanted anything like I wanted Darcy to return to me. Or maybe it was the waiting, her absence, the safety of wanting something without ever having to act on it, that I really coveted.

While she was away, we'd FaceTimed every day. Once, she'd Face-Timed me from the bathtub, a setting that felt so intimate to me, and my inner monologue was shrieking, "Act normal, act normal!" I spent so much time pretending to be chill with the things Darcy did, like when she texted me a photo of her pubic hair while I was at work "as a joke" (ha ha ha), or when she told me about how common orgies were in her high school, and I just nodded along, like *That must just be what growing up in Manhattan is like.* I always felt like she was testing me, or encouraging my romantic-leaning feelings, making me feel like we were on the same page, even if she knew we weren't. And I was always pretending to be fine.

It was late when she got home, and it was humid. Her two-story, one-bedroom apartment had only one wall-unit air conditioner on each floor, leaving my sweaty feet sticking to the hardwood floors as I pranced across the living room to greet her. When she arrived, I hugged her with the intensity of one million wives waiting for their husbands to come home from war, but there was a distance in her eyes that revealed she didn't feel the same. Darcy's birthday had been a few days earlier, and we'd planned to celebrate when she returned—or maybe I assumed we would celebrate, because she was my best friend and I couldn't wait to celebrate. Either way, it was eleven thirty at night, she had just gotten off a plane from a two-month trip, and I should've read the room. I should've seen where she was at. Maybe I did, but I was so excited, like a puppy that pees on you whenever you get home, that I just couldn't *not* give her the birthday presents before she put her bags down. Because I thought it'd be funny, I gave her a beer can helmet that I'd had since high school, plugged two cold beer cans into, and written *HBD DARCY* on its sides. She didn't seem too excited, but it didn't matter, because that was just the appetizer, the gag gift. I was saving the real present, the main course. I handed her an envelope with two tickets to a Jenny Lewis concert at the Roxy. She loved Jenny Lewis. I liked her, but I mostly listened to her for Darcy, because I wanted us to be able to sing in the car together. I spent hundreds of dollars I didn't have—at this point,

I was working as a full-time production assistant at Nickelodeon, barely scraping by—and I blew that money, money she could've farted out and not felt it, on what I thought was the perfect birthday experience. When she took the tickets in her hands, it almost looked like she felt bad for me, like only she knew these tickets and this experience were for *me,* like she had to keep up this jig of being peed on by the puppy. Then she told me she had met someone on her trip. He, too, was back in town. He was already on his way.

I couldn't understand it—why would she want to see this guy, this guy she'd just met, instead of me, who she hadn't seen in two months? She was the only person I wanted to see, and I had spent those long weeks cat-sitting for her, putting in those friendship hours, spending that Jenny Lewis money, giving up my stupid orange beer can hat. And then I was sitting in the back seat of some dude's ugly blue car, watching the two of them flirt in the Wendy's drive-through, knowing I shouldn't have accepted their half-hearted "no, come with!" invite. I thought Darcy and I would be staying up all night talking about her steamy Canadian adventure. Instead, I fell asleep in the bed by myself—I had nowhere else to go that late at night—and she slept with him on the couch downstairs.

I had never been so let down in my entire life. It was hard for me to distinguish what part of this visceral disappointment was me being possessive and gross, what part was her being a bad friend, whether either of us were being irrational, emotional, or both. At the time, I was obsessed with who was right and who was wrong. The truth is we were on totally different pages—she didn't make me give up my apartment to cat-sit for two months while yearning hopelessly for her specter. Regardless, I stayed up all night, the freezing-cold air of the wall unit bristling my cheeks as I stared at the ceiling, confronting something I'd done quite a good job of not confronting for a very long time.

"Is this about someone in specific?" Darcy asked between pulls of an American Spirit, sitting on the step below me on her front stoop. I sat with my arms wrapped around my balled knees, sobbing into the dark night, praying her neighbors didn't hear what I had just told her for the first time, what I had just said out loud for the very first time: *I think I like girls, and I don't know what that means for me.*

"No," I said, averting my eyes, wiping my nose, pretending to be fine. I was turning inward. "It's not about anyone specific." I reached for the cigarette.

"Please don't do this," I begged, holding back tears as Darcy blew cigarette smoke into the muggy open-air bar, drunk. Weeks later, she was still one of the only people who knew what I was struggling with. Darcy knew it was eating away at me. But something had soured between us. She knew what I wanted, knew I couldn't have it—not really—and this toxic bitterness developed. Maybe she was curious, or wanted to but couldn't go there. Maybe she resented my feelings for her, because our dynamic had shifted. She repeated what she'd just said, this time with more urgency, as if I hadn't heard her the first time.

"That guy over there keeps hitting on me," she said, blinking at me, leaning her collarbone closer, turning the corners of her mouth up into a venomous smirk. "Make out with me so he thinks you're my girlfriend."

She grabbed my face and shoved her tongue in my mouth. Every neuron in my brain fought to keep my eyes dry, to continue keeping up this charade that we were still just best friends, that nothing had changed between us, that I was fine and chill and normal. But I wasn't. I was being so dishonest. Maybe that's what she resented. That I wouldn't just come out and say it. And I wouldn't. Or I couldn't.

"Tell me you love me," she snapped, grabbing the car door before I could close her out of the Uber. The driver tried not to eavesdrop on the drama unfolding just outside—and partly inside—his perfumed black car. It was nearing one a.m. and we were on the corner of Santa Monica Boulevard and Larrabee Street, the heart of gay West Hollywood. I had just stormed out of Flaming Saddles, the gay cowboy bar, where I found myself standing alone, performing "fineness" again while Darcy snuck off to the bathroom to make out with a new fling, some poor guy who was as hopelessly in love with Darcy as I was. By this point, my friendship with her ex-boyfriend (and my ex-friend) Ian had fizzled, as he could sense that my relationship with Darcy had taken an intense turn, and that I'd begrudged him for being her number one over me while they were together. I felt betrayed by her, or left behind, or just jealous and sad. I realized that the guy she was kissing in the bathroom, Ian, and I all had something in common: we were all yearning for something that Darcy would never give us. Because Darcy and I *hadn't* fully crossed that line, and still considered each other to be "best friends," I felt as though we shared something even *more* sacred than one might have with a romantic partner. Romantic partners tend to come and go, but at the end of the day, your best friend is supposed to be that constant, the one who stays, the one you can run screaming and crying back to when your lover leaves. In this moment, I felt like Darcy had blackened that primitive, sacred agreement that we'd mutually notarized. But we hadn't. Neither one of us said what we were feeling, what we wanted, or what we didn't want. We just let it eat away at our bellies like rancid ulcers, until neither one of us could survive.

Just before I had stormed out, not wanting to wallow in a crowd of gays while Darcy had her fun, flirty experience anymore, she caught me by the arm and said, "Let me order you a car." So we waited for the car. I wouldn't look at her. When the car finally came, she wouldn't let me close the door.

"Tell me you love me," she repeated as I looked up at her from the leather seat, this time allowing myself to cry, or maybe I really didn't have much of a choice anymore. "It's my car. You have to say it if you want to take the car," she "joked."

"I love you," I muttered pathetically.

"Tell me you love me more than your mom," she added, laughing a little, as if this mom bit might lighten the mood. Still not wanting to acknowledge the Thing, whatever this fucking Thing was between us, not wanting to take any action, to push the relationship forward or backward or make any sort of move at all, choosing to continue withering in want, in yearn, in limbo, I told her I did. She said, "I love you more than I love my mom too. Now give me a kiss." The Uber driver peered over his shoulder. I caved. I gave her the last of me. She took it, swiftly and unrepentantly. She leaned over and kissed my slippery, salty lips. She smiled, satisfied, and slammed the door of the cage I'd built for myself.

A couple months later, Darcy ghosted me. Emotions continued to boil, and instead of letting our relationship reach a head and completely explode in a giant, unforgivable fight, she chose to pull the plug. In some ways, I'm grateful Darcy disappeared before I could say something I couldn't take back. Because that was the whole thing. I wanted safety. I couldn't move forward, because if I did, I'd have to grapple with all of the tough stuff I'd been repressing the better part of my life. Like, *really* grapple with it. Our relationship became toxic and jealous, and we grew it to a place that reeked of black, rotted death. One way or another, whether by cutting the cord or having it out, it needed to end. So it did. I started dating my first girlfriend. She started dating a new guy. We both loathed each other's significant others. Cut to black.

In yearning, or in wanting, there is infinite potential, a thousand different futures laid out before you, a choose-your-own-disaster, or hopefully, a choose-your-own-happily-ever-after. We want partnership. We want to feel seen and understood. We want to be loved. Wanting is good, it's healthy. It creates drive. And if you want something badly enough, you can create your own little carrot at the end of your treadmill, and grow the will to keep running. But at some point, we must learn to appreciate the things we have, to live in the present and not in the "want." Recently, I've discovered something troubling about myself, that it's the *wanting* that I actually yearn for. The only exciting part of life is the part where the Thing hasn't happened yet, where I'm still chasing it. When we want something, we're living in a fantasy of having that thing—whether that's a person, success, a new job, whatever—we can imagine endless scenarios in which having that thing will exponentially improve our lives. We're stuck.

I learned to live in the want from somewhere, one particularly nightmarish, phantasmagoric realm: the romantic comedy. Look, the romantic comedy is deranged. We know this. I barely have to say it. But I'm going to, because I'm brave. I hate how optimistic romantic comedies are. Having nosedived off the precipice of innocence and blind trust—surviving, but with a permanent crick in my neck—I can't fathom how adult human beings can view the world with any sense of optimism. The only way that could possibly make sense to me is if you've never had experiences. Have you had experiences? Have you gone outside? Great, then you should see the human condition as the horrifying nightmarescape that it is. Of course, I'm speaking as a Hurt Person, or as I see it, just a Person, and any logical Person who has had experiences and been outside must know that rom-coms are nonsense. But I don't actually hate rom-coms. I love them. I grew up with them, I believed what they told me, but they lied to me.

Movies have a way of viewing the toils of our hell-world through rose-colored glasses. But if your typical war movie wears rose-colored glasses, then romantic comedies are wearing zAnY, Disney Channel, "wOoOoOooAHH!!!" brightness-and-saturation-turned-to-100 fucking beer goggles. When you strip the rom-com of all its frills (the white women in scarves, the overbearing mothers, the gay men with two lines of dialogue that are like, "Bitch!" or "Oh, bitch!"), the most basic premise of any romantic comedy is this: yearning.

One of my favorite rom-coms, which also happens to be one of the most brain-poisony ones: *Serendipity*, the 2001 film starring John Cusack and Kate Beckinsale. Jonathan Trager (Cusack) encounters Sara Thomas (Beckinsale) at Bloomingdale's in New York City. It's the holiday season, and they're both trying to purchase the same pair of gloves. They banter—I can't remember about what exactly, but it's probably like, "I can't help but notice that you're a mediocre-looking man and are also white, like me. Are we . . ."—in unison—"in LOVE?!" Then they prance over to the restaurant Serendipity and continue their talks on heterosexuality and what it's like to have never experienced oppression of any form. After the spur-of-the-moment date, Sara gives Jonathan her number on a piece of paper, but it blows away in the wind, and Sara takes this as a bad omen. So, she suggests putting their phone numbers into the universe another way, only to be found if they're fated to reunite—she writes hers on the inside of a book, he writes his on a five-dollar bill—and they call it. "See you on the heterosexuality forums," they yell to each other (or something).

Years later, Jonathan is engaged to another woman, but he's still hung up on Sara, this other white woman he met at Bloomingdale's and talked about gloves with. Sara gets proposed to by some guy, but seeks the connection she felt with the first straight white man who, for all she knows, could be a serial killer! Just saying. Any white man could be. Both Jonathan and Sara's respective best friends try to talk some sense into them: "It's the year 2001, and it's impossible to find this person because MySpace is still two years out, and let's face it, you're not interesting enough or horny enough to be haunting AOL chat rooms or using the internet to gather information," the best friends say. "Just marry this other flop and get over it!" But obviously, neither Jonathan Trager nor Sara Thomas can forget about each other. All they have is that chance meeting that left them wanting more, that infinite potential. All they have is this *yearning*, this untethered, groundless feeling deep in their bellies that tells them they were denied something magical by the universe, and they just can't let it go. They need another hit. They need to touch each other's bodies.

The rest of the movie follows the two of them blowing up their lives with their partners in a desperate search, this roofless yearn for each other, until "serendipity" brings them together once again. While Sara waits for her plane to leave so she can fly home, the flight attendant gives her change in the form of one earth-shattering five-dollar bill. Having noticed that he's always fingering *Love in the Time of Cholera*'s first few pages but never buying it for himself, Jonathan's bride-to-be gives him one earth-shattering book on the night of their wedding rehearsal. Jonathan and Sara ultimately reunite, end up happily ever after, yadda yadda—it's a super-fun movie. I loved it growing up, and I love it now. But it's also *head twisting 360 degrees, eyes rolling back in skull* HORSESHIIIIIIIT.

That's where every great rom-com leaves you: before anything bad or traumatic or downright psychotic can happen. The couple yearns to be together, and then they are—CUT TO BLACK. Rom-coms, my earliest understanding of what love is, of what love should look like, told me that love is the chase; winning the girl, *that's* the finish line. But they did *not* tell me what the fuck to do after you HAVE the girl—you know, how to actually BE in a relationship for the rest of your life. So, in psychoanalyzing where my bad scripts about love stem from, we can see here, based on My Research, that rom-coms are brain poison, as far as learning how to do love and relationships goes.

Rom-coms being bullshit isn't news. But when you're a queer woman, there's an added layer of movie nonsense that you inhale, internalize, and repeat in your own life, which can be really harmful to your understanding of love and relationships. Rom-coms tend to be deeply heteronormative, and most of them end with some sort of consummation of this hetero relationship: a happy ending, a wedding, an assumption that the couple will be together forever. But what happens if you take a movie about yearning, and you strip it entirely of a happy ending, or even any sense of finality or closure? Well, you get a LESBIAN MOVIE.

There's a jarring difference between most Straight Movies, specifically rom-coms, and lesbian movies. Have you seen the movie *Portrait of a Lady on Fire*? Not a rom-com so much as a devastating ode to yearning, but unless you're extremely online, extremely lesbian, or both, you might have missed it. Released in the U.S. in 2020, *Portrait* is a French drama by filmmaker Céline Sciamma about two women in eighteenth-century France who fall yearn-over-heels for each other, even though they're both . . . GIRLS. I know, it's so crazy. Marianne, a portraitist, is hired to paint Héloïse, a wealthy woman living on an isolated island in Brittany. The mother of the wealthy woman, who hires Marianne, insists that Marianne must pretend to be Héloïse's companion, accompanying her on her daily walks to the sea, because Héloïse doesn't like to be painted. Marianne is tasked with studying Héloïse on these daily walks, then retreating to her quarters to paint the portrait in private, from memory. Along the way, the women fall for each other, they can't be together, their story ends in heartbreak, yadda yadda yadda.

There is so much that makes *Portrait of a Lady on Fire* identifiably queer. Outside of, you know, a romance between two women, we also have the presence of the sea, thoughts being provoked, and the contemplation of every decision we've ever made while gazing across wind-kissed sands and vaguely European rock formations. But when you strip *Portrait* of its lesbian frills, like *Serendipity*, it's just about yearning. But again, unlike classic Straight Movies, lesbian movies are often about yearning that ends in *disaster*, rather than triumph.

At the end of *Portrait*, the two women break up, and Marianne spots Héloïse years later across the room at a concert, where they're both overwhelmed with emotion as the orchestra plays a song that Marianne had once played for Héloïse on a harpsichord. Marianne still seems heartbroken, but finds some satisfaction in knowing their love happened at all. I know I'm meant to look at this ending as melancholic and beautiful, but honestly what the fuck? She's happy she was gay with someone she loved *at all*? She's begging for scraps of affection behind closed doors, and is supposed to be grateful she got to experience it for like two minutes before it was homophobically ripped away? Fuck that. That message doesn't necessarily incentivize me to fall in love with another woman, because out here in the real world, I can guarantee I won't be "glad it happened at all." I'm gonna be on the fucking floor banging my fists on the ground like a toddler. I know I have some maturing to do, but bear with me.

There are so many lesbian movies—ones that I saw when I was coming out that actually affected the way I view love and relationships—that end this way (spoilers ahead). *Blue Is the Warmest Colour*: Lesbian couple breaks up, Emma insists she can't be with Adéle despite having "infinite tenderness" for her, Adéle attends Emma's art exhibition and finds a naked portrait of herself there, finds some satisfaction in knowing that Emma will always love her despite their not being together. *Kissing Jessica Stein*, my favorite lesbian movie, brain poison: Jessica Stein and her first-ever girlfriend who she moved in with break it off because Jessica "isn't gay enough," but they stay best friends while Jessica goes back to men, and is happy she met her now best friend at all. Or *Lost and Delirious*, one of two essential Piper Perabo lesbian movies, which follows Paulie (Perabo) and Tori, two girls in private school who are happily in lust until Tori's sister finds out, leading Tori to gay panic and call Paulie an obsessive creep, and then Paulie KILLS HERSELF!!! THAT'S HOW IT ENDS!!! Where did I get the idea that love is strictly about yearning, or yearning followed by tragedy? Oh yeah, from like, the five lesbian movies that existed.

There are some '90s/2000s lesbian rom-coms out there that *do* have happy endings: *Imagine Me & You*, *D.E.B.S.*, *But I'm a Cheerleader*. I love these movies. In *Imagine Me & You*—a truly incredible British comedy starring, once again, Piper Perabo and Lena Headey as an iconic on-screen lesbian couple—the women end up together. It's a classic cameras-spinning-round-a-traffic-stopping-on-my-way-to-the-airport-kiss-set-to-"Happy Together" finale. Regardless, the whole movie is like a supercut of lesbian yearning, which is, of course, in its purest form, just glancing. Their eyes first meet as Rachel (Perabo) walks down the aisle at her wedding, but glances at Luce (Headey), who arranged the flowers for the ceremony. After that, it's like machine gun glances: G-G-G-G-GLANCE, until someone makes a move. The only thing that makes a lesbian movie a lesbian movie is this: The two women cannot be together, but god*dammit* they will glance. Whether they can't be together because of homophobia or—no, actually that's it, it's always homophobia. Society—back when we used to live in a society—told these women, "You cannot be together," and they said, *glance.*

So, I loved glancing. I loved yearning. All I wanted was more glancing, more yearning. Glancing is no longer just a commonality in lesbian movies, it's a real-life lesbian love language. Ask any woman who has ever stood across the room from another woman at a party and made eye contact with her and then never approached. We are *living* for these small moments, these confirmations of mutual lust, or these questionable confirmations that aggravate our desire for more, without ever actually having to act on the "more." Lesbians, in general, live in the yearn. We've been taught to.

This is how I came to understand what a romantic connection between two women looked like. In 2014, I was in love with my best friend, and I didn't need to actually act on it or kiss her or be with her to feel alive. While wondering, "Huh, am I gay?" and watching a bunch of lesbian movies that were like, "NEVER touch," or "Actually you can touch, but just once, and then leave," or "Touch and then die," the little propaganda aliens controlling my brain transmitted this message: *It's not about the destination. It's about the spark, and the yearn, and the roadblocks that exacerbate the yearn.* Gay people have been told, throughout time, whether that's through micromessaging in film and TV or explicitly in our own lives by our own family members or workplace, that what we want is wrong. That same-sex attraction is fundamentally "unnatural," or a "choice." And this script has seeped so deep into my bloodstream, it's been nearly impossible to suck it out, no matter how hard I try: the idea that I can finally want things, but I can never act on them, or have them. Or worse, that the suffering is actually good, that suffering and torturing myself were what was actually rewarding.

Wanting anything is embarrassing, but having something? It can't be done. Especially as a lesbian, but also just as a woman in general. Think about how vicious people (men—but really not just men) became when Hillary Clinton had the presidential nomination. Everyone was like, "It's not that I wouldn't vote for a woman for president—there's just something about her that bothers me. She's so power-hungry. I don't know, I can't put my finger on it." Or Taylor Swift, who, in her lifetime, has acquired *so much.* And when she first secured that bag, everyone was like, "I like her music, but she's so annoying—like, she just seems so manipulative and sociopathic— she'll do anything to be on top. I don't know, there's something about her that bothers me, I just can't put my finger on it." Or Anne Hathaway! I'll say it right now: Fuck ANYONE who pretended to think Anne Hathaway was annoying as soon as she was an accomplished actor. "Like, we get it, you won an Oscar—the highest honor that can be awarded to someone in your profession—why did you have to *cry*? She's so eager. I don't know, there's just something about her that bothers me. I can't put my finger on it." Grow up! But also, these are such pervasive reactions to women having things. What unites Hillary Clinton, Taylor Swift, and Anne Hathaway? That in an alternate universe they're living in a vaguely problematic lesbian commune and are besties—yes. But also: They're all women who despite being at the top of their fields have been vilified for being successful, or happy, or just for having things. For so long, rom-coms, pop culture, and pre-penicillin lesbian movies have told gay people to yearn, but not to act. That our actions might have real, potentially grave consequences. So we don't. We yearn. We wait for her to come home.

Writing about falling in love for the first time, even remembering it, feels like watching *When Harry Met Sally*; it's like, I don't get it—you can't be together because you're . . . friends?? That's it, that's the whole thing stopping Harry from being with Sally, or . . . ? I want to yell to young Harry and my more youthful self, "Kiss her, dipshit!" Or at least, "I see your yearning, how about I raise you . . . being honest with her?" Yearning is good and natural— but at a certain point, you have to fucking progress. You have to bust out of the cage of wanting you've built around yourself. It's not that I was wrong to have real, valid fears about the possibility of homophobic backlash. But I wish I didn't romanticize self-torture so much, or feel like the suffering was the correct feeling, just because it was the strongest one. I think I was just unimaginative; I don't think I ever envisioned a happy ending as being a possibility, or a choice. All I knew was yearn cage.

But there is life outside of yearn cage. Now I know there's more to a love story than simply being British, kissing in the street while your whole family watches, and blaring "Happy Together." Actually, there isn't—what I mean to say is, there's something more important than the yearning and wanting and internal suffering that comes with having a crush. What comes *after* the big kiss matters. What comes after joining a religious blood cult so you can hang out with your gay crush matters. Queer people, you don't have to pretend to be in an angsty Avril Lavigne music video anymore. Your life is so much bigger.

KILL THE CREATOR OF *ENTOURAGE* IN YOUR HEAD

THAT BEING "ONE of the boys" used to be a good thing is very funny to me. Can you even imagine something so harrowing, so chilling, as to pride oneself on an ability to connect with . . . men? Ask yourself: Does anything in this world feel as good as connecting with a woman? No, it doesn't. Women *fuck*. Not like, sexually. I mean, we do fuck sexually, but like, in a more grandeur sense of the word, women FUCK so hard. We're the best. We're magic. And yet "the boys," as an image, or a concept, have been revered seemingly forever, since America was colonized and co-opted by spooky white people, certainly. The idea of "the boys" represents, for most straight men, and many white straight women who have yet to ascend to misandry, the epitome of cool. Americans are seemingly always longing for "the boys" to be back in town, pining for their coveted return from wherever it is that the boys went (a decent college? Kohl's? The AMC network?), and celebrating when it finally happens, when the boys are back, draped in denim and an American flag, probably. When we speak of the "boys' club," we're examining spaces in which women aren't welcome—or they are, but with an understanding that they must become "one of the boys" in order to succeed, that they will only be validated, be considered a quantifiable or qualifiable worker, so long as they can blend in with and submit to their male leadership. It's revolting.

The cultural landscape is much different today than it was pre–women's liberation movement, or in the latter half of the twentieth century, or even when I was born in 1991, or ten years ago, or *three* years ago. So most people, people who are in the workforce today, or are old enough to die in a war (but not old enough to slug a White Claw!), or are part of any generation older than the one that's currently being groomed to lead America into a genderqueer, socialist, "Reparations Now" revolution, came of age in a time that demanded women reject the feminine in order to fuse with or capitulate to these storied "boys." As a fairly lucid adult, a feminist, and a scorched-earth Lesbian Agendaist, that makes my stomach churn. Call me radical, but I'm currently of the opinion that, to truly dismantle the "boys' club," or the idea that women need to become "one of the boys" in order to succeed or fit in or win, we must ban the boys from returning to town once and for all, and for the love of god, make sure they stay wherever they keep coming back from (a Kings of Leon concert? Colorado? Buffalo Wild Wings???).

In HBO's *Watchmen*, based on the graphic novel of the same name, the fictional drug Nostalgia is a cautionary tale. Manufactured by Trieu Pharmaceuticals, Nostalgia is a pill someone in the *Watchmen*-verse could swallow that allowed them to relive their own memories. In one of the show's most damning indictments of human nature, the creator of the drug, billionaire Lady Trieu, says Nostalgia was her biggest failure; it was pulled from shelves once users began to abuse it in an obsessive attempt to relive their most painful memories, leading to psychosis. Lady Trieu laments that she underestimated humanity's propensity to relive our most traumatic moments. I wondered after bingeing *Watchmen*: Would *I* be one of those silly little Nostalgia junkies, one who not only cyclically ruminates on her traumas but also obsessively consumes them, even if doing so contributes to the deterioration of her brain? Yes, obviously, fucking yes, of course. I do it all the time without the aid of fictional psychedelics; I just need my HBO Max login.

I have rewatched *Entourage* numerous times in my adult life, a show that not only was predicated on the existence of the boys' club but *endorsed* the idea that women are dumb, bad, empty bags of skin with holes. *Entourage* is one of these moments of scarring for me; it's a time capsule of toxic 2000s culture that boldly declared Men Good and Women Bad, and the only way to become Good is to become Men, and we must get rid of the Bad by disposing of anything that might lead one to believe that we subscribe to Women, or femininity (which, if I wasn't clear, is dumb and bad). *Entourage*, with all of its one-sixteenth-baked female characters who are expected to throw themselves at shitty men and are shamed as prudes if they don't or excoriated as "sluts" if they do, was one of those harmful shows that led me to believe that I, myself, was a thing for men to judge and grope. Later in life, I would shockingly uncover something quite outrageous: that I was actually not a *thing*.

When I was in high school, "the boys" would gather around their rich dads' flat-screens every Sunday to watch Vince bag another "slut," or to watch Turtle use his proximity to the "godlike" Vince to coerce another "dime" into a sex act she didn't want to perform. "The boys" would sometimes invite some of us dumb-dumb girls over to watch with them, which was supposed to be some magical treat for us, as if we were being *allowed* inside the walls of the exclusive gentlemen's room of the country club. *Wow, thank you for this gift, milord! Finally, we little women can know what it's like to be average-at-best-looking and oppressive, depraved sexual monsters!* I felt sick to my stomach watching those sixteen-year-old boys worship at the toes of Adrian Grenier or creator Doug Ellin or, worse, any of the number of men involved with *Entourage* who have since been called out as sexual abusers in real life (like Jeremy Piven, who played Ari, and director and guest star Brett Ratner). We girls would sit there and laugh along with jokes made at our expense, happy to be a part of something so ritualistic, so male, so "cool," as watching *Entourage* with "the boys." But laughing along with it, being "chill" with chauvinism, still didn't give us membership access to the country club, not really. We were, alas, still just *girls*. We could never *actually* be a part of it. We could never be sex gods like Vince or big-money bosses like Ari. No, those titles were reserved for "the boys."

I hated watching this show with these people, even then, in the moment. It repulsed me in ways I couldn't yet articulate. I just knew it felt awful to sit there, sandwiched between monsters-in-the-making on their parents' sectional couches, absorbing this telecommunication that girls were meant to be grateful to be on the inside, to humbly appreciate that these boys found us "cool" enough to watch their propaganda program with them. What felt worse is that afterward, not immediately, but sometime maybe later in high school, we were supposed to be equally thankful to be touched by these sixteen-year-old boys. That they could use us up whenever they wanted, then toss us aside like the chattel they saw us as, shockingly, didn't feel good. *Entourage* told them: You are Vince. You are hot and rich and talented and special and girls will flock to you, because that's what you deserve. Or maybe you're not Vince, but you're soft and intelligent and a good guy like E, and if you behave like a "good guy," then you're entitled to certain things (sex with women). Or maybe you're not as smart and "nice" as E, but you're at least a goof like Drama or pushy like Turtle, in which case you'll still get girls, but they'll need to be convinced, coerced, possibly even bribed. And if the girls don't like you—you as Vince, or E, or Drama, or Turtle—then they're prudes.

Any form of resistance we might've put up proved to them that we were all just prudes and sluts and dimes who were withholding this *thing* that all "the boys" were supposed to be *given*, as is their right in this world as hot, or rich, or nice, or goofy, or pushy boys—the commonality being they're boys, the "thing" being women's bodies. Sorry to get so dark so quick, but this is what it was like to move about the world as a teenage girl in the 2000s. It was hell, growing up in a world that wasn't ours.

So, why would I rewatch something as an adult that actively reminds me of what it was like to exist in such a dystopia? Doug Ellin painted a picture of a berserk, mirror-shards worldview of the version of "cool" he believed in, a male fantasy that preyed on the bodies of women and could only be successful with women's capitulation to such a world. But it wasn't berserk. Not really. It was hyperbolic, but it certainly reflected a very present, male worldview at the time. Maybe that's why I'm obsessed with *Entourage*, why I rewatched nearly the whole series in 2018 and wrote about it for *Vice*, why I made my girlfriend watch the pilot recently so we could point and laugh at it, because I can't even begin to process that I endured these episodes, this nightmare, at such a young and impressionable age. I'm transfixed by the show because it's one of those moments when things went wrong for me, where I can still feel the bulge of scar tissue. And the wound is much deeper than just a stupid fuckin' show created by a guy named literally "Doug." So, you can keep your Nostalgia, *Watchmen*; I've found another way to time-travel into psychosis.

After high school, I attended Ramapo College, a liberal arts college in New Jersey that was lodged in a wet forest between a boulder and a reservoir. Ramapo could've been an oasis, had it not been wholly populated by people who resembled the cast of *Jersey Shore*. Plus, it was a "suitcase school," meaning most of the students commuted and didn't live in dorms on campus. I hated it there. My proudest moment at this school, a school that I loathed with every hole of my empty skin bag, was when I was asked to write for the *Ramapo Underground*, the college "satire magazine" à la *The Onion*. I say "satire magazine" in quotes because it was a blog and it was not funny.

I met Noah in 2011, when I was a junior. He was the head writer of the *Ramapo Underground*, and we were introduced through our mutual friend who also wrote for the blog. I was charmed by Noah. He was the exact Jason Biggs–like archetype of a man that *American Pie* and other dude comedies sold to me as being a good guy. He was Jewish, with tamed, short curly hair; stubble that was always visible, even with a clean shave; long, brown eyelashes. He was handsome—but not unapproachable. He was funny in a warm yet vaguely misogynistic, assholey, I'm-better-than-you way, which, unfortunately, made me want to impress him even more, and not just because I wanted to write for the *Ramapo Underground*, but because I wanted him to like me. Because if Noah, the Jew god of this nonsense "comedy" blog, could like me, then that meant I was worth something. That would confirm something I had always suspected about myself but could never accept as truth without external validation: that I was funny.

I wrote a music blog at the time, which Noah took a look at. He liked my writing right away and offered me a spot on the five-person writing staff of *Ramapo Underground* (four dudes and me). I screamed internally and accepted. To celebrate the hiring of a Girl to the blog that no one read, Noah suggested that we make it official by attending a frat party together. *What a magnificent treat, milord! A party? Just for me?!*

Ramapo was a small school without any real Greek life, so a "frat house" was simply an off-campus house that a group of frat brothers rented together. Nineteen years old and still straddling that line of "please think I'm hot" and "please think I'm cool," I wore a skintight skirt, black tights, and a black tank top in wintry, forty-degree New Jersey. I was officially "one of the boys," but something in me—possibly the damage done to me by television shows like *Entourage*—still needed to be seen as a sex object to them. I knew that I could never truly be seen by these boys, be respected by these boys, if they didn't also want me. That was the power I needed to maintain over them: You should think I'm funny and smart, but you should also want to fuck me. Because if you don't want to fuck me, then I am worthless to you, and thus, this world. It's fun here, isn't it?

Surrounded by blue Solo cups, Ping-Pong balls, beer-soaked floors, and belligerent frat brothers, Noah moved closer to me, leaning against the sticky cream wall, shouting over the throbbing beats of Big Sean.

"You're really funny," he said. I smiled and sipped my Keystone Light. "I think you're the only funny girl I've ever met."

I beamed. I was thrilled. It was the only compliment I had ever wanted. It was the fuel I needed to move forward in my pursuit of a career and male validation. *Yes, finally,* I thought. *A man has confirmed I am funny.* And not just funny—THE ONLY. FUNNY. GIRL. I felt larger than life. I was finally funny, and not because I knew I was, or because all my friends and family members knew I was, but because this male student with a blog, this gatekeeper of comedy, confirmed that I was. I had made it. Fuck all you other girls. You are not funny. *I* am funny.

He leaned over again, even closer, and shouted into my ear canal: "Would it be weird if I kissed you?" *Oh, milord. Thank you. Thank you for this generous endowment. Yes, take my body and do what you please. You're a* nice *guy; you* asked *if you could take what's yours instead of simply taking it. Now you deserve your bounty. Kiss me, milord! After all, I am the Only. Funny. Girl.* (He did kiss me. We dated for a month and a half, until he ghosted, and I eventually stopped writing for the *Ramapo Underground*.)

Obviously, this is all insane. As a lesbian, I now have the luxury of being freed from the prison of desiring male attention. The mere thought of caring about a man's opinion makes my eye twitch. The concept of a "man" in "comedy" makes me shiver so hard that my bones splinter. That a man would even know what's funny is funny to me. Not only do I not care to be adored by men—I don't even want to be *perceived* by men. Stop perceiving me. Your opinion doesn't matter to me. But in 2011, it did. It really, really did. I genuinely believed that Noah had given me a compliment, not realizing how insidious his behavior was, not only because his words implied that women were commonly unfunny and men were inherently funny, but that I should *want* to be the exception, that I should join in on the bashing of unfunny women as the one who made it, the chosen one. I felt like that was true and real, that there was only room for one funny woman, that if I was going to be a funny woman then I had to be the BEST at being the funny woman. I didn't want other women to be like me. I wanted to be the exception. Being "one of the boys" had almost always been valuable to me. And as I had come to know in my teenage years, being fuckable was also of value. The combination meant owning a slice of power in a world that rendered me, just a dumb little girl, powerless. I had achieved what I'd set out to. I'm just lucky I decided, over time, to throw out everything I had ever learned about what makes someone or something "funny" and rewrite it from scratch.

College and high school, though different in many ways for me, were also very similar, in that I felt walled in, confined to one space, one people, one groupthink. After graduation, I was finally freed from the physical walls of school to explore new places, and to explore myself: who I was, who I wanted to be, what I believed in. Los Angeles was that bitch: a luscious, sprawling, wide-open meadow, rich with opportunity and boundless horizons. In L.A., it was easy for me to embrace my love of pop culture rather than reject it, as I was living in the very nucleus of celebrity, an environment and an industry that validated caring about who was being papped outside of Katsuya. I stopped seeing being interested in such things as "vapid" or "feminine" and saw it for what it really was (fun, exciting, political). I peeled back my layers, skin sheet by skin sheet, did the work of unlearning beliefs I'd grown comfortable participating in, and eventually came to find that, oh shit, I was gay as oat milk (oat milk is lesbian, and I'm not obligated to explain this to you).

Coming out as gay opened me up to a whole new realm of possibility, of people and art and movements to admire; I fell in love with femininity. Sure, I fell in love with actual women, like, the people. But coming out frees you in ways that I'm not sure any straight person ever fully experiences. Queer shame spans a spectrum. On the more dangerous and depraved side, you might place having a violently homophobic father, being beaten for queerness, being thrown out of your home, and being killed. On the other side of the spectrum, though one may not be actively in fear for their life on a daily basis, there's still this undercurrent of shame, this feeling of "I shouldn't be doing this," where holding hands with your partner on the street might draw stares, judgment, a vocal outburst. Being able to overcome all of this, this anxiety that ranges from learning to protect yourself to justified paranoia, no matter where you fall on the spectrum, is nothing short of a miracle. And by "overcome," I don't mean holistically overcoming it—no, internalized homophobia will haunt you like Ari Gold eternally haunts Lloyd—but "overcome" as in saying it out loud, lifting that weight, that burden off yourself, of your own volition. Coming to a place of peace with yourself enough to say, "The world has historically said I should not be *this*, yet here I am, *this*, and I'm great," is simply a mammoth feat of human strength. So when I came to reconcile myself with queerness, and found peace with it, I felt lighter in many other ways, ways that opened me up to new experiences, new interests, newfound appreciations. I decided I didn't just love women, the people, in a romantic and sexual sense, but I loved *women*, the concept, everything we represent in the world, our drive, our persistence, our community, and yes, the hobbies and clothes and principles we've come together and agreed to love and participate in. For the first time since, I don't know, probably since I was a five-year-old kid with a Yankees hat and all five Spice Girls dolls, I came to understand that being more or less feminine didn't make me more or less valuable. Or better yet, that being a woman—and being a woman who loves women—*is* more valuable to me. Plus, what do men like that's so "cool" anyway? *True Detective*? Mark Wahlberg? Cigars? Cigars are bad—I've had one before and either it didn't work or it was bad. The point is: if an activity or a show or a thing is only (or mostly) adored by men, that's a red flag.

Throughout my period of openness and curiosity, my mind left totally unarmed, primed to absorb, I fell in love with a TV show called *Orange Is the New Black*. The series was Netflix's flagship comedy-drama, released in the same year as their inaugural drama, *House of Cards*. *Orange* hit the streaming service in the summer of 2013, but I was aware of its existence much earlier than that. The show was created by Jenji Kohan, the same creator behind Showtime's *Weeds*. If *Entourage* was everything that was sick about America in the mid-2000s, *Weeds* felt like everything that was right. I had binged all eight seasons when I was in college, and promptly hung a poster of the protagonist, drug dealer Nancy Botwin (played by national treasure Mary-Louise Parker), in a bathing suit, in my room. I was enamored with Nancy's character, with Kohan's voice. It's so pathetic to realize that, at twenty years old, I was still gobsmacked by the image of a flawed, complex woman, one who's both bad and good, on my television. Nancy wasn't the first flawed woman on TV, but *Weeds* was a staple of 2000s pay cable for good reason. Shitty boys had *Entourage*; shitty girls had *Weeds* (although, obviously, I mean "shitty" in different ways, because *Entourage* promoted rape culture and *Weeds* just made it okay for women to sell drugs and fuck their dealers. These are not the same).

Around the time I was prepping to move to Los Angeles, I heard that

Kohan's next venture was set to be released on Netflix, and the show was about a women's prison. A Kohan superfan, I was desperate to be involved in any way I could. Obviously, being in the writer's room would've been a dream, but I just wanted to get near the set, to see inside Kohan's world; to get her coffee would've been an honor, a real excuse to use the word "milord" (and mean it). I googled as far down the rabbit hole as one could google about a show that wasn't out yet on a streaming service that hadn't fully launched yet, and came up with a whole lot of nothing. I found a general phone number for Lionsgate, the production company behind *Orange,* and used fake voices and fake job titles in hopes that they'd connect me to someone inside Kohan's production company. I IMDB'd the writers of the show and tweeted at them, praying they'd open their DMs to me so I could beg for a dirty towel Kohan had sweat on. But I got nothing. Watching the show was going to have to be enough. Coincidentally, *Orange Is the New Black* ended up being released the same week I moved to L.A.

I was sitting in a Starbucks about five hundred feet away from my new apartment. I didn't drink coffee at the time, and because I was and continue to be a giant baby, I ordered a caramel Frappuccino. Sarah, one of my roommates, and Chelsea, her sixteen-year-old sister who was staying with us for the summer, sat with me, tucked away in a corner, all three of us sharing a small circular table with the backs of our laptops at war. Chelsea had audition sides to read on her computer. Sarah was applying for jobs. I didn't have anything to do except stare at Angelenos, who really weren't much different from how I'd imagined they'd be. I mean, it's not an exaggeration to say that you can walk into any Starbucks in Los Angeles County and see two to four white men with Final Draft open, and one of them is probably wearing a Kangol hat and saying something into his AirPods like, "So get this: she's a detective . . . but she also has sex." I wanted to blend in, to seem like I too had scripts to be working on, or contacts to be contacting. So I opened my laptop, sucked down my salty-sweet icy treat, and then I remembered: *Oh shit. It's July 11, 2013. Orange Is the New Black* had come out today, which I obviously had marked in my calendar, but in the chaos of moving and having new-city brain, I had sadly forgotten. I launched Netflix, connected to the ever-lagging Starbucks Wi-Fi, and urged every muscle in my face to appear cool and collected.

The first few seconds of the *Orange* pilot include naked women kissing in the shower, and within the first couple minutes, you will see numerous sets of boobs bouncing around in the slimy showers of a women's prison. I slammed my laptop shut, terrified that Chelsea's virgin eyes might've already caught a glimpse of my depravity, or that her deeply Catholic, deeply lesbophobic sister might've noticed that I was a perverted sexual deviant who watched lesbian porn in public. I, a horny and questioning twenty-one-year-old watching a TV show on my laptop, was basically a man masturbating on the subway. I was sick, twisted, criminal. *Monster,* I thought to myself about myself, followed by, *Let's revisit this later.*

I waited all day until I could wave good night to my new roommates, cutting our first-week bonding time short, and creep into my dimly lit lair to watch my lesbian programs. And over the next two days, I stayed up through the night, soaking up as much of the day's free time as I could, and more moonlight, to absorb season one of *Orange Is the New Black* into my gay vortex. My roommates and I were so new to the apartment that not only was the roommate I would be sharing a room with still packing up her stuff on the East Coast, but Sarah and I didn't even have Wi-Fi set up yet; I obliterated my family's data plan by streaming all thirteen episodes on my greasy little iPhone, alone in my bedroom, like an adolescent violently masturbating in front of their glowing blue screen in their shame room. Anyway, I loved *Orange Is the New Black.* I wanted to slice it open and wear it as skin.

When the second season came out, things were starting to change for me. I had become super close (too close) with my best-friend-from-the-cult-turned-infatuation, Darcy; I had a few queer friends; and I was questioning my sexuality. My fixation with *Orange*, which once felt like a dirty secret, was now a mutually agreed-upon phenomenon; the show was nominated in twelve categories at the Emmys in its first year, of which it won three, and the show was extolled, if not totally adopted, by the queer community. I was very literal and unimaginative; I had seen the world as it was fed to me—a walled-in community of backward Kangol hats and creeps named Turtle—and I hadn't asked questions, I'd just assumed, *We are pawns in Doug Ellin's world.* But when I saw *Orange*, when I watched this heartbreaking, steamy, passionate romance play out between its two protagonists, Alex Vause (Laura Prepon) and Piper Chapman (Taylor Schilling), I realized that I had never seen something so . . . lesbian. Not once, ever, on TV or in real life. It's unsettling how matter-of-fact I've been at times in my life, unable to visualize what I might want until I witness it playing out on TV or in tabloids and think, "Whoa, cool." I didn't question the lack of lesbian or queer women and stories in film and TV because I had never seen them at all. I didn't question my own sexuality in high school because there weren't any (out) lesbians or queer women in my school. You can't miss what you don't know is there. I just figured that's how it was, here in the mind of Doug Ellin: LGBTQ people weren't prevalent on-screen or in real life (the former was true at the time; the latter obviously was not). But watching *Orange*, alone in my new bedroom in my new city, on the starting line of my new life, I began to really feel something gay wiggling inside me, slowly moving its way through my gut, into my lungs, and eventually, out of my throat and into the world. You have to be able to see yourself to see *yourself.* I didn't know that being a lesbian was an *option* for me, because I didn't think lesbians were *real*. They were simultaneously as real and as mythological, as threatening and as harmless as Bigfoot: they may or may not be out there, waddling through the woods hunting their prey, and may or may not be extremely dangerous. No one thinks, *Could I be Bigfoot?* Similarly, I didn't think any of the lesbian-skewing thoughts I had, like *My best friend is hot*, or *Can a girl be your boyfriend?* or *I think I'm lactose intolerant*, could mean anything other than that I was weird, or I just hadn't met the right guy yet—*not* that I was a cryptozoology fan fave. Seeing Alex and Piper on-screen, or really immersing myself in Alex and Piper, feeling my own emotional attachment to their story line, feeling excited by their chemistry in ways I hadn't before, cracked something open inside me. It was lesbianism, yes. But it was also love. Just pure love.

Fast-forward: For season two, in June 2014, I hosted an *Orange Is the New Black* watch party at my apartment. A few of my queer female friends attended, a few of my straight friends, but in the end, it was me and my bisexual friend who stayed up until one a.m. bingeing the show. I finished it the next day, and felt that sinking feeling—which was still new at the time, since Netflix binge-watching had only been around for about a year or so—of "Noooooo, *if I watch this last episode, I'll have to wait a full year for more!*" I couldn't wait a whole year to see more Alex and Piper. There wasn't a world that I felt comfortable living in where I could wait another year to see Alex and her arm tattoo grab Piper by the waist and kiss her. I knew what I had to do. I had to become *arms akimbo like a superhero* Gay.

Orange not only boosted representation of lesbians, queer women of color, and transgender women of color, it demanded space for all of us to exist on TV. And off TV! My understanding that lesbians were Bigfoot started to melt, morph, evaporate, and reappear in a new form: First, that Bigfoot was hot. Then, that Hot Bigfoots are everywhere. Then, that lesbians were *not*, in fact, monsters in forests (though we are PRESENT in forests), but were rather . . . people? And finally, that I, myself, was one of those people, and that I always had been—I just couldn't see it through my Doug Ellin–warped vision. There was no room, and *Orange* said, "I'll make room." And afterward, female queerness exploded on TV.

Before *Orange*, there was Showtime's iconic *The L Word*, created by
Ilene Chaiken, which was the first time queer women were given any significant amount of space on the small screen. Chaiken's show gifted us with the
ability to watch lesbians interact on a weekly basis; it was for queer women,
by queer women; it was sexy and hot, but not predatory or voyeuristic. It
was true to form (though sometimes soapy). There were also monumental
lesbian story lines on *Grey's Anatomy*, *Buffy the Vampire Slayer*, *Glee*, *Pretty
Little Liars*, and *Degrassi: The Next Generation*. But after *Orange*, after one
of its writers, Lauren Morelli, penned an op-ed about realizing she was
gay while writing for the show (and later marrying one of its stars, Samira
Wiley), after Laverne Cox was nominated for three Emmys, catapulting a
Black trans woman to stardom, other networks had no excuse: They *had*
to include queer women on-screen. Not just because if they didn't, they
weren't keeping up with competitive prestige television, but because the
people demanded it. For comparison's sake: In 2014, the year *Orange* was
first nominated for an Emmy, just two other shows with queer storylines
were nominated, *Girls* and *Modern Family*, both of which only featured
white, male queer characters. In 2019, *Orange*'s final airing year, a number
of queer-led shows were nominated for multiple Emmys, including *Pose*,
Schitt's Creek, *Killing Eve*, and *Fleabag*. In 2019, GLAAD reported that 109
LGBTQ series regulars were counted on streaming platforms for the 2019–
2020 season, 49 percent of whom were women, as well as 90 LGBTQ regulars on prime time broadcast networks, 16 percent of whom were women.
In 2014, when streaming services weren't yet being counted in their own
category, just 32 LGBTQ series regulars were counted, and they didn't even
bother to disclose how many of those *32* characters were women. Fucking
yikes.

What is coolest about *Orange* is not just that it made so many people
feel seen and loved—lesbian and bisexual women, Black women, Latinx
women, women who have been incarcerated, transgender women, women

women women—but that it was a show just for us, for women—more specifically, for queer women—that was celebrated widely. Wondering if the world was ready for *Orange* or if *Orange* made us ready is very chicken or the egg: it sat on the faces—sorry—the shoulders of giants like *The L Word* and *Queer as Folk*. Was *Orange* the most excellent gay show, and *that's* why it broke the dam? At the time, yes, it was the best. More broadly, I'm not sure it's the most outstanding gay female TV show in history, though it's certainly one of them. Whether we realized it or not in 2013, the timing was immaculate. We were open, ready, and lubed up, and *Orange* brought me—sorry, uh—us, to orgasm.

It was massively successful: Netflix reported in 2019 that *Orange* was its most watched original ever, with about 105 million users having watched at least one episode. *Orange Is the New Black* was the first show lesbian and queer women had that was mainstream cool. Queer women have always been cool, with our overalls, our baggy sweatshirts, our hiking boots, our plant-based milks. But *Orange* changed things on a grand, unanimous, mainstream level: it made lesbian culture fucking *cool*. Not just visible, but cool. Fuck *Entourage*—Hummers, a matching sports hat and jersey, and an inexplicably naked girl isn't cool. Floral tattoos, fingerbanging, and unbridled emotional attachment is fucking cool. Queer women didn't need America or the Emmys to confirm that for us, but the dam-breaking impact and significance of *Orange Is the New Black* mattered because of how it affected people, on a deeply personal basis. It's important to feel valued culturally, to be told on a grand scale that you have worth, when you grow up feeling the opposite. And feeling worthy? I love it. Can't get enough of it. Again, chicken or the egg: I said we were "lubed up" for *Orange*, but the show changed things so drastically for queer people. Two years after its release, same-sex marriage was upheld in the landmark *Obergefell v. Hodges* Supreme Court case. *Orange* and gay marriage aren't inextricably linked, but they're not *not* linked. The show illustrated a newer, better set of beliefs that I, and my allies, could adopt into our own unimaginative lives, replacing the skeletons and ash of the barren Doug Ellin–scape that so ravaged them. And once I was able to visualize a new framework of a new creed, my life got immeasurably better. All of our lives did. Bottom line: *Orange* opened doors for us, doors that were closed in many of our heads that we were too afraid to peek behind. And afterward, there was just no going back.

But then I regressed again. Over the next few years, I began to chip away at the shrine I'd built to Respecting Women, specifically queer women, and the things we love. I didn't even know I was doing it. Old habits die hard. In the few years following my first secret binge of *Orange*, I developed a following on Twitter for my writing and my lesbian jokes. In 2019, a friend of mine, in an attempt to explain or justify my success as an internet writer, or to make sense of it, told me, "You know why people like you? Because you have all the workings of Gay Twitter, but for lesbians," he said, "and no one else offers that." And my ego immediately agreed with him.

If you're unfamiliar, Gay Twitter is a gay-male-dominated corner of Twitter in which gay men meme pop stars, female celebrities, and themselves to death. Reading Gay Twitter has brought me immense joy; I've always appreciated how vilely mean and thrillingly funny gay men can be, and Gay Twitter is a space for gay men to really flex those muscles. The jokes are very, very mean, and very, very laugh-out-loud funny (unless you're one of Gay Twitter's past targets, like Millie Bobby Brown, Bebe Rexha, or Rita Ora). Basically, I live for Gay Twitter. I share the interests of these men—pop stars, Academy Award–winning actresses over forty, dark magic—and I also share their sense of humor. So when my gay male friend told me that I was, essentially, the Only Funny Lesbian, I was honored. I was thrilled to be so adored by gay men, a group of people I respected so much, who I thought were the epitome of funny. In a way, my friend was right: I tweet and write about the same things as gay men, with a similar bite or angle, but with the added service of writing about them from a specifically lesbian angle, of lust rather than appreciation. It made sense to me; queer women follow me because I can offer them this service of being aggressively, abrasively lesbian . . . and also be funny.

Obviously, once again, my credence was flawed. To be fair, we are a very self-serious people. Lesbians will not laugh at your jokes if they are even vaguely problematic (as we shouldn't!). Are our lives supposed to be funny to you? Are these plants I raised and repotted *funny to you?* Is this cottage I built with my bare hands and these coffee beans I acquired from a sustainable, vegan Latinx roaster in Echo Park just a JOKE TO YOU??? But just because we are dead serious and are probably all ten-thousand-year-old witches who have seen it all and think you're boring, does NOT mean that we aren't funny. That said, try to name ten superstar lesbian comedians off the top of your head right now. You can't! There aren't that many famous lesbian comedians. And that's not a measure of whether or not lesbians are funny, but whether or not the boys' club values us, or what we like, what we find funny, enough to elevate us to such a level. It's "one of the boys" syndrome all over again!

I wasted decades caring about what straight men thought about me. I don't believe the time period in which I spent valuing gay male opinions over gay female opinions was necessarily time *wasted*—just like I wasn't afforded the opportunity to spend time with queer women in my youth and teenage years, I also hadn't bonded with any queer people. Still, I was jarred by the realization that I saw more merit in being praised by the gay male community than my own community, one which I, once again, had convinced myself I didn't fit into.

When I was first coming out and exploring Being Bigfoot, there were times when I really did feel outcast, like I "wasn't like the other girls." Many of the jokes that were exchanged between women in my own community, jokes about ourselves as queer women, I just couldn't relate to.

I felt this distance between myself and the "old guard" of lesbianism, if you will: quips about Subarus, flannel shirts, cats, and U-Hauls that have been tossed about for decades. But as a twenty-three-year-old who had just sprouted her first gay feather, I couldn't relate to U-Hauling (progressing so fast with a new partner that you rent a U-Haul and move in together), or owning a Subaru hatchback for camping trips, or wearing stereotypical lesbian uniforms. The stuff I did like—pop music, famous actresses, gossip blog headlines from 2004—tended to align with what my gay male friends were into. So I assumed I was just "one of the boys" again, instead of examining what moldy jars of misogyny and homophobia I was keeping in my fridge. What stereotypes had I been fed about lesbians my whole life that made me resent them so much, that made me want so badly to be able to be gay without having to be fully, well, *gay* gay? To be a lesbian, but not *that* kind of lesbian. What's wrong with being *that* kind of lesbian, and what does "that kind of lesbian" even mean? I have Level 10 heteronormative brain rot.

Queer women don't have a lot of stuff that's permeated all areas of culture, is considered cool, and is also just for us, but know this: we are inarguably cool as shit. Look at Kristen Stewart: I'm not even her biggest fan, but in her Ray-Ban sunglasses, her ratty tees, her rugged denim, and her greasy, tousled hair, she radiates the same kind of timeless cool that was previously reserved for men, like James Dean in the '50s, or Leonardo DiCaprio in the '90s—and not because she's mimicking it but because she's redefining it. Stewart is taking up space in cool culture. She doesn't give a fuck about anything, certainly not you. She'll saunter right onto that *Saturday Night Live* stage and say, "I'm super gay, fuck you" (I'm going a bit off-script here). She'll star in a *Charlie's Angels* reboot as basically herself and say "Good morning Charlie, go fuck yourself" (or something); she doesn't care. Look at the new class of queer movie and TV stars we have today: Tessa Thompson, Zoë Kravitz, Sarah Paulson, Evan Rachel Wood, Kate McKinnon.

Look at our ancestors: Wanda Sykes, Rosie O'Donnell, Holland Taylor, Lily Tomlin, Queen Latifah, Ellen DeGeneres (who, once again, is friends with George W. Bush, which is insane, but for the sake of this list, we will KEEP HER), Jodie Foster. Jodie Foster has been wearing belted khakis and crew-neck T-shirts on-camera for nearly half a century. Have you seen *Contact*? Jodie Foster in *Contact* is lesbianism in its purest form, and has influenced decades of women's fashion. Now THAT'S lesbian representation.

To this day, I go back and forth between "I'm not that kind of woman," or "I'm not that kind of lesbian," and then baselessly claiming, "This is what lesbians are" (ex.: belted khakis, lactose intolerant, "I grew these coffee beans ON A SUSTAINABLE FARM BY MYSELF with my WIFE," etc.). After a lifetime of feeling stereotyped or pigeonholed as a woman and as a lesbian, it's both harmful for me to consume jokes like this, and cathartic to release them into the world and say, "I make the rules now. I'm gay, and these are the things that I like, so these things are gay. This is lesbian canon."

I went from "one of the boys" and "I'm not like the other girls" to "don't even look at me if you don't want to talk about how awesome women are, specifically Alex and Piper on *Orange Is the New Black*," to being "one of the gay boys," to throwing my moldy oppression jars in the dumpster. I'm tired of pretending the things men like are cool. I'm sorry, but cigars and the state of Colorado aren't cool. Kings of Leon? Not cool. The National? Cool *now* because Aaron Dessner produced Taylor Swift's *folklore* and *evermore*.

Remember, the thing about Lady Trieu's Nostalgia is: it was pulled from shelves once users began to abuse it in an obsessive attempt to relive their most painful memories, leading to psychosis. I understand these fictional *Watchmen* consumers, I really do. In using my own little nostalgia portal, HBO Max, I sought to view the past with some newfound perspective. I sought to understand when I formed this stupid worldview about women, where I got the idea that what men think of me is of value. But what's actually of value to me isn't what Doug Ellin thinks is of value. I mean, what does he like? Unironic zip-off khakis? Cop-ass Oakley sunglasses? Bongs shaped like dicks, but "no homo"? I can't relive this anymore—it's just so sad. Time to pour those Nostalgia pills down the drain. And by that I mean cancel my HBO Max subscription—$14.99 per month? What am I, an oil tycoon? Just give me a splash of oat milk and a girl in red playlist; I'll be good to go.

A BRITNEY SPEARS *BLACKOUT* —
NO, NOT THAT ONE

THE POWER THAT pop songs have cannot be understated. Their ability to transport us back to whatever reality we were living in at the time that song was marked with a memory: there's no quicker or more visceral way to revisit a particular feeling. What sucks is that you don't get to choose what songs end up being the score to the important moments in your life. You can try to. You can coo to your partner, "This is OUR song!" But I promise you, it's never going to be *that* song, the one you consciously choose, that fucking wrecks you when you hear it in a Rite Aid, or on the radio, or at a live show. You can't choose your trauma soundtrack; your trauma soundtrack chooses you.

I often wonder what song will be ruined for me next. What Top 40 hit that I currently love will one day loom over me, a striking reminder of one of the best or worst moments of my life? It's like a sudden natural disaster or a tragic death—you can't predict when it will happen, where you'll be when it strikes, or how profoundly it'll affect you. But nevertheless, one day, that Michelle Branch song you once adored might turn on you, haunt you in your sleep, bang down your door in the middle of the night, ripping down the walls you so diligently built to protect yourself only to be disarmed by *that* song and *that* moment it reminds you of. Isn't it . . . kinda cool? How dumb and fragile we are, able be wholly destabilized by the likes of . . . Katy Perry?

I was sitting on the dusty Persian rug in my teammate's living room, my face glued to the pink-and-purple glow of the television. MTV Hits was on. If you don't know, MTV Hits was a channel that diverged from the 2000s MTV programming with the promise of solely broadcasting music videos (as the original channel intended). Typically, after school, my friends and I would kick off our Uggs (yikes) and turn on MTV Hits, alternating between Bowling for Soup, gossiping, Usher, and gossiping. But on this cool, goose-bumpy autumn night in New Jersey, MTV Hits was the white noise in a room buzzing with the excitement of teenage girlhood. I was wearing a white-and-navy tennis skirt with a hooded sweatshirt. I was fourteen years old, a freshman in high school, and a sponge with gaping sponge holes. The older girls on the tennis team liked me because I could be loud and jocular, unlike the other timid freshmen. But most times I was an observer, soaking up my upperclassmen teammates' behavior and trying to mimic the good and dispose of the bad. I was such an empty canvas that it scared me, always afraid to show my hand, in that I had no hand, knew nothing about anything, and felt embarrassed to even be alive near such cool, older tennis girls who had done things like drink beer and get fingered.

I had taken tennis lessons since I was eight, and had played on recreational sports teams before, but this was my first foray into being on a *real* team, a high school sports team. And in high school, teams did things like "bonding." On the tennis team, it was tradition to host "bonding dinners" on the night before a match. Each night, a different tennis mom would host the squad and their moms, and the girls would eat pizza, gossip, sometimes ask each other weird questions like "Would you rather make out with a guy who drools too much, or throw up on a dick?" Our team bonding was pretty mild, paling in comparison to the other sports teams, most of which comprised Populars and Hots who hazed the hell out of each other. Why were the tennis girls so mild comparatively? Because we were a squad of fucking losers.

Except for this one senior girl, the girl who tore up the tennis team's history book and decided to rewrite it—she was the stuff of legends. Every once in a while, a Popular or a Hot, or a Popular Hot, would diverge from the Hot Girl sports (like field hockey or basketball) and conscript to the tennis team—it was rare, but it happened, and that senior girl, Tori, made it possible for Hots to play tennis. When I was a freshman, Tori gave me hope: All of my friends, who I knew were destined to be both Populars and Hots, joined the field hockey squad in 2004, leaving me behind as a Loser Not-Hot. Early into my first tennis season, I feared that I had made a life-ruining, irreversible mistake. After all, this was Tori's last year, and if she didn't pass the torch to another Popular or another Hot, or another Popular Hot, the tennis team would surely shrivel into obscurity, withering and dying a gruesome death with the Freaks and the Uglies. We were a cursed arrangement of quiet weirdos who played violin and stuck rubber bands in our braces. But Tori, along with her successor, Brooke, changed that.

Brooke was a junior, and she was magnetic. She actually defected from the field hockey team—the hottest team in the school. She was a revolutionary and a thought leader. Brooke was one of the only girls I've ever met who actually resembled how most teenage manic pixie dream girls are written in movies. She was unafraid, political, head of yearbook, a true independent woman who didn't give a fuck about how deserting the field hockey team would affect her career as a Popular. Brooke was so multidimensional it was intimidating. I remember one time—and this was truly the most hazing I ever had to participate in as a freshman—Brooke declared that she would dress up as Allison Reynolds from *The Breakfast Club* the following day, and whenever a freshman passed her in the hallway, we'd have to scream "Oh my god, it's the girl from *The Breakfast Club*!" Brooke just wanted to wear heavy eyeliner and all black to school. And she thought it was really, really funny. We did do it, and it was really, really funny.

But on this autumn night, Brooke sat across from me on the floor, fiddling with a toothpick in her mouth, one arm draped casually over a bent knee, the other arm leaning on a sofa cushion. She took up space. Paper plates speckled with oil littered the floor, the ghost of pizza still haunting the room. There were about eight other girls there, belching and belly-laughing while moms with wineglasses milled about behind a closed door. Somewhere between exchanged nuggets of gossip and soda burps, the room fell silent; everyone's attention turned toward the flashing lights behind the cupboard doors, where the TV glowed. Brooke and I were both watching, diligently, before the group joined in, noticing what was happening on-screen. It began with those six unmistakable synth hits. The poppy, percussive clap of hands. The sensual draw of the artist's breath. It was impossible to turn away once those sounds beckoned, demanding your attention. After those first stabs of audio, I locked eyes with the music video: Her orange, sticky skin. The Sun In–like glow of the apocalyptic sky. A desperate ache for one last drop of water. It was "I'm a Slave 4 U" by Britney Spears—an enrapturing song and moment for pop music, but a *war cry* for horny teens of the aughts.

All of us, as a team, watched Britney slither through her choreography, sweat traveling down the crease of her neck, her breathy mouth and lazy bottom lip calling for us: *Lust for me*, Britney's sweat beads beckoned. Both male and female dancers gripped her slick skin, pined for her, desperate for her to strike up an orgy, and all ten of us girls watched, even more desperate, too scared of our own hormones to look such heaving sex in the eye, yet too horny to look away. We were in a trance, hypnotized by Britney's pheromones, which were being transmitted through audio waves. And just before a detectable tremble could escape the back of a feeble, violin-playing freshman's throat, Brooke said it. She said a thing I'll never forget for as long as I live . . .

"I'd go down on Britney Spears. Easily."

My senses abandoned me. Taste? Gone. Smell? Nope. Touch? Fuck off. My pupils turned to gaping black holes as my neck craned 180 degrees to gawk in wonder at Brooke. My vision turned to a kaleidoscopic prism of both her and Britney's faces. My body remained on the floor but my soul escaped in wisps through my nose, then shuttled down a rabbit hole, throttling through a winding tunnel of Technicolor that ended in devastating blackness, a vacuum of sensory deprivation that one can only experience during their First. Gay. PANIC.

When I came to, half of my teammates were scream-laughing, clearly uncomfortable with but amused by Brooke's outrageous statement. Oral sex??? On a GIRL???? The other half of the girls trembled uncomfortably, unsure how to respond to such unthinkable words. Brooke remained unshakeable. She cackled with the girls but straddled this inscrutable line of laughing with you and laughing at you, neither revealing if she was serious nor being hyperbolic. The words thrashed around in my skull like booms in a cave: "Go down, go down, go down . . ." "Britney . . . Britney . . . Britney . . ." "LESBIAN!!! LESBIAN!!! LESBIAN!!!"

It couldn't be. How could one girl . . . go down on ANOTHER girl? It didn't make sense to me. Sure, I knew what lesbians were—I mean, culturally, I was aware of them and I had come to know that they were freaks. But there couldn't be lesbians . . . HERE. Not near me. Not in New Jersey. A LESBIAN? In New JERSEY?? I knew there were hundreds of Hot Singles Near Me, but LESBIANS?? It didn't make sense. Brooke had to be kidding. But what kind of sick Batman villain would say something so vile, so shocking—what kind of game was Brooke playing? What trickery had befallen Mountain Lakes, New Jersey? Here was Brooke, legendary Popular Hot who had already gone where no girl had gone before—as in, defected from the field hockey team—and who had more natural cool and confidence than anyone could possibly be born with. And she, this person I had come to understand as being a perfect archetype of a teenage girl, was expressing desire . . . sexual desire . . . toward another girl. I couldn't wrap my mind around it.

Those words haunted me all throughout high school. Here I had thought I wanted to *be* Brooke. But I knew for sure that I did NOT want to be a lesbian. I couldn't reconcile the two. I wondered: *Could you date boys, like Brooke did, and also be a lesbian?* (Yes, and I did that for years—it's very different from being bi- or pansexual.)

For years after, whenever I heard the song "I'm a Slave 4 U," I was blasted back to that moment, the first time I heard a girl make some sort of declaration of sexual desire about another woman. When those six bassy synth hits squirted out of the car radio and into my ears, I felt like Derek Zoolander fighting the hypnotic power of "Relax" (sorry to bring the character Derek Zoolander into this queer space). I was under the control of that memory, a memory that was objectively not traumatic, yet still shook me. I was so quickly and so easily transported back to that moment, to that feeling of my reality splitting at the seams, to the fear I had felt that everything I'd come to know about girls who liked girls wasn't just wrong . . . it was *lies*.

When I think about "I'm a Slave 4 U" today, I laugh. It's such a haunting and amusing reminder of what it's like to be fourteen, so unscathed, just an amalgamation of other people's thoughts that you've heard and accepted as truth, getting your world rocked every twenty minutes by some new piece of information, then trying to make sense of it. It's not shocking to me that a Britney Spears song could change a person. She's god—god changes people. I was, however, far less prepared to come face-to-face with a pop star whose song had also chosen me . . .

CRUSH ME AT THE FORUM

THINGS WERE NOT good with Kate. I knew that, despite trying to change it. We had been dating for three months, but she had broken it off a few times. The first couple of times, it wasn't *really* over. When she told me she didn't want a relationship or to call me her girlfriend, I played it cool. When she told me that this had all become too much for her, I drove shrieking and wailing to my friend Sam's apartment to flail around on his floor and insist she didn't mean it while he stared at me like, *Should I call an ambulance?* When I was sitting at a conference table at work, surrounded by coworkers, and that little gray iMessage bubble popped up in the corner of my computer to say "I can't do this anymore," all of the blood in my body turned to stone, but still, I hoped for the best.

That's how it works with these types of relationships, right? One person is in way too deep, offering all their horcruxes to their lover to hold and to crush, while the lover just walks in and out of their life as they please. The lover is like, "I want this," then, "I changed my mind," then, "I need you," and then, "I told you, I can't do this." And when you're the Me in this Hell Relationship, the giver of horcruxes, you just do what the lover says. You beg for scraps, you take her back, you watch her go, you decide that you believe in god so you can pray for her to come back, you take her back, you get fucking desecrated over and over until all your horcruxes are gone and you've become goo. That's what I did with Kate. I let her grind me up until

I was gone. And then she snorted me up like cocaine. And then she pooped me out. And then she flushed me. And then I lay in a sewer, rats weaving through the bits and bobs of my corpse. And then the rats ate me. And then the rats pooped me out. And then I went back to her. Okay? That's what happened.

When Kate texted me "I can't do this anymore," I stared at my laptop, catatonic, my face flushing, water beating behind my eyes, ready to deluge. I excused myself to the bathroom so as not to come unglued in front of my coworkers. In the stall, I called on my lizard brain to come through for me, muttering, "Do not cry, you stupid bitch" until the stone-blood in my face once again turned liquid and pulsed through my body. I lizard-brained through the rest of the workday, got in my car, and drove home, white-knuckling the steering wheel while participating in the most gruesome act of self-harm I've ever done: blasting the Chainsmokers. I was not of sound mind. I pulled into my driveway, and Kate texted me again, as I hadn't answered since she'd sent the text that morning. Her second text was simply a slanty-mouthed smiley face. I had given her all of my horcruxes in a ceremonial offering at her altar—though she did not ask for them—and she gave me a slanty-face emoji.

A few weeks of pitch-black depression later, Sam knew just what would cheer me up, because of course he did. Sam and I met a couple of years earlier at our mutual friend Debby's Fourth of July party, but it wasn't until a few months later that we'd really bonded. In the fall, we reconvened at Debby's. We sat cross-legged on her living room floor, and Sam craned his iPhone toward me to show me a *Vanity Fair* headline that changed my life. It read: "Mary-Kate Olsen and Olivier Sarkozy's Wedding Featured 'Bowls Filled with Cigarettes.'" Something in my body snapped, and I nearly coughed

up my guts laughing so hard with him about the image of "bowls" of cigarettes as a wedding table centerpiece. After that night, Sam and I began
texting each other Google Images of Meghan Trainor, and we've been close
ever since. Sam and I are in constant communication via text, even if the
communiqués are just paparazzi photos of pop stars, or memes that say
something like "I may be a dumb bitch but I'm also stupid" inexplicably
juxtaposed with a photo of Daisy Duck. Sam sees and understands my soul
in a way that feels extremely rare. At the time that I was breaking down the
altar I'd built for Kate, Sam also happened to be going through a devastating
breakup, and that mutual despair further trauma-bonded us.

Also, the last six months of my life had been chaos, and I was living with
my parents. They had moved from New Jersey to Chatsworth, a town just
outside of L.A. in 2014. Six months earlier, in the fall of 2016, I was laid off
from my job as an on-air cohost and producer at an FM radio show, the *Zach
Sang Show*. From there, I ran out of money, stayed with my friend Debby
for a couple months, moved in with my parents, moved into a damp studio
apartment, ran out of money again and also my apartment had bugs, moved
back in with my parents, went cuckoo for Kate, then came utterly unglued.
One morning in April, Sam called me, and I picked my thousand-pound
head off the patterned quilt in my parents' guest bedroom, and groaned.

"Hiiii," he flirted. "Work is giving me two tickets to The Pop Star at the
Forum this weekend. Should we go?"

"Um . . . yeah," I croaked. Of course I *wanted* to go. Fucking obviously
I would want to go to that. The only thing that would've seemed shady or
out of the ordinary would've been if I said "No, going to a pop concert is
not something I'd want to do." Pop stars are my favorite, more than actresses
over forty, more than long-forgotten CW stars. But I *was* being shady. Upon
accepting the invitation, I decided to hide something from Sam, a piece of
information that made up 99 percent of my real reason for wanting to—no,
needing to—go to The Pop Star at the Forum.

A month or so earlier, when Kate and I were still together, she'd told me that her younger brother, a gay, was coming to town, and she had bought three tickets to The Pop Star at the Forum, because he loved The Pop Star. At the time, she'd asked if I wanted to go with them, and I was like, ready to offer my firstborn to be able to go with her and a member of her family to The Pop Star at the Forum. Back then, I still imagined a future between Kate and I, and sharing an experience like that with her younger brother felt like the next step in a relationship I so desperately coveted.

So when Sam asked if I wanted to go see The Pop Star at the Forum, yeah, of course I wanted to go to the pop concert with my best friend. Plus, Sam was an editor at a fancy news magazine, so the tickets were free, and the seats would be incredible. But also, I knew Kate would be there, which meant I'd get one more chance to text her. But just about the concert. And definitely not about anything else, like my feelings, or reviving our relationship, or swearing a blood oath to each other.

Kate and I did talk after the "I can't do this anymore" text; after work that night, we texted back and forth until I was numb and fell asleep with my face crusted to my pillow. She had reached out numerous times afterward, trying to keep things civil and friendly, but I asked her for space, because if we really weren't going to be together and were supposed to be moving in the direction of friendship, then I needed some time to heal. Heal, I did not. So, when I texted her the day of The Pop Star at the Forum, my intentions were, of course, to respark the thing that had been resparked and fucking blasted by a fire hose a hundred times already. We kept it casual, and agreed to meet up in the aisles between the opening act and The Pop Star's set. It was *casual*, I told myself. But every time her name popped up on my iPhone, I recognized the emptiness I'd felt without it, the void I'd felt emanating from my screen, how much I missed seeing the little curves of her name appear in a blue glow, and the excitement that brought me.

Sam and I vibrated in the back of a Lyft on our way to the Forum, which sits in a deadlocked area of L.A. that absolutely sucks to get to, traffic-wise. By this point, he knew my real intentions—he had tried to cancel on me earlier in the day, and I basically held him hostage until he agreed to take me to see my ex-girlfriend who wasn't ever actually my girlfriend so I could torture myself one last time. I pulled on the loose strands of my hair, a nervous tic of mine. I picked at my face, another tic. I nibbled my nails, tapped my toes, lowered and raised the window—I was not well. I had the kind of palpable nervous energy that makes anyone in proximity to my shivering body nervous too. Sam was not happy with his decision to aid in my act of self-harm, which he was realizing, in turn, was harming him too.

We found our seats. I stared at all 17,000 seats in the house, wondering which one belonged to the person who made my heart flutter and shatter with each ping on my phone, which one belonged to her brother, and which one was supposed to be mine. Sam and I watched The Opening Act, a girl group we adored that nobody had ever heard of.

The Opening Act exited, the house lights came up, and I knew it was my time to walk the plank. Sam looked at me the way you look at your best friend through the back windshield of a car as she drives away to college for the first time. He wished me luck, but I could see the fear in his eyes—that sacrificial *I love you and I'm going to let you do this but only because you need to learn lessons the hard way, but oh god, don't do this* look. It was like he and the entire rest of the stadium were smart enough to know that this one would sting. But I didn't. Or I didn't care.

As it turned out, Kate was sitting in the section next to me, so we walked up the stairs to meet in an aisle that felt private enough that we could say what we needed to say while going mostly unnoticed, but public enough to feel protected by the crowd. When I first saw her, I managed to fight back tears. We hugged. We bantered. Whatever sound space wasn't filled with Top 40 intermission music was abuzz with the excitement of 17,000 young adult girls. It was easy to not talk about *the thing*, to distract ourselves from feeling, and instead discuss the trillions of conversations and moments being had around us. Until it wasn't. After a long, long while, the conversation lulled. A security guard asked us to find our seats, and we said our seats were nearby, that we'd return in a second.

And then she stared at me. I stared at her. The tears came back. She pulled me in for a hug, and I hugged her back. I could feel from the shake of her body that she was crying. I let myself cry too. I felt the grit of her denim jacket between my fingers, smelled the way her hair and skin always smelled, and tried to store it in my memory. I felt what it was like to hold on to her for what, it became clear in this moment, would be the last time. I don't know how both of us knew, but we did. In that moment, a pulsing energy tied our bodies together and whispered in both of our ears, "Say goodbye now." I felt everything I had ever felt for her: the love, the obsession, the hate, the sadness, the emptiness, all at once, just sitting there in my belly like blackness and glitter. The security guard turned to ask us once again to return to our seats, but stopped when she saw that we were two lesbians sobbing openly in a public space. I felt our tears mix between our cheeks. I felt her arms gripping my torso tight, like she had so many times before, like she never wanted to let go, even though she knew, deep down, that she would, that she would release me this time. And then, the lights went out.

The arena turned black. The jet-engine roar of thousands of shrieking girls rippled across the stadium, turning the stale energy of intermission to white electricity, like alchemy. In the pitch-blackness, a sprawling LED screen blinked awake, illuminating the human wave comprised of bobbing heads, and a countdown started. Thirty seconds. The sound of a gigantic ticking clock.

Girls and their boyfriends and their dads and their moms and their screaming little sisters bolted around us, bumping into our intertwined bodies in a desperate scramble to find their seats. Kate turned her head, her lips grazing my cheek, and locked her lips on mine. We made out through the salt of tears, the howl of fans, and the ticktock of the countdown. And then she pulled away. A voice bellowed through the arena, counting down the last ten seconds until show time. I looked at her, one last time, the white LED screen reflected in kaleidoscopic refractions in her tears, and she said, hurriedly, "I guess we should go." I forced a laugh through the lump in my throat and said, "Yeah." Our bodies split apart. Our fingers let go. We moved farther and farther away through darkness. The countdown ended. The stadium roared. I ran past the impatient security guard and toward the guiding light of Sam's face, searching for me, worried for me. I jogged down the stairs and locked eyes with him, and I was so laid bare, so exposed, he could see it all over my face. Nothing had to be said, but he said it anyway. Over the hum of excitement in the stadium, he shouted, "You okay?"

I shook my head and sat down in my aisle seat. At the same time, what was left of the remaining seated crowd shot to their feet. The stage lit up. The Pop Star appeared. And the first few bangs of bass rang throughout the stadium: it was her opening song, "All Good." The crowd was invigorated, enlivened, electrified, while I was depleted, gray, defeated. The crowd sang it back to her, because they loved it, because they were happy, because they believed it. And The Pop Star told us, "It'll be all good."

I saw the shimmer of her platinum blonde wig through the crack of indoor hedges as I walked toward the private room of the restaurant, and I stopped in the middle of the room to signal to Sam, *She's here.* I gulped.

Our friend Jess is longtime, childhood friends with The Pop Star. It was a warm December night in Beverly Grove, a little over two years since I had seen The Pop Star perform at the Forum. Jess was throwing a small birthday dinner at this new, vibey Japanese fusion restaurant on Third. Sam had recently discovered it, and it was delicious, despite being one of those Asian restaurants marketed toward white people as having an "unconventional" twist on Japanese food. (There was no twist. It was meat skewers and fish on tufts of rice.) But I'm garbage and I loved it. Sam and I had wondered if The Pop Star would be at dinner, but figured there was no way; Jess would've said something, right? If you're going to dinner with ten or fewer people, and one of them is the most famous pop star in the world, you have to warn the others, right? Those are the rules, RIGHT???

The thing is, I knew The Pop Star too, sort of. We had crossed paths a few times. When I first moved to L.A., I worked at Nickelodeon, where she launched her acting career. We didn't interact much. Once, as a production assistant, I had to drive her from our lot in Hollywood to do ADR (automated dialogue replacement—like a voice-over for dialogue fixes that need to be edited in postproduction) at a studio in Burbank. After a year or so at Nickelodeon, I became the social media manager for many of their channels. Most days, I'd walk to set seeking photo approvals from the stars of the show, including The Pop Star, so that I could post the photos to our channels. When I left my job at Nickelodeon to join a friend at the *Zach Sang Show*, The Pop Star came in for an interview. But when she arrived, it was unclear whether she remembered me from Nickelodeon—and by "unclear" I mean I never brought it up because I was scared of her, so I just sank into the back of the room and pretended not to be alive until it was over. (She definitely remembered me, right? We interacted on a weekly basis! We were coworkers!)

The Pop Star had become this figure in my life—or rather, I molded her into the shape of a meaningful figure. I ascribed meaning to every iteration of our relationship (using that word lightly), assuring myself that the way she kept popping up in my life was significant. When I moved to L.A.

and started working with her, her music career was just blooming. And I thought, *Wow, this is so cool, watching this person's meteoric rise first-hand. Maybe I'm meant to witness this so I can know for sure that I made the right decision to move to this "city of dreams."* Whenever I'd hear her first few popular singles on the radio, I'd always turn it up in the car, because it made me smile ear to ear. It made me feel cool, cruising down the 101 to my new job in my shiny new life in my dazzling new city with these cloudless skies and breezy palm trees. Her success, her new beginnings represented my own new beginnings, my own promised path to success. And when we met again at the *Zach Sang Show*, I thought, *Wow, look at us now, Pop Star. You were once but a Nickelodeon star, and I but a measly production assistant, driving to Burbank together, gabbing about boys and Halloween costumes. Now here we are: you, an international pop sensation promoting your new single, and I, a shock jock on this* Ryan Seacrest–*esque radio show for teens, withering in the corner so as not to be seen or perceived by you.* Of course, my third collision with her wasn't personal, but she did perform live at my breakup. That had to mean something, right?

When Sam and I sat down at the ten-person dinner table in the secluded back room of the "untraditional" Japanese restaurant, I felt my butt cheeks clench in that familiar way, just like they had at the *Zach Sang Show*. I knew, in that moment, that not only would I be extremely weird throughout this whole dinner, but I would also not look The Pop Star in the eye, for fear of not being remembered again, or maybe for fear of existing at all on this stupid earth. Existing continues to be embarrassing, and for some reason, she absolutely paralyzes me.

Sam and I were late to dinner, so we were seated at the end of the table, while Jess and The Pop Star and the scant few others we knew sat in the middle. We made small talk with this straight couple we'd just met and with whom we pounded a few rounds of something called "inside out sushi" (reader: it was just sushi). Toward the end of the dinner, people started shuffling around, and I moved to the other side of the table to talk to another Nickelodeon friend of mine. The Pop Star sat near us, and nausea passed over me. I wanted to engage with her, but I couldn't, like I physically couldn't look at her. I think she just has this effect on people: She's the kind of celebrity presence that sucks all of the air out of the room, demands your attention, rips a true tear in the space-time continuum. She's scary-whip-smart and funny. She's also extremely rich and powerful. That's a truly intimidating combo.

Regardless, throughout the night, I put all of this pressure on myself to talk to her at dinner, to try to make sense of our collision course, to maybe get some closure on the Kate chapter in my life. I don't know. I just wanted The Pop Star to mean something to me at that dinner, like she had in the past, or like I'd foisted upon her numerous times. But we barely talked. We exchanged probably eight words. At one point, I was telling an old friend about the toils of lesbian Tinder, and she jumped in and asked, "What's lesbian Tinder?" and I said, "It's just Tinder. But . . . with lesbians." And my friend, being a straight man, said, "I bet you get a lot of clit pics." And The Pop Star stared at me and asked, "Do you?" And I said, "No, I do not."

I left that dinner with my shoulders in my ears. I was so tense and so disappointed. Her music had been so present in these important moments in my past few years of life, and she was also this actual rising figure in pop culture, and the combination made me feel like I was a part of it, or like she was a part of my life, but she just wasn't. Maybe we did just happen to cross paths like ants on a sidewalk a few times. Maybe she has had some sort of impact on my life. Or maybe I'm just trying to assign meaning to every part of what felt like a massive, life-changing, magical, cinematic-feeling moment because that's what happens in the movies. That moment with Kate couldn't have been scripted more perfectly had it actually been the end of a dreary lesbian movie—it felt so big, like movie magic, so perfectly timed and melancholic and dichotic, the way the crowd's hearts rose and mine fell, and how I knew, I just *knew* that it would be the last time I ever saw or held Kate again. But the thing is: it wasn't.

Sorry to play into the Evil Homosexual trope, but I'm not being totally truthful; I'm an unreliable narrator. Months after The Pop Star at the Forum, I *did* see Kate again. We met up and hung out for a few hours. Then, another time, she took me on a date to get sushi and see *Hamilton* at the Pantages. *That* was actually the last time I ever saw her. But that moment didn't *feel* as big, because it wasn't as physically grand in scale. It was small. I felt small in it. Kate and I finally ended once and for all after she drove us back to her place after *Hamilton*. When we got out of the car, I naturally moved to follow her inside, but she stopped me and said she wanted to go to bed, that this wasn't a good idea, that I should go home. So she went inside and I stood in the moonlight on an empty, winding road in the Hollywood Hills, and I cried. It was so quiet, and so dark, I could hear nothing but crickets, a breeze, and my own muffled sobs. I was severely alone out there; I felt like I could disappear. I got in my car, drove forty minutes back to my parents' house, and cried the whole way there.

But when I think of how Kate and I ended, I think of that night at the Forum, with the hum of the crowd swelling around me, when my heartbreak felt supernova-big and important. *That* was the movie moment. *That* was the story worth telling. It was soundtracked—live!—for fuck's sake! And now that song, "All Good," so poignant at the time, is forever marked for me. I had no idea it would be.

As Sam and I stood on Third Street and watched that blonde wig disappear into the back of a black SUV, I waved goodbye, my hair blowing across my forehead with the breeze of the night, and The Pop Star drove away. Standing there, I felt so unresolved, so empty, so unfulfilled by this night and this person that I wanted more from, who couldn't deliver on my impossible, unfulfillable expectations. "Make sense of my breakup," I wanted to say. "Tell me why it happened at your concert, why I have to hear that song for the rest of my life and think of her, why that moment is inextricable from you and you from it, forever until I die." I mean, how often is it that someone gets to have dinner with the person who sings the song that breaks them into tiny shards of glass every time they hear it? That *has* to mean something, right? But it didn't. I tried to make that dinner matter, but it just didn't. It was a fantasy: My whole fever dream of a breakup with Kate felt so surreal, like the climax in the movie of my life. I wanted this dinner to be a bookend, to close that chapter in a consequential and significant way. I wanted my narrative of Kate to have act structure, to hit the appropriate beats and come to perfect conclusions, to give me a picture-perfect ending to my picture-perfect heartbreak. I wanted The Pop Star herself to reach across the table and say, "I see you. You've come so far. You're going to be fine." But that's not reality. You can't force this stuff. We never get to choose the moments that become meaningful to us.

I joined Sam in reality, and we walked back to our car.

STEP ON ME, JULIANNE MOORE

I'VE RECENTLY BECOME obsessed with *The Bachelor*. No, wait, don't stop reading—I promise it's not about *The Bachelor*, or any of the extended cinematic Bachelorverse shows that dangle limply around the two cash cows that are starkly juxtaposed by gender (*The Bachelor* and *The Bachelorette*). I mean, this show sucks, right? I love it. Whenever I tell people I've recently become obsessed with *The Bachelor*, or my favorite spinoff—the smuttiest one—*Bachelor in Paradise*, they act appropriately shocked: What does this show have for *Jill*, famously and intensely a lesbian? *The Bachelor* is the pinnacle of heterosexuality; it's quite literally not for me. Even when they try to veer into the reality that is the End Times, some girl will be like, "I like a man who can show emotion," and I'm like, THAT'S your measure of excellence? THAT'S where your brain has stopped progressing? You want to date a person who can show an emotion, I—That's so bare minimum, it's— Wow, we are living on separate planes. But that's exactly why I like these shows. The only straight people I know are my parents. For me, watching *The Bachelor* or *The Bachelorette* feels how I imagine aliens feel watching humans go about their little lives. Like, "Damn, they're still doing this shit?" It's a glimpse into a long-lost world, not just the world of heterosexual dating but of heterosexuality as a form. It's a case study: What do these people like? What makes them tick? What's still considered "hot" or "romantic" to them? I mean, the show is popular because there are so many (white) people out there in America who still participate in these long-lost gendered dating "norms," who watch this show and actually *relate* to it, who see these contestants and are reminded of their sweet and simple high school boyfriends who smelled like orange Trident gum and didn't have interests and said things like "Thank a cop today." Perhaps that part of it is comforting to me too, reminding me of my teenage years when I was blissfully ignorant and inherently believed that humanity was worth saving. The show is a numbing agent, a perfect dosage of dullness. But above all, what fascinates me most is one "norm" in particular. There's this recurring phenomenon in which each Bachelorette, or any female contestant on *The Bachelor*, says she loves a man because he reminds her of her own father.

That's weird, right? Am I being insane or is that weird? Sometimes I fear that I'm *so* gay that I can no longer even understand or level with people who experience this caliber of heterosexuality. But the longer I watch *The Bachelor* shows, the more women I see whose eyes well up when they say, "He treats me just like my dad does," or even "He physically resembles my dad, who is fucking hot" (paraphrasing), the more I desperately try to examine if there's a Sapphic equivalent to this clearly Oedipal complex these women are suffering through. What would make a straight woman want to fuck her dad? The easy and obvious answer is that, bubbling not far at all below the surface of these statements, lies a "daddy issue." But, like everything in the world of queer dating, things are often different for queer women. I'm sure tons of queer women have daddy issues. But I can say with certainty that nearly every queer woman I've ever met has some semblance of *mommy* issues. I'm sure all these *Bachelor* girls don't want to *actually* fuck their dads—does having mommy issues lead to lesbianism? No. Does being a queer woman mean you want to fuck your mom? No. It means that mother-daughter issues are complicated, perhaps the most complicated relationship available in the human experience. I think every woman, not just queer women, has a labyrinthine relationship with her mother. And it's obviously quite common to seek partnership with a person who reminds you of the person you've always idolized or sought the most attention from, and perhaps from whom you didn't receive said attention in the amount you desired (i.e., Mommy or Daddy). This isn't news—I'm not stirring up any genius new psychological developments here. But you know what does seem to be somewhat new? Or at least has burst through the earth's crust and exploded like a geyser on social media over the past few years? Queer women who want to get their backs absolutely blown out by actresses over forty years old. Lesbian mommy culture has exploded online in the past few years, and as an active participant in Lesbian Mommy Twitter—a sprawling and ravenous group of women who want Cate Blanchett to step on us—I want to explore this space. See, I promised this wouldn't be about *The Bachelor*—it's about Cate Blanchett. And Lucy Liu. And Rachel W—We'll get there. It's about the mommy phenomenon—The Phemommynon?—and what makes queer women horny.

My mom recently revealed to me in an alarmingly casual manner that I was accidentally malnourished in my first few weeks of life. She said she and my dad took me to the doctor when I was two weeks old because I seemed to be colicky, but what they found out was that she was so exhausted she wasn't producing enough milk, and I wasn't being fed properly. I was legitimately starving. For weeks. She told me this during the pandemic, when my girlfriend and I were over to eat dinner, and then breezed past it to tell me about someone I went to high school with's mom who is QAnon. It was so nonchalant that I just kind of snort-laughed and moved on, like "You learn something new every day!"

But the next day, I started processing what my mom had told me. I was like . . . did I just completely uneventfully come to understand my entire personality? Did my mom just breezily explain my whole life to me in a sentence? That, since just two weeks old, I've been—and I'm saying this with absolutely zero shred of hyperbole—quite literally starving for female attention? Jesus fucking Christ, Mom. What have you done?

For the record, my mom is and was a great mom—and clearly it wasn't a big enough deal that it affected my physical health. But what about my psyche? My desperate search for female attention (or maybe just nutrients? Okay, sorry, I'm done) is the string that's tied together my three decades of life. When I was a toddler, I was obsessed with my cousin's extremely hot babysitter and was stoked whenever she'd hang out with us; when I was in elementary school I ratted out my own babysitter for inviting her boyfriend over (I have been a jealous, toxic lesbian truly since I was five); I used to say things like "Baby Spice is so cute—I wish she was my mom"; in seventh grade I purposefully misbehaved in class so I could sit in detention and "bother" Ms. Williams every day after school; in eighth grade I performed a similar obnoxious feat with my math teacher, Ms. Long (later I would find out this kind of attention-seeking playful nudging is just called "flirting"); every one of my friends' older sisters were like gods to me, these hulking, Amazonian princesses that made me want to bend the knee and whisper "my liege" as they sauntered past me on their BlackBerrys, blasting Sisqó or whatever. And why not? They were bigger and better and hotter and more experienced than me—why not bow to your friends' older sisters? WHY NOT?

So, since childhood, I've been obsessed with older women. I think it's pretty common for kids to be "into" adults in their lives, like babysitters, teachers, friends' siblings. But the difference is, when you're closeted, you can't say it out loud! All the boys in my eighth grade math class said disgusting, sexual stuff about Ms. Long—but I couldn't chime in, even with something as delicate as "I would buy Ms. Long flowers so fucking hard." I couldn't chime in on kiss-the-teacher discourse for twenty-three years! It's no wonder I found myself here, on Lesbian Mommy Twitter, desperately asking Rachel Weisz to hurl me through a cement wall with the strength of a *Westworld* bot. I spent decades repressing my thirst—the word "thirst" here is confusing because, again, at two weeks old, I was actually starving. But now that I'm out as gay, professionally gay even, and wholly supported by my loved ones, it's like the floodgates have burst. My thirst pours out of me like deluges of water gushing from a recently opened dam. I don't even think wanting Angela Bassett to shred me like printer paper is about sado-masochistic yearning—maybe a little, sure, but it's more about the degree to which I feel this long-repressed desire to pine over older women. Also, like the Amazonian Princess older sisters of my youth, they're taller and cooler and better than me! It's like, I'm just a dumb, useless husk of a gay—and you, you're Academy Award–winning actress Julianne Moore (or the captain of the basketball team and have made out with multiple guys). You, Julianne Moore (or Caroline, tall senior sports captain goddess), *shouldn't* like me. We have nothing in common! I'm not your equal. I'm not worthy of your time, your seasoned, gilded time. I don't even want you to give me sexual attention, or any attention—you should just toss me to the curb like the trash that I am. You should step on me.

Who threw the first brick at Stonewall? Who first tweeted or posted to Tumblr "Step on me, Mom"? Questions that may always plague us. If you're unfamiliar with queer thirst Twitter, or the phenomenon of horny fans asking hot celebrities to "step on me," first of all, welcome. I don't want to be like some boomer explaining internet language in a cringe way, so let me just give a brief overview and offer some examples. There's a trend on social media, mostly specific to a fan/celebrity dynamic, in which fans ask the people they're fans of to assert dominance over them. One of the more common outbursts is "Step on me, Mom"—"Mom," because whoever you're a fan of and whoever is "taking care of you," more or less, is now your mom, ideally—"step on me" because you're trash and deserved to be stepped on by your new mom. Does that make sense? The outburst comes in many different flavors, some more violent than others: Brie Larson, punch me in the face—in *Captain Marvel*, Brie Larson punches an old woman in the face, which, to many fans, felt very "one time she punched me in the face—it was awesome" (*Mean Girls*). "Rachel Weisz, please choke me"—in *The Favou-*

rite, Rachel Weisz pins Olivia Colman against her bedpost and chokes her and it's like, okay, obviously that's something *I* want to happen to *me.* So, we're really out here pioneering.

I'm less concerned with firsts and more interested in why the Phemom-mynon happens at all. After all, sexually worshipping someone much older than you is a phenomenon that's existed in many formats, for a long time. In the 2000s, the era of elder sexual worship I came up in was the era of the MILF (or the DILF). I remember being young and not feeling empowered to participate in either MILF or DILF culture. While my friends were all obsessed with "daddies" like George Clooney or Viggo Mortensen, I felt confused by their cravings. I would try to chime in like, "Mmm, yeah, look at his . . . jowls?" I didn't get it. What was there to like about someone as old as my parents? Gross! I was still trying to process the Lawrence brothers—I didn't need to figure out attraction to older men on top of that. And on the other side, 2000s MILF culture was perplexing. MILFs were charac-terized as these hypersexualized, tits-spilling-out-of-triangle-bikinis ladies who were meant to look like they aged out of *Playboy*—Stacy's Mom, Jen-nifer Coolidge as Stifler's mom—just very catered-to-men-type looks that I couldn't vibe with. I mean, don't get me wrong, Jennifer Coolidge is the GOAT, but there was something about the image of "MILFs" in the aughts that made me feel like men were constantly and consistently shocked that a woman over thirty-five could be hot. Or that men thought the only way a woman over thirty-five could have sex appeal was if she was dripping in traditional, male-gazey sex, with tons of makeup, teased hair, frilly lingerie, and "I got these for my husband" implants. I'm not even anti any of those things (makeup, big hair, frills, plastic surgery)—I got a large mole removed from my neck in middle school, which severely reduced my bullying and improved my quality of life, ok? I am PRO plastic surgery—it's just that the idea of doing any of it to please a man makes me green around the gay gills. And the notion that in order to be hot, an older woman would have to physically transform her body to mimic that of her younger self didn't make sense. None of this was hot to me.

I used to think I was just too young to "get" why George Clooney was appealing, or why boys were supposed to drool over women who looked like Stifler's mom. But queer sexual awakenings often happen in more arcane settings, in clandestine corners where one might not think to look, because what's hot to a queer person sometimes isn't what's spoon-fed to heterosexual people as hot or romantic. Before the dam burst, most living queer people have had to piece together, build, and define our own narratives, what *we* think is hot, what *we* want in a partner, what *we* consider to be romantic, how *we* express desire, how *we* receive it. It's like, one day you're thirteen, saying, "Uh, I guess George Clooney has a thick voice?" and the next you're walking out of the 2004 sci-fi thriller *The Forgotten* and saying, "I don't know, I just think Julianne Moore is a REALLY good actress," then refusing to shut up about HOW good of an actress for months.

If you've never even heard of *The Forgotten*, you're truly not alone. I don't know if I know anyone, besides my mom (who I saw the movie with), who has seen this aptly named film. I've seen *The Forgotten*, a sci-fi mystery about a woman named Telly (Moore) who is suddenly told that her children never existed, dozens of times. And yet, I still couldn't really tell you the plot of *The Forgotten*. The plot never mattered. What mattered was that Julianne Moore was just a really, really good actress in this movie—like, she's so cool and her hair is so long. She just really cares about her kids and seems like a good person, you know? Is she in other stuff? I really liked her character but I feel like I should watch more of her movies, just to be sure that she's a really good actress. Her jaw is so strong! I wonder what she smells like?

What I'm saying is, Julianne Moore as a concerned mother in a truly "forgotten" 2000s movie was hot to me. So many of the things I found to be, um, let's go with "exciting" since it wasn't quite clear to me at the time that what I was experiencing was horniness, could not be further from what had been traditionally defined to me as "sexy." Much of what I liked was actually quite maternal, but definitely not in the Stifler's mom type of way: Whoopi Goldberg safeguarding her fellow nuns in *Sister Act* was hot. Shannen Doherty as a protective older sister in *Charmed* was hot. Miss Honey adopting a child and creating the blueprint for cottagecore living in *Matilda* was hot. Kirstie Alley adopting a child and tending to a man's head wound in *It Takes Two* was hot. Geena Davis leading her team and being butch in *A League of Their Own* was hot (okay, I think this one is like, objectively, indisputably hot). To me, *this* is MILF culture. Moms are just hot! Older women are just hot, and not because they're shape-shifting and taking the form of a twenty-year-old girl; they don't need frosted lip gloss or chunky blond highlights or whatever weird shit was thrust upon "MILFs" in the aughts.

You know what's sexy? Being cared for and held and consoled. Safety and warmth makes me horny. I'm broken, sorry!! Queer women, this is my message to you: No one genuinely loves women more than us, right? No one can define what makes a woman hot better than other women. And to any millennial queer women who are reading: We, the children of 2000s MILF culture, need to redefine what a MILF is, take back the night, revert to a time when Mrs. Robinson was the epitome of hot—except we cannot just lust after Mrs. Robinson, we must also ask Mrs. Robinson to stab us. Maybe we just leave the bone-chilling MILF acronym behind and start anew. Because women like Cate Blanchett, Regina King, Sandra Oh, and Gillian Anderson are not "MILFs"—they're so much more than that. Maybe they're more like a MILFEM—Mother I'd Like to Fucking End Me. Or maybe they are MILFs, if the acronym stood for "Mommy I'd Like to *Fear*."

On the "end me" of it all, there's also an element of shame involved. This is why when straight people participate in "kill me" thirst culture, I'm like, no, you don't get to do this. Wanting to die is OUR thing. I don't ever want to see a straight woman on the timeline say, "Brad Pitt, murder me!" Like, there's no grand admission in a cishet woman declaring that Brad Pitt is attractive. You don't need a violent outburst to let people know that you like Brad Pitt, *Danielle*. In thinking about how badly I wanted Caroline (my best friend's older sister) to drown me like a dead rat, or how much I want Gillian Anderson to break my ribs with a splintered baseball bat, there's this inherently queer element of shame, or worth, or lack thereof. Queer people are told from a very young age that their desires are wrong, or twisted, or depraved, which creates a shroud of shame around our desires, and it follows us like a shadow-self throughout our lives. There is the version of "me" that thinks I'm attractive and intelligent and worthy of love, and then there's my shadow-self, my queer shame cloud, which tells me that basketball queen Caroline (or Julianne Moore) could never love something as sick and broken as *you*, you disgusting little twerp. So, in asking Kathryn Hahn to vaporize me, isn't there a part of me that feels like that's what I deserve? That the kind of love or sexual attention I deserve is one that physically injures me? Like, a trade-off: you can have your revolting sexual desires, in exchange for instant death (as seen in *Lost and Delirious*). In asking to be vaporized, I'm taking *back* that shame, *owning* it instead of continuing to be controlled by it. So back off, Danielle. Nobody cares that you think Adam Driver is hot. And you know what? Adam Driver will NEVER hit you with his car, because no one's ever told you that finding Adam Driver sexy is weird, or that you're unworthy of love and deserve violence for simply existing. You don't GET to be hit by Adam Driver's car . . . Does this make sense?

You know what, I swerved a little bit there, I'll admit it. I guess what I'm saying is, MILF culture is a space I'd like to queer, and to queer the MILF space we *must* ask older women to trap our souls in cursed lockets, sentencing us to an eternity of misery. I'm just a girl, standing in front of Julianne Moore, asking her to step on my face and crush it. I don't even need a face. In fact, I'd be better off if, where I once had a face, I instead had the outline of Julianne Moore's footprint. Step on me, Mom!

I KNOW THIS NOW

Dear Younger Me,

It's me, you. I'm in the future! I hear you're twenty-three right now. Haha, that sucks. Or, I don't know, parts of being twenty-three were cool, like there's small stuff you should appreciate. For example, you don't feel any back pain yet, right? You can like, still do a cartwheel and feel fine and normal the next day? That's so nuts, wow. Your muscles will turn on you faster than you think. And oh my god, Rihanna is still releasing music, yeah? God, you're so lucky. Damn, twenty-three. It's 2015, then. I hope this letter finds you well, and by "well" I mean fucking hot, with all your youth and freedom of movement and wealth of new Rihanna music. But the reason I'm writing is because I know this letter certainly will not find you well, because I know exactly where you are in this moment in time, and I know you are very, very unwell. Listen, Me, I know that things feel like they've gone really, really sour. Maybe you don't feel like you have anyone you can talk to about this. Maybe you feel like you won't make it out of this moment alive. You will. But let's talk about it.

Sometimes I think about when we were thirteen. Our first kiss. Remember that? For years after, you'd be so mad at yourself for blowing your first kiss on

Dylan Summers in Julianna's basement playing spin the bottle. How trite! We were always such a romantic, playing our Justin Timberlake CDs and sobbing, wondering when someone would love us the way he loved Cameron Diaz and Britney Spears, or when we might get to love someone like Cameron Diaz or Britney Spears. (By the way, he is a douche. Wait till you see the *New York Times*'s Britney documentary.) We romanticized things. We built up this grand idea of what a first kiss was supposed to look like, based on all the movies we'd seen and sweet stories we'd heard about that first kiss that's impossible to forget. And yet, ours was so forgettable. Had it even been with someone we actually liked, it still could never have lived up to the impossible expectations we foisted upon it.

We were thirteen, sitting in a circle of other horny thirteen-year-olds, in my friend Julianna's massive basement. A few pecks were exchanged. But we never got the chance, the bottleneck never flew our way. Mad, feeling robbed, we spun the bottle while everyone was dispersing, moving on to the next thing, playing foosball, gossiping, popping in a recorded tape of *SNL*, in the hopes that someone else was still there, still horny, also refusing to let their first kiss melt away with the night. And he was. As the bottle slowed, we locked eyes with Dylan Summers, the only person left, then followed him into a dark corner. There, we smushed our tongues around in circles. It was exhilarating, quick, and hollow. When it was done, just a few seconds later, the two of us walked away without saying a word. And that was it. The first kiss vanished, with no shot of a do-over, or of something better, something meaningful. It was just some guy from class that we almost never spoke to and had no real interest in speaking to again.

We saved our virginity too, didn't we? The second it happened, I remember feeling like, *That's it? And if that was it, then oh my god, you dumb-dumb, you could've done this with anyone.* Twenty years old. Twenty years old! We felt like it would *never* happen, like we'd resigned ourselves to a future of being incel grandmas, rotting away with our feral cats in a shack in the woods, all because we wanted it to be with someone who "mattered." It didn't even have to be love! Just someone we even a little bit cared about. The thing is, we didn't care about anyone, even a little bit, ever! Our best friend Taylor—yes, miraculously, you are still friends with her now! A true feat of human strength that a person can stay best friends with someone they befriended at eight years old—would always say, "You just haven't met the right guy yet." I mean, she had always had it so easy, with her long, lanky legs, her shiny brown curls, and those bright brown eyes. We knew she would lose her virginity first—she got her period first; she started dating her first boyfriend, the hottest guy in the school, freshman year—she was always one step ahead. And we were always like, but why haven't *I* found someone who means something to me? Taylor has, everyone else seemingly has.

And then it was the summer of 2012, and we were entering your senior year of college. You were mortified by every sexual encounter you'd had there. Virginity didn't matter anymore—why was I acting like some Christian flop whose body parts were too holy to be touched? It's a vagina, not a sacred tomb! Seriously, WHAT was I protecting our vagina from?? (Spoiler: men—I was protecting it from men.) But how many more humiliations would I have to suffer through to feel the thing I'd always wanted to feel? To close the deal on the horniness that'd ravaged our body since Pokegutzgate?

And so, on that summer night in 2012, it was Lena Dunham Guy: some guy we went to high school with who ironically wore Hawaiian shirts, who you had nothing in common with, just like Dylan Summers. But you were both drunk, and you were both *there*, and your parents were away that night. So you took him to our childhood bedroom, which was embarrassingly still slathered in stuffed animals, rainbow polka dots, and Britney Spears paraphernalia—actually, it's not embarrassing. What was in his room? Floor crumbs and a football? He opened the condom, you immediately started thinking about where to throw away the wrapper and condom so your parents wouldn't find them, and then you did it. While thinking about throwing away the condom. And it was just . . . I don't know, over. Finally. It was neither good nor bad. I just remember feeling so relieved that I could finally put virginity behind me that I was *high*. I was so excited to call Taylor in the morning and say, "I'm finally like you. I've finally caught up. I can finally talk about sex now and feel like I'm in on something that everyone else I've ever met is." Or what's better, I can start having sex with whoever I want, now that the hump of the first hump is finally dead and gone.

God, that sucked. All those years of waiting to feel what ended up feeling . . . fine? Wait, why am I telling you this again? Don't you already know this stuff? Oh, right. You're twenty-three. You've slept with a few guys now. And you're dating the last one, Brian. And you're having so many mixed feelings about him. Or maybe they're not mixed. Your instinct is telling you that your feelings about him are dramatic, so you're ignoring them. Don't ignore them, Jill. Right now, you're asking yourself if there's something wrong with you. There's not. There's something wrong with him.

Something else is happening too. It's the one source of good in your life, but it's also the scariest. Her name is Darcy. Your new best friend. You love her so much. No, like you *really* love her. It's okay, you can say it. Sometimes you sit around and think, *Is it normal to love your friend this much? Am I obsessed with her? Am I creepy?* I know you just asked your therapist that for the first time too. No, don't put this letter down—I didn't mean to embarrass you. It's okay. In hindsight, it is *mildly* funny that you felt so much for Darcy that you were scared you were obsessed with her in an *American Psycho*–type way—like you would've rather come out as a psycho-killer than a lesbian. But first loves really do feel like an obsession wrapping itself around your neck and pulling tight. I'm proud of you for telling your therapist that, however misguided it is. I'm proud of you for going to therapy at all. Despite knowing no one else who goes to therapy, you can feel that something big is happening with you, and you don't feel like you can trust anyone in your life with it. You don't even know what "it" is yet. But it's there, and clawing to come out, and now it's ready to break through. Let it. It's okay. Ahh, I hate thinking about this part. But it's important.

You just got back from Palm Springs with Darcy, right? God, that trip was so much fun. Wait, no it wasn't. It was searing. The degree to which you felt everything in this moment in time made you think it was the happiest year of your life—you weren't happy. You were transforming. I don't know how to tell you this next part about Darcy. But think about this weekend again, really think about it. You squinted at the golden-hour California sunlight, reaping orange all over your and Darcy's skin, bobbing up and down through the dusty hills near Joshua Tree, listening to the sweeping, ethereal sounds of Lana Del Rey. Out there, on that abandoned, snakelike road, you were completely alone with her, and you felt magnificent, like nothing had ever been bigger or better or more special, like this desert road was carved into this mountain just so you and this girl could speed across it. It was intense. That was the high.

The weekend had lows too. Like when Darcy kept FaceTiming her boyfriend, because she missed him, even though she was with you. You didn't miss anyone. She was the only person you needed to be with, and she was right there, on the patio of the Ace Hotel suite she booked for you to share. You watched her while she spoke to him, smoking a cigarette, wearing that ridiculous sun hat. She was the closest, most intimate and emotional relationship you'd ever had. That had to mean something, right? She suggested you call your boyfriend while she called hers, and you'd forgotten you even had one. And while she sat there flicking her cigarette, ash falling over her tanned, long legs, your belly filled with dread at the reminder that Brian was back home, waiting for you to return, and your stomach churned and churned, knowing that on the other side of this weekend, you would have to confront something really, really big, and really, really scary, or two things that were. And all this—the magic of being in Palm Springs, watching the pink-and-orange sunset turn dark purple and navy, being with Darcy before anything changed—would be unreachable forevermore.

Why didn't you miss Brian anyway? He had recently come to Passover and met your grandma, the only time she'd ever met someone you were dating. Taylor and your other childhood friends from New Jersey came to visit and see your new L.A. apartment, and they cooed about how hot Brian was, and how sexy it was that you met him at work. You, the postproduction assistant; him, the strong, tall production assistant. He used to say irksome stuff like, "Girls shouldn't be allowed to be production assistants because they're not physically strong enough to carry equipment," and you used to think, *What a fucking asshole*, or he'd say offhandedly, "I can't believe this company is run by women. It's like a bunch of chickens running around with their heads cut off." And you were like, "That's kind of fucked-up to say, isn't it?" Ugh, you're so close, Jill. I want to say I wish you saw it sooner, but there's just no map for how to endure something like this, or how to stop it from enveloping you. Actually, there is: Women are told that so much of Brian's behavior is normal, par-for-the-course male ego, rage, sexuality. It's not. You're going to learn that very soon, and then you're going to be angry with yourself for not knowing. Don't be. Be angry at the world that told you to weather it, and told him that he was right.

That night, when you got back from Palm Springs, you were so exhausted, emotionally and physically—it was late, after ten p.m. You kept running the events of the weekend over in your mind: sharing that big bed with Darcy, feeling so safe, yet so uncomfortable, but not for the same reasons you felt uncomfortable sleeping next to Brian. He kept texting you that he was going to come over, and you kept saying, "Tomorrow, I'm tired." But he wouldn't listen. He never listened.

He came over, despite your wishes. While you were unpacking, he threw your clothes around, trying to be playful, saying he wanted to "distract" you. It wasn't funny. You were at the end of your rope. He pressed his body weight against you, trying to kiss you, and you said, "Tomorrow, I'm tired." You told him exactly what you wanted: to shower after a long day in the sun and go to bed. He asked if he could join, and you said no. You got in the shower, safe for a moment. And then the door opened. He walked in, already naked, his penis erect, and you thought, *Please not this, please not now*, and tears welled, for so many reasons. Everything changed overnight—or, it changed over many nights, and after this weekend, there was just no pushing it down anymore. It was here. The questions you'd been asking your therapist were dead-on. You weren't "obsessed" with Darcy. You were in love with her. What did that mean? What could a thousand more weekends like Palm Springs look like? What if you could be happy? And if you liked Darcy, did that mean you didn't like men? Is that why you also realized you didn't like Brian? He opened the shower door and stepped in.

He pressed himself against your back, rubbing himself against you. You said, "Brian, I'm so. So. Tired." He pushed you against the wall. His breath picked up. The heat poured down on your face, which was already hot with tears, and flush, and fear, and physical and emotional exhaustion. Again, you said, "Brian, stop. I don't want—" And he shoved himself inside you. And he was so much bigger than you, towering over your small, vulnerable body in this slippery tub. All you could do was steady yourself, make sure you didn't slip and fall. He didn't care that you were crying. You had been here so many times before. You tried to push him off, but he didn't want to stop, so he kept going. Finally, you pushed him off and got out. He followed.

You dried off, put a pair of underwear on, and got into bed, facing away from him. He crawled in next to you, pulling your underwear down. You said no again. It didn't matter how many times now. He started to rub you. You said, "What the fuck, Brian? I said I'm not in the fucking mood." He said, "Jeez, okay," backing off as if he actually might listen for once. He quickly resumed. You said, "You're doing that thing we talked about. You're pressuring me again." He said, "I'm not pressuring you. I'm *convincing* you." That's what he always said. He was "convincing" me. "Trying to put me in the mood." But it wasn't "convincing." In therapy, you'd revisit these moments.

Like the time you were sobbing in bed, overwhelmed with your job, and he curled up behind you, and you were crying so hard that you didn't feel him take his pants off, and he pushed himself inside you from behind, startling you, scaring you, while you were crying. What kind of person does something like that? Or the time you were on your period and said you weren't in the mood, and he ran upstairs, grabbed a condom and lube, came back down, and told you that this would be the perfect time to try anal. He held your hands down and pulled your pants down and your playful-yet-fearful "Brian, no's!" turned from nervous laughter to soul-crushing begging. This language he would use, it was never "convincing." It was sexual coercion. You'd ask your friends if their boyfriends ever behaved this way, expecting them to say, "Obviously—men are horndogs!" But they'd just stare at you, horrified, and say, "Jill . . . no."

One time, Brian even told you that he was scared that a girl he was intimate with in college would accuse him of rape, and you asked why. He told you that she was blackout drunk, and halfway through, she began asking him to stop, but he didn't. He said he "couldn't." He said, "You have no idea how hard it is to stop when you're enjoying it." But she wasn't. How do you enjoy something that someone else isn't enjoying? You thought, *He has no problem "enjoying" when I'm not—that's not good, right?* But then he started to cry, and your teachings said, "Comfort him." At the time, you thought you were comforting him because you loved him and he was scared, but you were in survival mode—a man had just told you he'd had sex with someone who was begging him to stop, and he consciously kept going, despite or in spite of her. He was describing a rape. You did what you had to do to stay safe in that moment, to not react, to get out alive. You're so close to this realization. You'd tell your therapist about this too: Brian said, in a hypothetical situation, if he was locked up in prison for decades, never seeing or touching a woman, and then a woman was locked in a room with him, that he would rape her because it was human nature, sexual deprivation, male libido. You asked your friends about that one too, and that really scared them. Soon, you'll look back on these moments and think, *He told me so many times, to my face, didn't he?* And you'll hate yourself. You can't, Jill. I'm older now. I know this now. There was something wrong with him. Soon, your therapist will spell this all out for you. She will have to be the one to tell you that you have been raped.

How could I blame you for not knowing? Or for writing off a gut feeling as being dramatic? You weren't given the tools to deal with something like this, or even to understand it. Your understanding of rape and sexual assault is so narrow right now, because why wouldn't it be? When you hear the word "rape," you think of gruesome, violent, bloodcurdling screams, villains holding victims at knifepoint. When you think of a victim of sexual assault, you think of scared, battered women shivering as they tell their story to Mariska Hargitay. And those kinds of scumbags, those predators, are thrown in prison, where they should be, where shows like *Law & Order* say they should be. But what about predators who walk among us? Who blend in as "good guys" or "just an asshole"?

In a couple of years, I promise that you and the whole world will have a reckoning with this, with rape, sexual assault, the spectrum of sexual harassment, coercion, and abuse, and a culture that continues to write off sexual transgressions and aggressions as unpunishable. The reckoning won't change things right away, but it will start a conversation that needs to be had, badly. In this moment, you're twenty-three years old and no one has told you that, yes, you can be raped by your own boyfriend. When your therapist tells you, you're going to stare blankly and numbly at her. You're going to think, *Rape? Isn't that a little extreme?* And you're going to ruminate on this word, and your current understanding of it. You'll think of the stories you've seen, a rape revenge film like *Kill Bill*, and think, *My story is nothing like that.* You'll think about watching *Gossip Girl* as a teenager, when Chuck Bass attempts to rape Jenny Humphrey and he's momentarily reprimanded by his classmates but ultimately continues to be regarded as one of the hottest, most coveted guys at school. He's painted as an "asshole," not a serial sexual abuser. These are the kinds of experiences that have become not only extremely common among women but extremely minimized. Since 2017, many, many pieces have been written about how *Gossip Girl* alone normalized abuse. Your entire generation has internalized TV moments like this—the culture never made a big deal of it, so why would you? Brian *is* an asshole. Is he a *rapist*?

Yes.

I don't want to overwhelm you. I just want you to feel what you're feeling in your belly and trust it. I know you feel like you're floating ten feet above your body in this moment, next to him in bed, fighting him off, staring at a fleck of dust on the wall so you can focus on something, anything, to just get through this. And you're thinking, *I'm going to break up with him tomorrow.* That's good. I remember driving to his house after work and doing that. It was scary, but it was one of the best things you've ever done for yourself. Right now, you're lying there thinking about her, thinking about him, and you're asking yourself this terrible question. You're thinking, *Why don't I like this? Why don't I like when he touches me? Maybe this really does mean I'm gay.* No one should ever have to ask themselves, "Am I gay? Or was that sexual assault?" But right now, you are.

You didn't enjoy it because it was rape. It felt awful because you never consented to it. All those times, you never consented, and it made you hate him. But because you were simultaneously enduring another taxing emotional experience, you conflated the two: It's not that you hate sex with Brian, which proves that you're a lesbian. You hate being sexually abused by Brian. And yeah, there is something else, it's just unrelated. You're not a man-hating lesbian, or a failure for not having a successful relationship with a man, wondering if you should try women on for size. I wish these two transformative life events didn't overlap, but they did, and now they *are* intertwined. Yeah, you are gay. You're going to have to deal with this now too.

But you will deal with it, swiftly and gracefully. I know, because I did it. Your parents won't care. In a couple of months, you'll drive forty minutes to their house in Chatsworth for a casual dinner. Over Thai food, you'll say, "I think the next person I date is going to be a girl." They'll say, "Oh, okay," and then, "Pass the pineapple fried rice?" And after that, things are going to be so much easier, so much freer, so much safer. After you tell your friends and your family, it's going to get so good. It's still going to be intense and scary, but it's going to be awesome. I understand why you are, but I'm begging you: don't ask yourself this harrowing either-or question. Both things are true. You are gay. You are also being repeatedly sexually assaulted. You're not turning toward women because of a poor experience with a man. You just happen to be in love with your best friend, at the same time that you're suffering through an abusive relationship with a terrible person, regardless of gender. Jesus Christ. I don't know what to say to carry you through. Let me try.

Based on every movie I've ever seen about time travel, I know I'm not supposed to tell you any of this, but I have to share what happens in the future—it's going to pull you through, I know it. The promise of a bountiful gay life is on the horizon. Follow the rainbow, literally!

Here's how it's going to go down. You're going to cry and tell Darcy you like girls, and it's going to feel like burning a hole through your chest. She won't care. You're going to tell Taylor, and she's going to be momentarily weird and see that you're panicking, so she'll try to "talk you off the ledge" by saying sometimes relationships between women can feel intense, that doesn't always mean you're gay. You're going to get mad at her, because you were trying to tell her your truth, and she wrote it off, despite her intention in trying to calm you down. You'll tell her again, and she'll be like "All right, that's chill." You're going to tell Maddie, your sister. She's going to balk at you and say, "You would NEVER go down on a girl, come ON," like it's some sort of party dare. A few weeks later, she'll realize that you just came out to her and she'll settle down. And then, things are going to get HOT.

In a couple of months, you're going to hook up with a girl for the first time. Yes, you already know her, she's your friend. After a big group dinner and an after-hours hang at some dude's house in the Hills, you'll go back to her place, act very weird and coy and pretend you're not there to do what both of you know is exactly what you're there to do, continue to tiptoe around it mercilessly, and she'll eventually look you dead in the eye and say, "Okay, you tryna fuck, or?" And you'll nod. At this point, unfortunately, you will have smoked too much weed because you were anxious, but the weed will have backfired and tripled your anxiety—oops! Anyway, it'll be INSANE and scary and INSANE. Like your first kiss and losing your virginity, it won't mean anything—but fuck it, firsts aren't really your thing. Just be okay with that. You touched a boob, and that's fucking crazy. Good for you. Nobody came, but you overcame, if you feel me. Wink.

After that, you'll stay friends, pretty much never mention it ever again, and you'll kiss a lot of other awesome girls. And some really freaky ones too. And you're also going to FINALLY FEEL SOMETHING when your skin touches another person's skin. That alone, I promise, will fuel you and carry you into your thirties. Dude. Not to be weird, but you're going to make a girl orgasm, and it's going to be fucking bananas. Stop smirking! I'm not smirking, you're smirking! Dude. Nice. Girls rock. Girls fucking SLAP. Okay, what else is there to look forward to . . .

GIRLS

So, it's mostly just girls. The important thing is: you're going to learn that sex and dating can actually be fun. One time, you'll fly to New York for a friend's birthday and end up fleeing to the bathroom to make out with this girl you met in college. You'll spend the night together and it'll be fun and flirty and sexy—so much so that you'll fly back to New York to do it again.

Oh, oh, oh! And then, at one point, you'll be sleeping with two girls who live in different states, and you will feel like an international assassin, or something, someone who has go-to people to hook up with based on whatever city they're in. But it's fine, because none of you are super invested and you've all been honest about it. One weekend, they'll both tell you that they're in town, and you'll see both of them and feel like a terrible person, but in a hot "I'm a main character in an HBO show" way.

After suffering through numerous circumstances where you and another woman want to kiss but both fall victim to fear of admitting desire, I promise you, you *will* start flexing that muscle—the "kiss the girl" muscle. And let's be real, while the "will they / won't they" relationships—of which you'll have, like, six—feel fiery and exciting and dangerous, they're ultimately extremely unfulfilling. Know THAT. But you'll get it out of your system quickly, and the faster you do, the better off you'll be.

One day down the line, you'll meet Emma, your first real, true love and long-term relationship—I know, dating a woman whose first name is your middle name: fucking dyke shit. You will be electrified yet harrowed by your past experiences of dating in L.A., of using dating apps, or worse, dating someone you met on Twitter dot com (bone-chilling). You'll finally be ready for something real, for someone who lives in the same state, for something more fulfilling than HBO cringe-sex. Emma will have hardly any pictures on her Hinge profile, but the text banter will be good. Once you give her your number, the first text she ever sends you will be a photo of her birth chart. How did she—That was so quick—I don't—But you will say to yourself, "Fine," and ask her on a date. You go to this dive across the street from your apartment (you're so lazy! Wow!) and you will be so nervous around her that you get diarrhea on the date and disappear into the bathroom four times. Later, she'll tell you she thought you were calling a friend and trying to get out of the date, fearing it wasn't going well. Nah, it's just IBS.

You and Emma will kiss—just kiss—for weeks. It will drive you mad. But she tells you up front she wants to take things slow, so you never question it. While you're kissing, you think, *Wow, this feels like my whole body is melting,* and *Please touch my boob, please god, touch my fucking boob.* The first time Emma takes her shirt off in front of you, you will feel like you're falling off a skyscraper. And it will just keep feeling like that for a while— through asking her to be your girlfriend, through telling her you love her for the first time. Eventually there will be a pandemic, which makes it hard to feel that caliber of pure ecstasy, but you'll still be so in love with Emma that— Oh fuck. I wasn't supposed to tell you about the pandemic. Uh, forget about that part. No, I said "Panem . . . ic." Like in *The Hunger Games,* they live in . . . Panem. Being with Emma feels like living in . . . *The Hunger Games . . .* It's . . . *Panemic . . . ?*

Moving swiftly along—there's more stuff to look forward to in the future too! Look look look!

CATE BLANCHETT IN SUITS

Some other stuff, hmm. Okay, you're in 2015. Oh my god, you know Cate Blanchett? In the VERY near future, she becomes a lesbian icon (no, she's not gay, she's just a gay *icon,* it's—well, it's complicated). She's going to wear all these stunningly gorgeous suits that will make your stupid gay jaw hit the floor every time you see them. Oh yeah, and soon your brain is going to turn to "stupid gay brain" and everything you see will be filtered through the numbing pleasure of unhinged lesbian thirst. No, trust me, this is a good thing. Anyway, Cate Blanchett in suits—something to look forward to.

BLAKE LIVELY'S HAIR STILL INTACT

OH! You like Blake Lively, right? Okay, she still hasn't cut her hair and it still looks fucking amazing??? That's not a big one, but you know, something to keep in mind.

MILEY CYRUS IS JOAN JETT NOW

Miley Cyrus, as you always suspected, is out as queer now. How cool! At one point, she gets a mullet and wears a lot of leather and does all these rock covers and basically becomes Joan Jett, which slaps. She does this hot-as-fuck music video with Dua Lipa—Oh, that's right, you don't know Dua Lipa yet. Omg.

DUA LIPA

DUA LIPA.

OAT MILK

Wait, you haven't even had oat milk yet, have you? Holy fuck. Oh whoa, I forgot that you started developing a dairy allergy in 2014, so you're like, *newly* not eating ice cream and so, so sad about it. Girl, don't even worry. Oat milk is coming in to wreck your shit (in a good way). IBS hive, this is OUR time.

TWO TAYLOR SWIFT ALBUMS IN ONE YEAR

It's 2015, which means *1989* is still your favorite Taylor Swift album, oh wow. Jesus, so much has changed in the world since 2015. What's it even like there? Do people still think Anne Hathaway is "annoying"? Damn, this is crazy. Do you know who Sarah Paulson is? Oh no . . . Are you, like . . . *very* into Hillary Clinton right now? Oh gosh. Let me reel this in for a second.

I guess what I want to say to you is this, young Me: Remember that "It Gets Better" campaign? They lied: Things actually do get quite hard for you after this. But, as you from the future, I can promise that you're *better off.* Dumping Brian is one of the most important things you'll ever do for yourself. Coming out as gay is *the* most important. Right now, it seems scary, I know. But trust me, this will be the most freeing, healing, terrifying, awesome, excruciating, magnificent, supermassive thing you will ever do with your life. And you know what? The experience is all yours. No one can take that away from you. Are you going to have to learn how to feel a sliver of control over your body again? Yeah. You will. Is your relationship with sex going to morph and suffer? Yeah. Big time. But then it really will change for the best, and you'll be better off. You're going to meet so many women who make you feel so many things, who make you feel sexy, and safe, and dangerous, and alive in ways you didn't know were possible for you. They're going to rip your heart out and stomp on it, but that's okay. Listen. After this, you never see Brian again. You quit working at Nickelodeon soon, and you never, ever, ever see him again. Not in passing on the street, nothing. He can't hurt you anymore.

And I'm sorry, but Darcy is not your person. I know you want her to be, but she's not. The whole relationship has been kind of toxic and painful, hasn't it? She's not good for you. Someone will be.

You have so much left to experience. I need you to try to keep going. It will be worth it. You're going to fall in love. You're going to have beautiful, tantalizing, HBO—fuck it, HBO MAX—sex. So many women will teach you so many things about yourself and your body. Sex is hard. Having a body is hard. Having it violated, feeling your autonomy stripped away is gutting. God, I just want to take it all away from you, but I can't.

I'm sorry you had to go through this. No, you'll never forget what happened. But you'll move through it, and in doing so, you'll find strength you never knew you were capable of achieving. In reclaiming your own body, defining your relationship to sex, and taking back autonomy over both, you will come into your power like never before.

I see you, right now, in your striped T-shirt and your black overalls with your Ray-Ban sunglasses. You're fucking feeling yourself. In a few months, marriage equality will be upheld in a landmark ruling. You'll log on to Twitter, and you'll have so much to say, and you'll be scared of what people will think of you, but you'll also be excited to finally, *finally* shoot off some ghastly thirst tweets about Julianne Moore. I want that for you.

Hey, younger Me. I'm proud of you. I'm sorry. You can let it out now. And don't hold back. It's okay to let it all go.

Love,

Me

KISS ME, MURDER ME IN THE WOODS

HE HELD MY hand and pulled me through the humid woods. Our hushed, eager laughter hummed beneath whispering insects and crunching twigs. The rush of holding hands with my first crush, a person I liked who actually liked me back, was unlike any hit of dopamine I'd ever received. Weaving through the towering pines, hopping over rotted tree stumps, Jack and I finally arrived at our destination: a clearing between trees, far away from the other kids, tucked away, hidden. It was a secret spot built just for us to kiss in.

His brunette bob shimmered in the moonlight. He shook his hair out of his eyes and smiled at me. He caught his breath. I didn't quite catch mine. The darkness swirled around me. Time slowed. Looking at him, looking at me, every burbling feeling of exhilaration and crush and anticipation screeched to a grinding halt. *I don't want to do this*, I thought, and my heart twisted in my chest. The romance of the navy night sky, blinking white stars, and sweeping tree branches gnarled. The disfigured fingers of the brown vines wrapped around my throat, constricting my breathing. The wall of trees closed in on me; the soil beneath my pink Converse sank. Jack's stare pushed on my chest until my breastbone cracked. Bone slivers poked my heart, candy-red blood spurted from my mouth, trickled out of my eyes. I had wanted to come here. I had wanted my first meaningful kiss. I had wanted it to be him. But now everything was wrong. I was trapped, there was no choice, I had to kiss Jack, and there was no getting out of it. I felt the heavy weight of sexual expectation looming over my shoulders like a sinister, all-enveloping shadow. My big moment soured, mutating in front of my eyes from an endearing coming-of-age tale to a slasher flick. Jack inched toward me. *Run*, I thought. He moved closer. *RUN NOW*, I thought, and my body answered: I bolted back through the trees, bounding over damp rocks and black puddles. I felt the judgmental whispers of gossiping insects and the disappointment of the old wise pines on my back. I ran and I ran and I ran, back to the house, back to the safety of other people, back to being alone.

A few years ago, I'd casually and flippantly say things like "I would *never* go back to being a fourteen-year-old girl." For obvious reasons: the horror of tough mounds forming behind your nipples; growing to hate everything about your body and personality that makes you unique; thinking a first kiss will be the most foreboding experience you'll ever endure . . . But as I move through today's wicked world, finding newer and larger things to fret over each day, and newer and larger questions to keep me up at night, I find myself longing for horrors of yesteryear: experiencing my would-be first kiss with a boy; fearing that a bolt of lightning would strike a tree outside, plunging it through my bedroom window and into my chest; shrieking through a scary movie about Kate Hudson getting her eyes and mouth stitched shut by a poltergeist. Doesn't it all sound pretty . . . nice?

You might recognize the latter reference to *The Skeleton Key*—or you might not, because why would anyone know this Kate Hudson–fronted horror movie from 2005, which has a score of 38 percent on Rotten Tomatoes, and which the *New York Times* called a "gumbo of fluff." But I know this movie, I know it *too* well. I was fourteen years old when a popular girl invited a bunch of kids over to watch *The Skeleton Key* in her living room. Her mom was super lax, probably too lax, so everyone knew this was a perfect chance to make out. I did not make out. While all of my friends cozied up to their fourteen-year-old boyfriends in mesh shorts and zip-up hoodies, my eyes stayed glued to the TV, my body shaking like porcelain plates in an earthquake. I hope you all enjoyed the taste of gluey Goldfish stuck to the back of your boyfriends' molars—I, on the other hand, didn't sleep for *months* after watching *The Skeleton Key*, okay? MONTHS. Every night, I would close my eyes and wait for sleep to come, and all I saw was pretty, bubbly Kate Hudson with her thin lips sewn together like a decaying wound. When my mom asked me why I couldn't sleep, I told her there were spirits of black death floating above me in my bed, because there WERE. This movie opened a portal to hell and sent the fear of Hades searing through my skull. When I tell people that I'm still plagued by Kate Hudson's performance in *The Skeleton Key*, they always laugh and say either, "Really?? THAT movie??" or "I don't know what that is." I wish I didn't know what *The Skeleton Key* was either. The thing is, when I was a teenager, I took horror movies *very* seriously.

Until recently, a core tenet of my personality was hating scary movies. Thrillers, slashers, hauntings—I loathed them all. Since I was a kid I've hated being afraid. The pursuit of happiness already felt grueling; why would anyone purposefully try to derail it? Why not, if given the chance, eschew any negative feeling forever? I remember what my teenage friends used to say about horror movies. It was a good excuse to cozy up to their Goldfish-molared boyfriends. It was "fun" to be scared. That being afraid, temporarily jolted out of comfort, was "thrilling." I couldn't understand the concept of "frights." Roller coasters made me cry and puke. A Kate Hudson movie sent me into a six-month mortality spiral. Being afraid wasn't a game to me—I saw horror movies simply as warnings. They were bullet points to add to the ever-expanding PowerPoint presentation in my head of Things to Be Afraid Of. When I watched the stupid *Skeleton Key*, a movie about a woman who stays on a New Orleans plantation and becomes enveloped by the ghosts of hoodoo-practicing slaves (yes, this horror movie from 2005 is—shocking to nobody—racist), I became certain that I too was sleeping in a home that wasn't mine and I too should respect any possible lingering entities. This was something I didn't know I even had to be afraid of, but was glad that I now knew so I could stay hypervigilant for vengeful New Jersey ghosts. I couldn't experience fear as a fleeting emotion like so many of my teenage friends. Each time a brother-fucking West Virginian incel popped out from behind a tree and a blond girl screamed her way to a gory death, that fear stuck with me, seeped into my bones. My floor-length scroll of things to "beware of" grew ever longer.

That all changed in my life pretty recently. I have what is known in the LGBTQ community as a hot goth girlfriend. She's spooky as shit and loves graveyards and ghastly horror films. During quarantine, my hot goth girlfriend moved in with me, and suddenly, I had nowhere left to run, and neither did she: I had no choice but to start watching movies that Emma actually liked, instead of the forty-eighth comfortable rewatch of *Taylor Swift's Reputation Stadium Tour*. It's called "compromise," apparently.

We eased our way in. In March, Emma and I watched the 2020 thriller *The Invisible Man*, starring Elisabeth Moss, because as a lesbian, I'm quite familiar with the concept of suspense: "suspense" is inherently lesbian. Lesbians are consistently rigid with tension, sexual or existential, feeling a sustained sense of doom on the horizon. We are constantly, ceaselessly . . . awaiting. Do not ask what we're waiting *for*: we are bracing, we're lying low, we will be ready when it comes.

Next, Emma and I dove into erotic thrillers, a genre I'm actually quite familiar with and have always enjoyed: sexy thrillers are somehow always about a psychotic bisexual woman with a vendetta—and if they're not, then they're bad. While the "depraved bisexual" trope paints bisexual women as conniving and manipulative, which is offensive, the depraved bisexual trope is also . . . how do I say this . . . hot. Think about all of the best erotic thrillers: *Basic Instinct*, starring Sharon Stone as a sociopathic queer crime novelist who spends her time gazing over sea cliffs, plotting, and killing men. *The Roommate*, starring Leighton Meester, Minka Kelly, and Aly Michalka's belly button ring, which gets RIPPED OUT OF HER BELLY BUTTON BY THE MOVIE'S KILLER. What a perfect plot point. Every post–*The Roommate* writer, retire bitch. *Chloe*, one of the many queer works of Julianne Moore, who stars as Amanda Seyfried's object of lesbian obsession—yes, Amanda Seyfried, who also stars in the best queer thriller of all time, *Jennifer's Body*, which is about being lesbian-obsessed with Megan Fox, even when she's possessed by a demon, *especially* when she feeds on the flesh of men. I mean, these are cinema classics (Criterion Collection, call me, I just want to talk). So, once Emma and I reacquainted ourselves with some of the classics—also *Wild Things*, also *Single White Female*!!!—okay. After bingeing all of these sexy thrillers, I was feeling particularly brave, and decided it was time for a reckoning, to confront the scares I'd eschewed in my teenage years. It was time . . . to watch Tara Reid and Eliza Dushku and Jessica Cauffiel and, yes, even Rumer Willis scream and die.

Luckily my work was laid out for me: an assistant editor and friend of mine at *Vulture*, Jordan Crucchiola, once compiled a comprehensive list of turn-of-the millennium horror movies. I crossed films off that list like a killer with a half-baked motivation and a crossbow. I watched everything: *Swimfan, Scream, The In Crowd, The Faculty, Disturbing Behavior, Teaching Mrs. Tingle, Soul Survivors, Urban Legend, Urban Legends: Final Cut, Wrong Turn, Valentine, Misery, House of 1000 Corpses*. Then I watched some of the late-aughts hits, like *Sorority Row, Cabin in the Woods*, and even *Prom Night* (*Prom Night* is misogynistic and sucks, but something we—as a culture—don't talk about enough is the significance and calming presence of Brittany Snow, so I felt I should mention it). And goddammit, these movies were addictive, like sticky-sweet candy-coated time capsules of a long-lost era. Watching Katie Holmes furrow her brow was as relaxing as devouring a bag of Hi-Chews. At one point, I looked around, and all I could see were layered camisole tank tops, choker necklaces, and perversions of denim; all I could hear was Mark Hoppus's bass and teens calling each other "freak show" and "skank." I craved more gummy, euphoric comfort.

It's hard to talk about turn-of-the-millennium horror without talking music. That punk-pop-meets-slasher-rock flavor was such a perfect tonal compliment to teen horror. Diablo Cody knew exactly what she was doing in *Jennifer's Body*, writing in a fictional emo band ("Low Shoulder") fronted by a predatory, familiar-looking, black-eyelinered lead singer (Adam Brody). Not for nothing, but the Low Shoulder song "Through the Trees" absolutely bangs. Watching Adam Brody bring the house down—no, like, they actually burn the dive bar down while playing their rock song—with his saccharine faux-emo lyrics and tenor was such an underrated snapshot of 2000s teen-agerhood (especially white suburban teenagerhood).

So I reached my grubby hand deeper into the Hi-Chew bag. I listened to everything that made me feel even remotely emotional between 2000 and 2009. I slammed play on the opening lyric of "The Reason" by Hoobastank ("I'm not a perfect person"). I listened to it over and over and, like muscle memory from my teenage years, thought, *Man, life will break you.* I sat in a lawn chair, wore a black hoodie and my "I'm in a mood, don't talk to me" sunglasses, streamed Green Day's *American Idiot* album, and let a single tear trickle down my cheek. Billie Joe Armstrong sang, "'Cause everyone's heart doesn't beat the same / It's beating out of time," and, like muscle mem-ory, I thought, *Nobody gets me. Nobody gets ANY of us.* I drove the freeways at night, sailing through black mountains and light-polluted skies, blasting "Perfect" by Simple Plan. I shook my head and thought, *Fuck you, Dad.* I love my dad; we have a great relationship. In the fall of 2020, something had clearly broken open inside me—streaming Simple Plan in earnest as a grown adult woman is not a sign of, uh, stability. Not quite ready to confront whatever was clawing at me, I melted back into the faux-angst of white teenage suburbia. It was so soothing.

For a while, I relaxed. The only thing I had any interest in doing was watching Eliza Dushku sprint through the woods, or Tara Reid scream in her muted, husky voice, or Denise Richards (period). I listened to Good Charlotte and American Hi-Fi and Sum 41 and raised my middle finger to the cruel, conformist world. I screamed, "I'll never be like you!" Mmm, more candy. I went to 7-Eleven and bought Milky Ways and M&M's and Swedish Fish and Dr Pepper cans. I turned the TV on in the middle of the day, where Rachel Maddow was wishing Donald Trump a speedy recovery from the coronavirus. I zipped my Fall Out Boy hoodie up to my chin and shook my head. "Sellouts," I growled.

At some point, I stopped participating in my life. It was pointless to. All I wanted was candy. I wanted to feel that "fear" I endured in nearly kissing my first crush in the woods. I wanted the anxiety I felt watching *The Skeleton Key*, or the melancholy of listening to Green Day as a teen and feeling misunderstood. But the candy eventually made me feel nauseous, a sign from my stomach that something was off, that maybe I should stop. I didn't care— I didn't want to be *here*. *This* sucks. Those things sucked so much less. I wanted to be *there*. I just wanted to forget about the real terrors I was feeling: fear that the barbarous circumstances of the pandemic would break me and Emma apart; that a love I'd worked so hard to attain and maintain would wither and fade; that my parents could die so much sooner than I'd imagined and we hadn't resolved things that needed resolving; that I was almost thirty and could barely afford to feed myself and my cat; that my ambition was slipping away; that making art felt like nothing to me anymore; that my friendships had crumbled; that I had. I couldn't bear it all, I couldn't bear *fear*. Like my brave teenage friends, I just wanted *frights*.

Every day in the pandemic felt like being a pile of goop that had to be scraped off the floor and shoved in the freezer in a human-shaped tray to solidify. Then I'd reemerge to lug my frozen ice-block form through all the motions of performing humanity: making myself little breakfasts and writing my little words and watching my little programs. The hours of the day alternated between absolutely horrifying and excruciatingly dull. Nothing was sure: Not the results from my COVID-19 test, not the presence of trees on planet Earth, not my life, not my parents' lives, not my love. During the pandemic, the long list of anxieties I'd been keeping in the PowerPoint presentation in my mind since I hit puberty turned to mucky, globby, papier-mâché mush. The list wasn't real; each bullet point was a haunted hayride, a Tower of Terror—it was fear tourism. As an adult with real things to dread, I could finally watch Tara Reid scream and run and plead, and I would feel absolutely nothing. It's much easier to watch horror or thriller or slasher movies as an adult than as an anxious teenage girl. It's also easier to watch someone get stabbed in the woods when real life feels like a sacred tomb has been pried open, releasing a plague on humanity. When the shroud of death looms over your country like a thundercloud ready to burst, being murdered in the woods falls down a few notches on the list of anxieties.

I miss when things were as simple as Jack and I being "perfect" for each other because our names were a famous nursery rhyme. I miss when terror had such easy fixes. Back then, kissing was scary. Watching Kate Hudson's possession was distressing. My understanding of what could be scary was so narrow. At the end of the day, I had the privilege of running home into my mommy's arms and she told me everything's going to be okay, and then it was, even if it wasn't.

Now fear is always there inside me. It's a low-burbling dread creeping around in my stomach every day, and it makes me sick more days than not. Almost having my first real kiss and then running away from my nursery rhyme–perfect first real love blew, but it was only sixty seconds long. *The Skeleton Key* sucked, but it was only ninety minutes. I love horror movies now! I love watching Megan Fox eat a man's skin. If it grows too gruesome, I have the luxury of looking away! I used to say, "I'd never go back to being a fourteen-year-old girl." But now, as a conscious, adult woman in the world, I look at *gestures around at everything* and think, actually, growing up again, and learning how to hate everything about my body and personality that makes me unique . . . sounds kinda nice, all things considered.

Maybe I had to get a really, really bad bellyache to make me clean up all the Hi-Chew wrappers. I might be becoming an Old, growing obsessed with the past, longing for the "good ol' days" of my youth. Or maybe I needed to remember that some things are *known*. The past has been written. I know how every story from the 2000s ends. I know how the story of almost kissing Jack in the woods ends. I know that it made me anxious, but that I survived it. I know that I'm still here and breathing, which means that I didn't get murdered in the woods in the 2000s, unlike Emmanuelle Chriqui in *Wrong Turn* (RIP).

The present, for any person who's alive in any moment in time, is scary, yes. But in this *current* moment in time, almost nothing is known. I lie awake, wondering when the next earthquake will rock me, when a wildfire might spark in the hills outside, which people I love might die, or if Emma will still love me when it's over, if it's ever over, if either of us even survive, if I don't blow up our relationship in a misguided attempt at self-preservation. Living in the present is just too delicate and appalling for any human brain to comprehend or reckon with. Everything about being alive today, with so, so, so much human suffering, feels like an abomination. I just need to remember that this too is being written.

It's no wonder we so often reach for our youth and our past like it's the last bastion of peace and tranquility we'll ever know. It was the "good ol' days" because we survived it, because we know that we did. Horror movies feel like a warm hug because they make us long for the days when we were sure we'd live, when things were simpler because they were known, but also because they just *were*. I want to listen to Michelle Branch and eat Gushers and let my mom rock me to sleep while I cry. I want to go back. Please, god, take me back—even if it means reliving every painful moment of being four-teen and having a first crush, which is so embarrassing, or eating so much candy that I throw up on my Fall Out Boy hoodie. Please just take me the fuck away from *this*.

I was so afraid back then—of crushes, of disappointment, of living. Now I know what happens. It's not scary anymore. Neither are the horror movies. In fact, they're an extraordinary release of anxiety. I don't know which is more soothing: the final girl surviving, or the sweet release of finally getting chopped to fucking pieces. Either way, it's over.

THE CURRENT LESBIAN CANON, AS IT STANDS

NOWADAYS, QUEER TEENS have no idea how good they have it, with their lesbian-outfit Instagram accounts and their dreary homophobia movies and their JoJo Siwas. Back in my day (2003), finding something gay to be horny over was like navigating the Oregon Trail. You'd have to run home from school and sit in front of the TV for hours waiting for the "Me Against the Music" video to play on MTV, just so you could get a *sliver* of gay, and that would be your *only* shot at seeing gay that *whole* day. No quietly streaming Netflix on your laptop in your room, no saving photos of Cara Delevingne and Selena Gomez showering together to camera roll, no "every Jamie and Dani scene in *The Haunting of Bly Manor*" compilation video on YouTube. Just a single queerbait moment of the day with absolutely no idea when it would come or ability to plan for it. Just sit and wait for Britney and Madonna to flirt. Oh, you have to go to the bathroom? What if you miss it? No, you'll be fine, just go. You missed it. The flash of a moment where Britney pins Madonna against the wall and they almost kiss is gone. Sorry you ate too many SunChips and got diarrhea and blew past the only possible lesbianism you could find today. You died of dysentery. You missed the gay; try again tomorrow.

Yeah, admittedly, things aren't "perfect" or even "good" today, given that 99 percent of lesbian movies are still about two women who hate themselves hiding behind a harp together and being like "I would die of tuberculosis for you" or whatever. But still, we *have* lesbian movies (and lesbian-outfit Insta-gram accounts and JoJo Siwa and YouTube compilation videos). The breadth of Sapphic art, and what can be considered Sapphic art, expands with each passing day. But in a vacuum of explicit queerness, generations of queer peo-ple were left with no choice but to celebrate the implicit. The instinct to col-lect the implicit—despite having an oeuvre of explicit queer art today—has not disappeared. And that right there, the ever-growing list of implicitly Sap-phic stuff that we've culled from the absence of gay, is called lesbian canon.

Quick explainer, if you're like "lesbian canon, the whomst, now?" canon is just another word for "official." In fan fiction, the word refers to the "offi-cial" storyline that the fanfic is based on. But with so little "official" lesbian content in the ether, the concept of such has become an in-joke. Anything can be "lesbian canon"—a person, a television show, a concept, an object, a song, your DAD. If a queer woman identifies with or feels "seen by" an art, a person, a thing, then that item is lesbian canon. If it's still not clicking, I'll give you an example, before diving into the current lesbian canon, as it stands. The best possible case I can think of is Neve Campbell. Neve Camp-bell, as far as the official public records show, identifies as heterosexual. But doesn't she just . . . seem really lesbian? And not even like in an explicitly "has definitely hooked up with women" way. But her energy, her essence, her breadth of work is so, so queer. There are other elements that could, of course, contribute to making someone or something lesbian canon. Like, Neve Campbell played queer in (one of the greatest movies of all time) *Wild Things*, alongside Denise Richards. So like, her work technically is or has been queer. But like, her character in *Scream* seems gay but isn't . . . right? The way she speaks, the way she has bangs, wears tank tops, that she typi-cally plays a tomboyish hot goth girl and existed in the '90s—these are all factors that would lead me to believe that Neve Campbell is queer. But she isn't! Neve Campbell is probably not gay. But she *is* lesbian *canon*.

That said, where are historians on this? Why is no one recording the thousands and thousands of things that queer people have declared lesbian canon for posterity? Years from now, when a teen opens a book, hoping to learn what is or isn't lesbian canon, how will they know? They won't. No one else is doing this work, so I have to. I won't call this the *official* official recorded list of lesbian items, but this is at least *my* official list of lesbian items. Again, these are things that aren't officially gay but SEEM gay, and thus are: lesbian canon.

LIQUIDS

- Oat milk.
- Vape juice.
- Blood (all types).
- Coffee.
- Tea.
- Hot water with lemon.
- Elderflower syrup.
- Anything lavender flavored.
- Rosewater.
- Dakota Johnson's brand of sex wax candles (once liquefied—if they're solid, doesn't count).

FASHION

- Bad fashion: Vests. Tevas. Zip-off shorts. Shapes of clothing that shouldn't exist and actually seem like a mistake.
- Good fashion: Denim. Leather duster jackets. Dressing like you're a hot vampire and/or in *The Matrix* and/or a Sith Lord.
- Track suits (exist between bad fashion and good fashion).

THE ELEMENTS

- Water.
- Earth.

- Fire.
- Air.

PEOPLE AND THEIR BODY PARTS

- Neve Campbell at every age, especially with bangs.
- Winona Ryder—wore a lot of leather and denim in the '90s. Also shoplifting because you're bored is gay.
- Eliza Dushku simply existing.
- Shiri Appleby.
- Jordana Brewster.
- Sandra Bullock in *The Net*.
- Julia Roberts in *Mystic Pizza, Flatliners, The Pelican Brief*.
- Michelle Trachtenberg in *Harriet the Spy* and *Gossip Girl*.
- Linda Cardellini truly just breathing in any movie or TV show.
- Basically every brunette actress who was popular in the '90s/2000s.
- Parminder Nagra (fucking obviously—*Bend It Like Beckham* is lesbian arthouse cinema, as far as I'm concerned).
- Lucy Liu and her lesbian paintings (Lucy Liu has, somewhat inexplicably, been painting and exhibiting Sapphic art for the past few years, but has never explicitly come out as queer—it's quite opaque, and being a mysterious artist is lesbian).
- The Olsen twins smoking cigarettes.
- Regina King has queer energy in general but specifically her shoulders and toned arms are lesbian.
- Brie Larson's back muscles are lesbians.
- Blake Lively's moles are dykes.
- Meagan Good—can't explain it, but she was a true gay girl mood in the '90s/2000s.
- Devon Aoki.
- Kaley Cuoco's hair.

- Emma Roberts saying, "Surprise, bitch."
- Rachel Weisz, obviously.
- Rooney Mara staring from across the room.
- Sleep paralysis demons.
- Thandiwe Newton is just very powerful? And being powerful is lesbian.
- Eve, the hot rapper, but also . . . Yes, *that* Eve.
- The Jonas Brothers.
- Awkwafina, who is cool, and cool is gay.
- Rosie Perez.
- All witches, real.

FICTIONAL CHARACTERS

- All witches, fictional.
- Gerri from *Succession*.
- Beth Harmon (who slept with a woman in *The Queen's Gambit* but it's grazed over—I thought the least I could do was certify her as *canon*, because if nothing else, her energy is Sapphic as hell).
- Xena and Gabrielle.
- Bent-Neck Lady from *The Haunting of Hill House*.
- Hela from *Thor: Ragnarok* (duh).
- Lola Bunny.

PLACES

- Moon (like THEE Moon, but also all moons).
- Castles, especially windy ones, freezing ones.
- Seas.
- Precipices.
- Big Sur.
- Art museums.

- History museums.
- Angular homes (art is lesbian, so an art home is gay).
- Oregon.
- Towers (all).
- Six Flags Magic Mountain (Six Flags is homophobic but Magic is gay).
- Piers.
- Forests.
- Lakes.
- Peaks.
- Valleys.
- Mountains.
- Deserts.
- The equator is a big lesbian.
- The Golden Gate Bridge is a lesbian.
- All alleyways.
- All bookstores, especially enchanted ones.
- Anywhere that's enchanted—magical forests, mythical underwater communities, etc.
- Wendy's drive-throughs (not really, I just love Wendy's).
- The internet.
- Mission Control or control rooms.
- Server rooms.
- Boiler rooms.
- Rooms.

APPS

- TikTok.
- Twitter.
- Calculator app.
- 7-Eleven rewards app.

ANIMALS/PETS

- Owls, hawks, and most birds. The hobby of birdwatching too.
- Rats, ferrets, chinchillas, guinea pigs—owning some sort of rodent is something a lesbian does in their youth.
- Cats.
- Fish, otters, anything in oceans, lakes, or rivers.
- Moose.
- Furbys.
- Tamagotchis.

WEATHER

- Storms.
- Snow/slush/ice.
- HAIL—extremely lesbian. It's like getting fisted . . . by nature.
- Gray skies, all sinister clouds.
- Light rain.
- Pouring rain.
- Marine layers.

CONCEPTS

- Invisibility—to *feel* invisible, to *be* invisible? To blend into nature? Lesbian.
- Anxiety.
- Warmth.
- Magic.
- Shapeshifting (which is basically the lesbian act of code-switching, but with your Form).
- Science (but not math).
- Flight (not like planes, but wishing you could fly is lesbian).

- Threats.
- Socialism.
- Communism.
- The concept of a "flop era."
- Suspense.
- Betrayal.
- Revenge.
- Paying in cash.
- Or saying, "Do you have change for [amount]?"
- All of the months except for January.
- Myths.
- The space-time continuum and sci-fi-adjacent stuff: black holes, the multiverse, the big bang, existence in general, parallel universes, evil twins, doppelgängers, etc.

BLESSED OBJECTS

- Every book.
- Nondairy ice creams and plant-based dairy products.
- Unjustifiably expensive candles that smell like wood.
- Every suit worn by Blake Lively.
- Every piece of clothing that has ever touched Cate Blanchett's skin.
- The drums that Shakira played.
- All microphones.
- String sections.
- Woodwinds.
- Fashion mullets (regular mullets are not only heterosexual but *violent*).
- Stamps—implied long distance, sending letters . . . very queer.
- Robin Wright's many wigs.
- The movie *Aquamarine* (2006) starring JoJo, Emma Roberts, and Sara Paxton.

- Arcs, like the boats.
- Actually all boats are lesbians. Did you know there is a boat called a "cigarette boat"? Sorry, who are "cigarette boats" even for if not rich lesbians?
- Actually all boats *except* the *Niña*, the *Pinta*, and the *Santa Maria*. Fucking colonizers.
- J.Lo's coat from *Hustlers*.
- Rihanna's Versace coat from the "Bitch Better Have My Money" performance at the iHeartRadio Music Awards.
- Trench coats.
- Weighted blankets.
- Cast-iron skillets.
- Charcuterie boards.
- Bonnets.
- Every word that leaves Zendaya's mouth.
- Paparazzi photos of Brad Pitt.
- Swords.
- British accents.
- Magazines.
- Cool Ranch Doritos.
- The *reputation, folklore,* and *evermore* albums (because of the yearning, the depression, the woods, the energy of waving a fist at someone from your past like "I'll show you!").
- Every Maggie Rogers song.
- Tattoos.
- Tiny sunglasses.
- Message notifications.
- The way British people sign written messages "x".
- The tuna sub from Jersey Mike's, Mike's way (being really into sandwiches is gay, too).

- Bagels.
- Songs that are playing at CVS.
- Educational podcasts.
- Vibes (like vibrators, but also . . . vibes).
- Curio cabinets.
- Antique dressers.
- Armoires.
- Hair.
- Rosamund Pike's vape in *I Care A Lot.*
- Kate Winslet's vape in *Mare of Easttown.*
- Nail clippers (wink).
- Boxes (wiiiiink).

I won't keep you, but the list drags eternally on, like a desperate lesbian ache. Just know that it's constantly changing, morphing, being added to, being thoughtfully debated and heavily policed. And if the list is amorphous, then the list itself is queer, because being malleable or in a constant state of flux is also gay. I'm so happy that postmillennial generations have so much visible and available queerness to consume and relate to, whether that's stanning JoJo Siwa or falling cavernously into the algorithm of lesbian SmithTok (in which lesbian blacksmiths sensually meld swords) or suggestive Sapphic PotteryTok (they finger the pottery). I'm lucky to exist somewhere between both worlds—having weathered the grueling conditions of being gay in the '90s and 2000s, which left queer people so brain-poisoned that we walk around saying things like "Wind is gay now"—and safely and comfortably saving photos of St. Vincent and Cara Delevingne to camera roll. Now, every saved image of Annie Clark feels like I successfully dragged my wagon across nineteenth-century America. I'm a pioneer, baby! (Pioneers are lesbian.)

CLUELESS AT CHATEAU MARMONT

ANY EAST COAST transplant living in Los Angeles will tell you that the single worst part of living in a perpetually optimal, warm and sunny climate is that it comes at a cost: we can't wear coats. In New York, a coat can be your entire personality: you can wear your chosen jacket or vest or coat every single day of your life, until it becomes a part of you, until it becomes *your* signature coat. You can have a closet stuffed with a wide range of woolly coats and leather dusters that you can sift through, calculating which piece of outerwear might perfectly fit the occasion. In Los Angeles, you wear a stupid white T-shirt, black jeans, and Dr. Martens every day, even when you're sweating, even when you're freezing. In Los Angeles, you pray for the day when you can wear your favorite coat that you only ever get to wear when you're in New York: the loss of coat culture is staggering. So in L.A., when the temperature affords you the opportunity to wear a coat, you fucking take it, and you fucking remember it.

February 18, 2020, was one of those nights, a brisk and memorable evening in West Hollywood that called for my favorite coat to be worn. And it wasn't just because of the temperature. No, the temperature was the invitation, a wormhole that allowed me to enter a coat-wearing dimension. And sure, I could wear the black denim jacket that I'd recently decided was my 12th organ system, like it was any old day, but it wasn't. This was a special night that demanded my most special coat: a heavy black-and-white graphic coat that seemed fancy because its geometric shapes were so bold, but was in fact from Forever 21. February 18, 2020, was a date night, a rare jewel of one, the kind of date night that feels conjured out of a spell book or stolen from the pages of a cheesy YA romance that makes you think, *That would never happen.* It was the night of the *Emma* movie premiere, which I had two tickets to, as well as two vouchers for the after-party at the illustrious Chateau Marmont, a bougie and historic Los Angeles hotel, the very nucleus of the Sunset Strip. And the aforementioned date on my arm would be my girlfriend of eleven months, who is named . . . Emma. Yes, I had been given the gift of bringing the person I was in love with, named literally Emma, to the premiere of Autumn de Wilde's 2020 remake of *Emma*, on a date. If this night didn't call for the wearing of coats, what would??

Emma and I met on Hinge, but I like to think we met the same way most single people meet: by half-consciously lumbering through spaces where other sad people lurk, hoping to connect with something, anything— a lover, a person, a dark force—yet nihilistically prepared to fall into bed at the end of the night, defeated, alone, back to usual. We had been casually dating—or, inviting each other over every Sunday to pretend to watch *Game of Thrones* and kiss—for about a month and a half before it became serious. I was completely obsessed with Emma from the beginning. When I arrived at Residuals, the dive bar we'd agreed to meet at in Studio City, I saw her sitting on a bar stool, drinking a beer, facing away from me. I hate dates—they make me sweat both internally and externally—but I took a deep breath and approached her, my feet sticking to the black floors, souls shrieking—uh, I mean *soles* shrieking—as I went. When I reached her, she turned around and our eyes met. I felt a little twist in my stomach, a lock in our eyes, that paradoxical yank in my brain that screeched, "Look away!" while every muscle in my eye sockets felt lodged in quicksand, glued to her sea-green eyes. The eye contact knocked the wind out of me, so much so that I stumbled on my opening words, struggling to string a sentence together that resembled

"I order beer now too," and then played catch-up with sending words from my head to my mouth for the next hour. She was pretty in a way that was jarring, that felt like a crossover between the intimidating goth girl in your school who could crush you beneath the weight of her black tactical boots, and your camp counselor whose hair is delicately braided, who's quiet yet assured and is also somehow Dakota Johnson. But more than anything, I felt something so powerful, so unspeakable between our eyes. I couldn't look away.

Over the course of the first date, we both collected data about each other to tuck away for later. She worked in postproduction and visual effects as a producer. I was "extremely online." She discovered I loved pop culture, like *really* loved it—like, have a Spice Girls tattoo and would write a fanfic novel about Zoë Kravitz wearing a beanie in a Zoom video that aired during the Brits while she was honoring Taylor Swift with the Global Icon Award. I discovered Emma had no clue what was happening in celebrity media or on Twitter—which is so classically cool—and was into music I didn't know actually existed, sounds that could be categorized by or described as "local artist," or "industrial," or "rock" (not sure if I spelled that last one right). She loved Rob Zombie movies and I loved any piece of floating garbage starring Tara Reid. She wanted to have intellectual conversations about books and history. I wanted to have iNteLLeCtUaL cOnVeRsAtiOnS about the cultural significance of Vanessa Hudgens's outfits at Coachella. She wanted to take spooky ghost tours for date nights, and I wanted to take her to the Fonda to see a brand-new pop star that no one's heard of perform songs about cell phones. Her taste was anti-establishment, and I was the Man. In some ways, we were Martians to each other. Still, I felt drawn to her, like her heart was sand and mine was the sea and I wanted to mash them together. She was sweet, endearing, easy to talk to, and quietly funny—like, the kind of funny that surprises you, because she doesn't advertise it or commodify it or monetize it into some sort of sad "look at me" career (wink).

In our first year of dating, our lack of common interests roiled from time to time, but was always pacified by that unmentionable force between us, the dark matter that kept us glued to each other. Plus, we did find common ground, and patches of crossover, like the movie *Jennifer's Body*—the poppy, colorful 2000s thriller that fused Emma's love of the sinister with my thirst for Megan Fox. There was other stuff too, but mostly *Jennifer's Body*. During that first year, it became clearer and clearer to me that we were "different," whatever that even means. I was so visibly a *Clueless* girl, and she was an *Emma* bitch.

Even though I'm more of a *Clueless* girl, I'm still as much a fan of the Jane Austen story as any basic white woman who pretends they can read. I knew the *Emma* premiere would be an incredible opportunity to flex on my girlfriend, who I'd been with for almost a year and didn't *really* need to flex on, but still. It would also be a once-in-a-lifetime opportunity to take tons of photos of her with her name up in lights, something she'd have stashed for future profile pictures and avatars forevermore. Plus, I wanted to feel like the sugar mommy I always imagined I'd be. I felt like the high-couture Serena van der Woodsen inviting a little Brooklynite Gossip Girl into her world, one of luxury, fame, and notoriety. This was my very own arbitrary yet exclusive yet vague "fundraiser"—which every good CW teen show seems to have an unjustifiable number of—and I was on the list.

Wearing our coats, ready to take on the night, Emma and I walked up to the DGA Theater Complex on Sunset Boulevard, home to the Directors Guild of America, which houses a series of theaters usually reserved for "screenings, premieres, and special events," per its website. Emma's thick-heeled black boots clomped against the cement as we walked and gawked at the scene unfolding before us, which contained much more commotion than I'd anticipated: dozens of photographers and their flashing lights and grizzly voices, yelling for an actress to *look this way*; policemen halting us in our tracks, demanding we step back, as the sidewalk was reserved for the red carpet; an excruciatingly long line of people waiting to get into the theater, periodically diverging from the line to sneak a glimpse at whoever was being beckoned to *look this way*.

"Wait, you didn't tell me this was the *premiere* of the movie," Emma said, though I had, in fact, told her that this would be the premiere of the movie. Otherwise, why would I have said that we should wear coats and boots? (This is how lesbians dress up.)

"Yup," I said proudly, happy to remind her how *impressive* this date was, by anyone's standards. Then I turned to the bellowing police officer and said half-authoritatively, half-trembling with imposter syndrome, "Will you point us toward the press check-in?" He immediately stepped aside, clearing an opening toward the theater's entrance, allowing us to bypass the impatient crowd of moviegoers who were not as special nor as important nor as prioritized as I was—the Press, who needed to urgently pick up my tickets from will call, rather than wait in line like some sort of sickly plebe. *I deserve this*, I thought. I couldn't waste any of my precious time doing something as measly as standing near other people. After all, I was the Press—ever heard of it? Emma's eyes widened as we stepped in front of the line, partly because she was impressed (or embarrassed) by the Access I'd been given, mostly just relieved that we didn't have to endure the absolutely harrowing experience of waiting in a line or the searing, existential distress of watching people arrange their bodies for a photograph.

You might be, justifiably, wondering *why* I was given tickets to a movie premiere, and you'd be right to question it. Now, I'm not a journalist or a reporter, though I've written a few pieces that could loosely be considered journalism. I would barely even call myself a critic. The freelance work I've done has mostly been humorous commentary on films, television shows, or albums. I say this not to discount myself or the work I've done, but rather to insist that I am not a Serious Writer. Most times, the pieces I write are titled "Women of *Big Little Lies*, Ranked by How Much I Want Them to Step on Me" (*Elle*), or "Kate Winslet's Movie Love Interests (If They Were Sandwiches)" (Decider), or "I Am Rachel Weisz's Pig" (Bustle). I'm telling you this because my inflated ego about skipping a line was completely unwarranted. Over the past few years of being a full-time freelance writer, I've realized that half of freelance writing is writing, and half is scamming. And a small percentage of the scamming is learning to be moralistically okay with scamming people, because as a freelancer writer, you are constantly, 150 percent of the time, being taken advantage of and scammed. Therefore I have, many times, asked around for a contact on a specific film or show (via other friends in media, or cold-calling production companies, studios, and PR companies) and asked to attend an advance screening or premiere, wholeheartedly knowing I will *not* be reviewing said film or show. And I have also, many times, not felt bad about flat-out lying to Kara or Alexandra or Chelsea in PR, because if I can't have healthcare, a 401(k), or financial stability ever, then I should at least get to see a fucking movie for free once in a while. Fuck you, capitalism.

If you work for a major media company or magazine or Are a Big Deal, you might receive invites to such premieres, events, and screenings without making any fuss. But freelancers, who are always out there flailing in a zero-gravity indoor skydiving chamber of despair, stuck in an endless loop of reaching out and circling back and following up, typically have to do the legwork themselves in order to secure an invite so they can see a movie, so they can sell an article, so they can write about the movie, so they can have electricity. As a freelancer, it's extremely common to get snubbed by publicists, who want to fill screening or premiere seats with Important Bodies, or at absolute least, bloggers who will write obsequious reviews of their client's movie. That said, freelancers who can't *guarantee* coverage on a film in a specific outlet aren't prioritized. They'll ask if you're "on assignment," and if you reply "no," they will likely stop responding to you. Admittedly, there are definitely ways around this: being *very* nice, and lying. But it's important to maintain a delicate balance: if you're lying, then you'd better deliver "Alexandra," or whoever, coverage after they let you into their stupid movie. That's where my scam prospers: figuring out what movies I can attend for free, how much I have to lie without ruining my reputation, and also securing a plus-one so I can bring a date. Again, I only tell you this so you know that my presence at the premiere of *Emma*, as well as my girlfriend Emma's, and my scoffing at the thought of waiting in line with the sickly gen pop, was utterly unjustified—I would not be "covering" *Emma*. Or at least not the movie . . . *smirks like a disgusting old man*

Emma and I took velvety, raspberry-colored seats in the dim, red-hued theater. Like a mom at graduation, I leaned back into the cushion of my chair, held my iPhone sideways, and pointed it at Emma, motioning for her to take a photo with the sprawling, glowing projection of her titular name on the silver screen. She beamed-through-pain at me like *did you get it*, and then more urgently, as if to say *can this please stop*. I sloughed off the snooty, jaded Hollywood types—the ones who you can tell just by looking at them that their throats have been ravaged by cigarette smoke long ago—who were sneering at us for taking photos. Then we sat back, removed our coats, and grinned: *Here we are, at our big Hollywood date, doing what teens in YA novels could only dream of doing.*

The movie was fine, but ultimately who cares.

Afterward, we walked back to my car, on a sidewalk that seemed ghastly bare given the bloodbath it had endured earlier. I drove us down the street to the famed Chateau Marmont, which, let's be honest, was the main event. I pulled off of Sunset and up the little hill that houses the luxury hotel, threw my car up into park for the white-sleeved, vested valets to take over. For days now, Emma had been clamoring about how excited she was to go to the Chateau—even though she grew up in Southern California, she'd never been. She was fascinated by the architecture, the rich history of the building, and all its secret, spooky compartments, both its storied real ghosts and the ghosts of old Hollywood glamour that still haunted its humid walls. I was just excited to rub elbows with celebrities and show her how cool I was for knowing my way around the Chateau Marmont.

I had been to the Chateau twice before: Once to have a sixteen-dollar cocktail when I was a doe-eyed, twenty-one-year-old production assistant—I had just moved to L.A. and wanted to feel like I was a part of Hollywood, though I so clearly wasn't. And once to accompany my best friend, Sam, a writer and editor of a bougie news magazine, to a different postpremiere after-party. There, he told me, "I have to go say hi to Amy Adams, will you come?" I shook hands with Amy Adams. I nodded and laughed at all the perfectly choreographed beats while Sam talked to Amy Adams. I stared at her orange hair and deep blue eyes, my teeth and butt cheeks competing for which could clench the hardest.

Before I started dating Emma, Sam and I did this a lot. Between the last of the forty times I went back to Kate and when I finally met Emma, I spent two years dragging my knuckles through Hollywood in search of stimulation, validation, and stuff to fill my holes with. Sure, I crammed some of my physical holes with food and sex, as one does, but mostly, I was seeking plugs to my existential holes. I roamed around listlessly, lost and empty, seeking fulfillment in my love life, which felt perpetually doomed and grim. So I turned toward something that felt like it was blossoming, like if I squeezed it hard enough it might pop out some pus-like validation: my career. I figured I had to give a person something to latch on to: Without a big, shiny career, a name for myself, or a house in the Hills, I was translucent, invisible, unworthy. It was impossible for a woman to reach out and grab on to someone who wasn't there. But if I made myself important enough to a bunch of important people, if I could ensure that my presence was coveted, then I could bring glow to my skin, solidity to my form. Then, and only then, could I meet a woman who could reach out and grab hold of me physically. And then, and only then, would I stop feeling spiritually like Swiss cheese.

Sam was much more successful than I was. He had all of the invites to all of the premieres and parties and events, and all of the critical acclaim and interpersonal adoration from venerated Hollywood figures (including Amy Adams) to go with it. When we'd met on the Fourth of July at Debby's house, I had just come out as gay and was on my third-ever lesbian date, in a state of paralyzing lesbian shock from receiving sexual attention from another woman, so when Sam and I were introduced, I barely even looked him in the eye. I had no idea what he was talking about in the conversation we had. About a month later, he and I ran into each other in a grocery store. He stopped me and said, "It's me . . . Sam? We met at Debby's house? On the Fourth of July?" I had no idea who he was. I truly had never seen him before in my life.

Months later, we were cackling over "Mary-Kate Olsen and Olivier Sarkozy's Wedding Featured 'Bowls Filled with Cigarettes,'" and then we were fast friends. Though Sam seemed eons ahead in his career to me, we were in similar enough boats: writers trying to break into TV and film, obsessed with the stupidity of L.A. and the celebrity culture it houses, and absolutely bogged down by our own respective inexplicable sadness. Sam too was seeking plugs for his holes.

Both wholly unfulfilled, lumbering through the streets of West Hollywood like dead-eyed gay zombies, we were a perfect pair. For two years, Sam took me to dozens of events that made me feel special and relevant and important. We would traipse in and out of Hollywood's Cinerama Dome, a hotspot for premieres, then walk down the street to the bougie after-parties, where we'd histrionically perform the theater of being too jaded for this heartless city. We'd say, "Ugh, how long do we have to stay here?" Or "Oh no, here he comes," when some other media gay would approach us. We'd flirt with publicists named Kelly or Mackenzie or Christine. And then we'd leave, saying, "Was it just me, or was Katy Perry like, VERY chilly to me?" Or, "Why doesn't Lana Del Rey *ever* look me in the eyes?" It felt like some hazy *Sex and the City*–meets–*Entourage* fever dream: two best friends tearing through desirable rooms with drinks they'd never touch (Sam is sober, I barely drink) and foods they'd never eat (I have allergies, Sam is keto), cackling with once-famous WB actresses, grumbling with publicists, and asserting, each time with more rage, "I'm JILL" to a gay man I've met fourteen times who is somehow at every event but who cannot see my face.

But the truth was that Sam and I had so much fun, and I loved it. I loved vaping outside the ArcLight and rubbernecking the red carpet. I loved gossiping about which publicists were secretly a fucking mess, or speculating about why Jennifer Love Hewitt was here. It made me feel relevant and important and special, but it also made me feel close to Sam, and loved by him. Trafficking in celebrity spaces and pretending we didn't like it was clearly a shared love language of ours. It was fun, being bonded by this, a series of experiences that were objectively dumb but clearly something both of us had wanted to do since we were young, sitting in our bedrooms, waiting for our lives to change, watching a python writhe on Britney Spears at the VMAs, thinking, *I need to be there.* It felt good to be a part of this duo, this two-headed monster that spoke the same meme-language, wanted the same things (human connection, personal peace, attention from Amy Adams), and was harrowed by the anxieties of daily life. I felt like I had an ally in Sam, someone who liked the same stuff as me, who was pursuing the same distressing career as me, who I knew would protect me and take care of me through the scariness and loneliness of a city that repeatedly tells you no.

Now that I had Emma, some of my holes were finally beginning to feel plugged. Sure, I didn't have the house in the Hills yet, but I had made a (admittedly small) name for myself, and I had invites to fancy-shmancy parties. This date night felt like the cherry on top of my love cake: I had fought for a love like this. I had trained with giants (Sam) in bringing a plus-one to big-time movie premieres. I had walked myself off the precipice of dread, and walked straight into Emma. And now, I was going to reward myself. I was going to be Aladdin and show her the world: shining, shimmering, fucking splendid. This date would be the final piece to the puzzle.

When Emma and I stepped out of the car, paparazzi cameras flashed at us—not zealously, but enough that it felt extremely jarring. Photographers always wait by the valet outside the Chateau. They take pictures of everyone, because if they don't recognize someone immediately, they can save the photos and put names to faces later—or, if the person turns out to be just a scam-artist writer like me, they can delete the photos. Emma was immediately overwhelmed by the pops of light, but I grabbed her hand and decided to act like this was normal, this was a thing that people had to deal with, and it's not at all out of the ordinary because, well, this is just how life is here. I told her it would be less hectic inside as I flashed our tickets to the appropriate people and led her into Le Chateau (this is what everyone calls it, trust me).

I walked her through all the rooms that I was familiar with, having been to an after-party at the Chateau one (1) time: the corner Prohibition-era-looking bar room, stuffed with gawking, squawking gluttons; the velvet-couched room that housed cheese-and-grape plates and a photo booth installation with a real photographer; the open-air main room with more bars, more finger foods, directors, actors, influencers, and an activation station where you could inexplicably and absentmindedly get your initials stitched into a handkerchief while you swilled your wine and people-watched. We trudged through each room, and past a very short Elijah Wood, which elicited a very small whisper from Emma: "Frodo." I saw one person I knew, an old comedian guy named Paul who I'd met a few times and had empty interactions with, who repeatedly introduced himself to me, which made me feel more numb and dead inside each time it happened. When I spotted him, I said to Emma, "There's that comedian guy Paul what's-his-face." She nodded, offering me an "Oh yeah." And I added, "Yeah, I kind of know him, but he never remembers who I am." She nodded.

As we passed through it all, we both grew more and more rigid with unease, becoming acutely aware of how few places there were to sit or rest or even pause in any one space. There was nothing to latch on to: no familiar hands to grab and say, "Thank *god* you're here," no perches to stare at people from, no corners to hide in. It was all so open, yet so stuffy, so filled with cheeses I couldn't eat and drinks I didn't want and sweat that wasn't mine and people who looked through us instead of at us, searching for someone "better." There were no small crowds gathering around us, no necks craning toward us, and so we just faded into nothingness. I wanted to interlock fingers with Emma and show her the world on my magic carpet, but instead there was nothing to show, and no one to see, and nothing to feel. We were wallpaper. After we manically secured two glasses of red wine—simply to have something to do with our hands—and two handkerchiefs stitched with our respective initials, we retreated to the room of velvet couches, praying there were still little fruits left on the cheese-and-grape plates. I was desperate for somewhere to sit, away from these people, away from this unexpected hollow feeling.

We sat on the soft cushions and stared into space, desperate for something to ground us and bring us back down to earth. Emma examined the decorative wallpaper. I watched influencers take photos at the photo booth, then look at the thumbnail with the photographer, grimace, and say, "Okay, one more," holding up a line of people waiting to do the same thing. This was supposed to be a dreamy date night. But neither of us even had much to say. I just wanted someone special to approach me and spark up a conversation, to show Emma how cool and wanted I was, how much I fit in here, how this could be her spectacular, new, shiny Hollywood life that I'd worked so hard to become a part of, that we could share with each other. I picked at a warm grape and sighed.

Paul entered the room and looked my way, and Emma and I exchanged a knowing look: he was finally going to remember who I was, to say hello, because he too didn't know anyone else here and felt awkward. He walked right up to me, and I froze, waiting for him to say something, to show some sort of recognition in his glossy eyes. And then he said, "Are any of these cheeses dairy-free?" And I just . . . evaporated.

"I don't know," I conceded, feeling like a flickering hologram onstage at Coachella. He snatched a grape off the gilded tray and walked away, leaving Emma and I alone. I saw Emma's frown, her darting eyes, her furrowed brow, how badly my socially anxious girlfriend didn't want to be there, at this place she'd been "dying" to see for so many years, and I felt like an asshole. Why, for even one second, did I think this busy, buzzing Hollywood setting was the kind of place that would make Emma smile? I wanted to smash my head into a wall repeatedly and yell, "Stupid! Stupid! Stupid!" Finally, we put our glasses down and retreated, making a grueling, tedious journey of *sorrys* and *'scuse mes* until we were outside again, in that brisk Los Angeles air, in our stupid coats.

I drove the curves of Laurel Canyon back to the Valley, one hand on the steering wheel, one on the stick, still trying to look cool, then over-thinking my hand placement and dropping a fist into my lap, and thought, *Am I really this superficial?* I was baffled by my own hubris and shallowness. Is an after-party at the Chateau Marmont really where I thought I'd feel at home, or welcomed, or even a part of? This wasn't what I wanted to show Emma, or what I wanted her to think was important to me. And what's worse? She didn't even care about this stuff. She never had. She's never given a fuck about luxury hotel dates or white-sleeved valets or rubbing elbows with Frodo. In fact, she was mortified by the faux-glamour of it all. Emma likes history and ghosts and silent films. She wanted to submerge herself in the rich history between the Chateau's damp walls, read historical blurbs about its beginnings, touch its artifacts, allow herself to be dazzled by its design. She wanted to feel the lingering phantoms of ingenues in mink coats and cat-eyed sunglasses who once smoked skinny cigarettes by the pool and threw up in porcelain bathtubs upstairs. She wanted to corner a musty bartender and ask if he'd ever felt a draft outside the bungalow where John Belushi died. That, to her, was exciting and glamorous, and anything else—getting our initials inexplicably and absentmindedly stitched into a handkerchief—was just a poor imitation of what used to be great. What's worse, I came to see the same; these kinds of things aren't very exciting, they're actually really dumb.

But it was me who was lured into the cloak of couture. It was me who had been duped, unable to let go of the idea that the environment is what makes things flashy or sexy or exciting, rather than the person you're with. Here was this woman who already loved me, who had loved me for almost a year now, *without* the luxury hotels or the white-sleeved valets or the Frodo. None of the things I'd tried to plug my existential holes with had really worked, and now they were haunting me, looming over me like the Chateau Marmont ghosts of ingenues themselves. Emma had finally fulfilled me in ways that were meaningful. I removed my hand from the stick, like I was still trying to look cool for no reason, and grabbed her hand. And as I held it, I recalled the photo I took of her in front of her glowing titular name on the silver screen. The Emma that mattered was the one who was smiling at me. She was what was important, not the other Emma, and she was so painfully there, staring me in my dumb face.

Of course, in staring down my own superficial bullshit, I was forced to reflect on my friendship with Sam. Although I never had to ask myself the question: "Was our relationship predicated on gratuitous yet empty Hollywood filth?" Because no, of course it wasn't. Your friends are supposed to share the same brain-dead interests and hobbies as you. I think about how many straight men I know—okay, I don't know that many straight men, let me rephrase that—I think about how many of my dad's friends I know who seem to be bonded by some sort of blood pact on the simple premise of liking sports. Or poker. Or chips. I think about how many rooms I've been in where a bunch of women are huddled over a phone, giggling about memes while their male partners watch football, eat "buffalo dip," and yell. I think of the concept of a "boys' trip" or a "weekend with the boys" or whatever, and I picture a wife rolling her eyes at her oaf partner as he sits in a basement with his "buds" (straight men can't just have "friends" or they'll be gay), chugging beer, playing cards, talking about basketball, and listening to . . . Bruce Springsteen? I don't know. And then I think about Sam and I, two people who are wholly removed from the lost world of heterosexuality, yet still bonded by liking the same stuff.

During the pandemic, I drove to Palm Springs to meet Sam for two nights, à la a "boys' weekend," and while the activities differed greatly (so fucking greatly), we still performed the timeless act of a boys' weekend: I needed some time with my best friend to lie around and do our smooth-brain activities that we loved doing. We sprawled across the couch watching thriller movies about sorority girls being hunted in 2009, or about Kathy Bates as a psycho killer. We drove around screaming the lyrics to Brooke Hogan songs, bopping to obscure millennium-era girl groups, turning the volume down on a song by *American Idol* season two contestant Kimberly Caldwell to say, "This is a masterpiece. This should be in a museum." I cooked us chicken and crispy brussels sprouts. We soaked in the pool and talked about our bottomless well of desperation and how awful it is that just over two hundred years ago, electricity was invented, and now we spend all day staring at poison boxes, comparing ourselves to people instead of feeling our feelings. We did a virtual bougie L.A. workout class on yoga mats in the bathroom. We cried, cackled, set our intentions, and assured each other we were fundamentally good. Sam understands me and supports me in unique ways that no one else on this suspended rock does. I cherish our relationship so much, and if we were less fortunate, and were both straight men in heterosexual relationships, doomed to a connection predicated on sports balls and buffalo-flavored dips and brands of beer, I know our souls would still be bonded by the kind of invisible forces in outer space that push two alike clusters of atoms together. It was never the fancy parties or the "why is Katy Perry glaring at me" or the access that mattered—it was our connection that I valued.

I feel utterly fulfilled by and inspired by and bonded to Emma for totally different reasons. Maybe friendship requires some kind of shared dogshit interests, and what brings you together with romantic love is less describable, the kind of magnetism that pulls two sets of skeletons toward each other, whose bones want to smash together and hold hands without a full understanding of why. Emma and I certainly share some interests and hobbies—bisexual pop stars, thriller movies from the 2000s, being Intense White People who buy river shoes so they can walk across the river in Big Sur—but we're also extraordinarily different. At first, this really scared me, and her too, that we didn't share all the same interests; we feared it meant we were incompatible. But when she's not near me, I feel curdled and fetal. She makes me want to blow myself up so she can collect all my dust and hold it in a locket against her chest. What's that all about?

I let my insecurities about our material differences aggravate our *Emma* date night. I thought I wanted all the trappings of these sparkly pop culture experiences, and that our braving them together would bond us. But we were already bonded. She already loved me. I felt it when we met, like we were melting into each other before we even knew we should be, or why.

And Sam too—minus that blip in the grocery store—it seemed like we were giggling together before we even knew what we were giggling about. The pop culture "things" never made me feel whole—connection did. Connection isn't predicated solely on liking the same pop culture stuff; connection is simply star stuff. The more sense we try to make out of it, the harder we'll fail. It just *is*.

As I stared at the passing palm trees and the snakelike canyon road, so specific to L.A., I was reminded of the movie I'd just watched, or shall I say, I was reminded of the movie *Clueless*, a version of the story I could understand more clearly (honestly, the *Emma* movie needed subtitles because I could barely understand a word those toothy British people said). I thought about Cher Horowitz, the *Emma*-inspired character, and her misplaced priorities—wealth, popularity, status—and how her belief in them repeatedly leaves her hoisted by her own petard. In trying to make Tai popular so people would like her, or in courting Christian, the hot, rich new guy who turns out to be gay, she just keeps falling on her ass. People already liked Tai, without the hair dye and crop tops and elevated vocabulary. In being so shallow, Cher not only sours her relationship with her new best friend but also nearly misses out on dating the love of her life, Josh. Josh, who she initially wrote off for being dissimilar to her—because he watches CNN and reads books and cares about social justice. Josh, who doesn't give a fuck about the who's who of Beverly Hills. Josh, whose eyes Cher stares into and sees swirling pools of universe and devotion and stars. In the end, Cher grapples with what she really values, and as it turns out, it's not the Alaïa. It's love. I shook my head. I was "totally clueless."

THE BEAST

IT'S A STICKY summer evening in L.A., and Kim Kardashian, who appears to be at an extravagant ranch, has tweeted a photo of her daughter's Friesian horse, of which she claims to own fourteen. Face hovering an inch in front of my body due to hypercaffeination, I quote-tweet her before even thinking or breathing and write, "i can't afford healthcare," for no other reason besides that it's true. In the first five to six months of quarantine, this has become my new normal, drinking drip coffee until I can feel my body existing in two realms at the same time, scrolling through apps, and melting down over celebrity media. Six months into quarantine, I've decided that two things are true: We live in hell, and celebrities shouldn't be allowed to have phones. Someone must take all of the celebrities' phones away until they can be trusted once again to proliferate content that's appropriate during this deeply tragic global moment.

I never thought I'd see the day when pop culture finally ate itself, but it's happened. Midpandemic, or rather, extremely early on in quarantine, pop culture collapsed under the mammoth weight of celebrities' brain rot. Celebrity media has always made me feel airy and chipper, even the (admittedly) vacuous and menial corners of it: in high school, I liked reading blogs and scanning paparazzi photos, seeing what Miley Cyrus's *official* Millions of Milkshakes shake contained, seeing which Famouses were photographed outside the once-cool L.A. restaurant Katsuya. But in the pandemic, even the most seemingly self-aware celebrity posts seem to be exactly what I've always argued pop culture wasn't: a vast black hole of emptiness. Pop culture and celebrity are reflections of social trends and cultural moments, and when the current moment is the actual End Times, then pop culture simply shows us how broken everything is: our country's systems, our own unfillable voids of need and want, the intersection of the two. Seeing dumb posts from someone like Kim Kardashian used to be entertaining, but now it aggravates something black in the soul, a blooming fear that just can't yet be put into words.

In the first few days of quarantine, in March, Ellen DeGeneres made a series of videos on her phone, saying things into her front-facing camera like "I'm bored," trying to mimic what her audience might be feeling. She took up puzzling, lay upside down on her couch, FaceTimed Justin Timberlake, and posted it all from the confines of her mansion. Things soon got worse. The cast of *High School Musical* and adjacent has-been casts of 2000s movies and TV shows filmed themselves lip-syncing their old songs, using that One Thing That Made Them Special Ten Years Ago in a desperate grab for attention (in a time when nobody was capable of giving them attention). There was Diane Keaton, and whoever she forced to film her, in a boomer-humor Instagram "sketch," in which she drags bags of clothes down the street, attempting to donate them to Goodwill, only to realize Goodwill is closed due to the pandemic. She dubs in a poorly edited, odd voice-over of her faux-realizing that the Goodwill is closed. Maybe the real take wasn't good enough. It's unclear and bizarre.

As I watched celebrities do what they thought they did best, perform and entertain, I grew more depressed. Seeing inside their beautiful homes, a glimmer of desperation in their eyes as they felt the audiences who once validated them slip through their fingers—it all felt too hard to watch. I used to want to be them. Now I just feel bad for them. I feel bad for me, as a person in a small, dark apartment I can barely pay for with just my girlfriend and my cat. But I feel bad for them, knowing that whatever they thought they achieved, whatever piece of their souls they exchanged for a more comfortable life, didn't work. They're widely regarded as special, unique, successful. Yet they're still so visibly, plainly unfulfilled. Why?

Every day my pandemic schedule looks like this:

>7:00 a.m.: *Shoot awake gasping for air, remembering I live in hell.*
>
>7:01–7:30 a.m.: *Seethe.*
>
>8:00 a.m.: *First and second coffees.*
>
>9:00 a.m.: *Blind panic.*
>
>10:00 p.m.: *Wake up from depressive fugue state, reenter my body, and wonder how I got to watching season six, episode four of* Alone *on Hulu with my girlfriend.*
>
>10:01 p.m.: *Hang out with my sleep paralysis demon because I can't sleep and why not? We're both here.*

A new rom-com about two lovers being stuck in a time loop was released on Hulu, and I can't bring myself to watch it, as I'm stuck in my own time loop. Every day, I doom-scroll through social media, consuming bleak celebrity posts, interspersed with an unending stockpile of traumatic events. And the more trauma I consume, the more rage I procure, and the angrier I get, the more feral I become. Less than a decade ago, I was obsessed with seeing what Vanessa Hudgens wore to Coachella. Now I'm learning about meat temperatures, botulism, and how to properly clean my cast-iron skillet. I'm basically Jodie Foster in *Nell*.

Writing anything during the pandemic is difficult. Doing anything productive feels counterproductive. I've always been driven by this invisible charge in my body, this electricity that rippled through me, that pushed me toward "achieving my dreams," achieving something spectacular, something I could be remembered for, that would both immortalize me when I'm gone and prove I'm special while I'm here. I've never taken a day off to question it, because I knew this was right: drive, passion, the pursuit of greatness. This is what we're all born to do. We are born to pursue. I've always wanted a large house and a comfortable life. I never wanted my future children to experience the anxiety of struggling to pursue survival, making money, providing. But when the world came skidding to a stop, so did this electricity. Seeing inside Ellen's stupid mansion that she's "bored" in creates tension in me, creates fear: fear that not only has my desire to succeed, to achieve bigness, evaporated, but I might be right to let it go.

My ego faltered. I sank further into depression. I rose higher into rage. I grew despondent at the accumulating American death toll, furious at my government for its role in such, ill while reading headlines about Gigi Hadid's $5.8 million Manhattan home. I felt hair growing on the back of my neck, like a werewolf about to turn. My soul felt mushy and vulnerable and open to change. Then, in July, something cataclysmic happened.

I awake to the sound of my phone buzzing against the surface of my bedside table, and realize the phone has actually been vibrating for quite some time, but I've been ignoring it. Something terrible must've happened, I think. Are my parents sick? Is the Great Class War beginning? Did Donald Trump finally die? (Just kidding, FBI, if you're reading this.) I lurch for my phone, but I'm a beat too late. My lock screen says I've missed three consecutive FaceTime calls from my younger sister, Maddie, and it's only six thirty a.m. Maddie loves to FaceTime me in the morning, a successful annoy-with-love tactic, while I'm groggy and vexed that I still exist. But even her most genuinely obnoxious pop-ins are at least around eight a.m. Something has to be wrong. Her fourth FaceTime rings in before I can call her back, and I answer immediately. Squinting through crusty, contactless eyes, I hold the phone two inches from my face and say, "What's wrong?"

"Bro." She smirks, knowing she woke me, and I sigh a breath of relief: clearly, no one is dead. "BRO," she repeats, holding a closed fist to her mouth, positive she's going to be the first person to tell me what she's about to tell me.

"What? I'm sleeping," I groan, as Emma turns over to see what terrors the world, or my pest of a little sister, might have in store for us today. Emma and I had been looking for an apartment together in March, just before the world shut down. Soon after, she moved into my apartment with me, and has since become accustomed to such pesky phone calls from Maddie. I think she even secretly enjoys them.

"Have you seen Twitter?"

"Just tell me," I say, impatient.

"Taylor Swift just announced a surprise album. It comes out at midnight," she says, widening her smirk to a toothy Cheshire smile. I stare at her. I turn over my shoulder to look at Emma. I turn back to Maddie. I think, *I'm too tired to care about this.* I thank her for telling me, hang up, and drop my head back into the warmth of my pillow. I sigh. I roll over and begrudgingly check my phone. I see Taylor's announcement on Instagram: It's true. Her surprise eighth studio album, *folklore*, drops tonight at midnight, and the internet is abuzz. *Fuck*, I think. *Not now*, I think, possibly about being too tired, possibly about the nightmare world the album's about to be born into. I email my editor Dee at *Vulture*, who I've been working with for the past year—an angel who pays me to write fan screeds about my favorite artist, Taylor Swift. Dee responds almost immediately, and I read her response in the voice of Samantha from *Sex and the City*: "There you are." The day, I think, might have mercifully disappeared into the abyss;

now it's Taylor Swift Day, a day that has come only once every year or two (or three) for the past decade. And there's something else too. The theme of the album, from its visual aesthetic of Swift solemnly wading through a forest to its rustic contributions from Bon Iver and Aaron Dessner of the National, is the woods. The thorny, ruthless, bloodthirsty woods. The thickening were-wolf hairs on my back stiffen.

Taylor Swift Day is supposed to be special. Taylor Swift Day is meant to be planned meticulously, anticipated heavily, and the release is magnifi-cent. If you've ever been a fan of an artist, then you know what a bounty it is to receive a full album of new music. And once you receive the music, you get to talk to your friends and your community—in this case, the Swifties—about it. In a time when CDs, vinyls, you know, music that you can touch and feel with your fingertips and hold against your chest while you're cry-ing and pass along with handwritten footnotes in Sharpie, are long gone, the only thing that feels even remotely physical about music is the discus-sion that follows. Trust me, I still buy Taylor's albums at Target, but without the flesh of the merch to grip tightly, the only thing that makes music feel real is the part that connects you to others. But in this moment, like the actual moment when I'm scurrying across my apartment, chugging iced coffee, trying to rush myself through the prerelease preparation ceremony, a grueling mental and emotional process, how can I reconcile Taylor Swift Day, or any major music release that means something to me, with the waning of my own personal enthusiasm about pop culture, and my own feral state of existence?

You have to understand, in case this wasn't already clear: I LOVE Tay-lor Swift. I love everything about the phenomenon that is Taylor Swift, from the actual songs, to writing about her rumored love affairs and the reveal-ing Easter eggs in her music, to the polarizing public figure she's become. Every element of past discourse around Taylor Swift—who she's dating, why I think she's a sunbeam of light, why others think she sucks, why her word on American politics is revered and loathed and dissected tirelessly—is fascinating to me. She's my favorite subject, from an intellectual perspective and from the point of view of the nosy child in me that's been bewitched by pop culture and celebrity gossip since I saw photos of Lindsay Lohan and Samantha Ronson "getting cozy" in 2008. Pop culture, music, the combination of both in Taylor Swift, has been such a source of positivity for me for so long. But now, as my body vibrates with cold-brew paranoia, the existential angst of being alive in the year 2020, and the actual mass death event happening outside my apartment door, I just don't know how to hear music that might actually make me feel something. I don't know if I can handle feeling anything at all.

Later that night, at nine o'clock Pacific, I turn off all the lights in my apartment, dig through my closet to find and ignite a Taylor Swift votive candle that Sam gave me as a joke but is not a joke to *me*, lie down on my floor, and listen to the album. Emma sits on the couch and gapes at me. The first song is about love lost, and it makes me feel sad—I don't want to lose love. Especially not now, please not now. My werewolf mane quivers. The second track too is a tearful, nostalgic review of heartbreak—is the whole album going to be like this? (Spoiler alert: yes.) My sanity wavers. Claws burst through my knuckles. By the fifth song, a breakup track so brutally raw and tragic, I feel searing emotional pain and self-loathing rupture through my chest. I can't hold it in anymore.

Emma runs shrieking into our bedroom and slams the door shut, throws a dresser under the door handle, and searches for something, a candlestick, ANYTHING, as I scream into the moonlight, allowing every pent-up quarantine emotion to come rip-roaring out of me, out of the monster I know I am. I can't let her see me like this. I tear the front door off its hinges and bolt into the night, galloping far, far away from here, deep into the unforgiving woods to hide my true, disgusting, hairy self: a beast. No one could ever love a beast.

[12:46 A.M., JULY 25, 2020]

"It's me," I say to the camera on a tripod I set up just outside my shelter. My face is covered in dirt, my hair home to twigs, my hands bloodied. I touch my face, seeing its scratches in the camcorder's small monitor. "It's, uh, twelve forty-six a.m. The spell wore off. I'm fine, just a little shaken." I look at my log-and-pitched-tarp shelter. "I just finished setting up camp for tonight. I'll check back in soon. But for now, it's just me out here. I have some stuff to figure out." I throw up a peace sign and turn the camera off.

[9:04 P.M., AUGUST 29, 2020]

"You know what's insane," I say to my camcorder, which sits on a tripod near the entrance to my log-and-stone cabin, where I've been living in complete isolation for the last month. I pick shreds of boiled rabbit meat off the bone, my elbows resting on my muddied, weathered knees. "Capitalism breeds a fascination with the extraordinary."

"What do you mean?" I reply to myself.

"Think about it. Think about some of the things that Americans have lionized and sensationalized in the past: Celebrities. Billionaires. Serial killers. *Aliens*, even! What do we value? We value anything that errs on the edge of extreme: massive success stories, anomalies, people who stand out, the extraordinary, the abnormal."

"Huh," I say, picking a piece of fat out of my teeth with a loose bone.

"We all want to be different, to be remembered, to be the exception, because that's what capitalism tells us to value."

"Right," I say, catching on, standing up and crossing to my bed (a rock). I wag my finger like a scientist approaching a whiteboard, on the brink of discovery. "Capitalism tells us from a young age that we have to pull ourselves up by our bootstraps—in order to succeed, we must be extraordinary at our craft, no matter the cost, because someone is always working harder, and you have to be the best, or you'll be nothing. So in order to achieve that end goal of success, of happiness, we must be *special*. We must be the exception. The ideology trains us to pursue such a status." I drop my head and cross my arms, pushing my bare, infected feet into a power stance in the dirt. "We were obsessed with serial killers because they are fascinating—it didn't matter that what they were doing was sick. They were new and interesting. They were original. They stood out. We loved it."

"It's sad, though," I respond, "what it does to people."

I nod. "It is."

[5:39 P.M., OCTOBER 24, 2020]

"Why is being normal even bad?" I say to a deer skull tied to my wall with squirrel tendon. The dim red blinking of my camcorder's recording light flashes on the back of my head. The pink and orange and purple of the sunset peek in through the holes of my shelter left uncovered by leaves and mud. It's been months of loneliness and isolation. Body fat has melted off my bones like butter. I miss my life, I miss Emma, but I can't go back now. I'm a beast. What if I hurt her?

I sit down on my chair (also a rock), pick up my whittling knife and a fresh block of cedar. I shave the wood against my thumb.

"Growing up, it was so hard to be yourself, like your real true self, without feeling judged," I say. "Everyone around you—teachers, parents, movies, music—tells you to be yourself, that there's nothing better in this world than being unique. And yet—"

"It's impossible to be yourself," I interrupt. "Especially as a self-conscious child. Which every child is." I stare at the cedar sculpture, which is already finished, and realize this is the thirtieth one I've carved of Karlie Kloss.

"The only thing that felt even remotely doable growing up was blending in. We tell our kids to be superstars, to be astronauts, ballerinas, the president of the United States. Pursue your dreams, and dream big. Reach for the stars. And yet . . ."

"The kids who actually pursue those things are painted as weird."

"Or as gay," I say. I nod, standing up to again wag my finger and stare into an invisible algebraic equation.

"So we want people to be special. But when people pursue the path of specialness, embrace their originality, invest themselves in this pursuit, we condemn them. Burn, witch, burn!" I shake my head.

"Because we're jealous? Because we're afraid of them? Because they're a projection of our own mediocrity? Or a projection of our own lack of *desire* to be anything more than . . . 'normal'?"

"And then the people who actually 'make it' are rewarded. They're rewarded with fame, money, attention, and immortality," I say, leaping into an urgent pacing between the rock that is my bed and the rock that is my chair.

"So we should strive to be different . . . But if we do, we're called 'weird' or 'gay.' Yet those who bravely push through the near-impossible membrane of criticism that comes with being unique really *are* rewarded. It's a paradox," I say, breaking a sweat from pacing due to lack of caloric intake.

"And in the pursuit of uniqueness, of specialness, of immortality, we often trade off the things we've known since the dawn of time are essential to the human condition." I stop dead in my tracks, reaching the frontier of discovery.

"Love," I mutter. Tears well in my eyes.

I think about Emma, who I left behind when I scurried into the woods. I think about our first date, when I clumsily stood on my tippy-toes to kiss her and she blushed, caught off guard by my awkward stab at a first kiss, and then I blushed, caught off guard by how much I was feeling. About the first time we spent a full day together, lying around in Echo Park on her buffalo-plaid picnic blanket, laughing, picking at vegan food. About driving her home, working up the confidence to put my hand on her knee for the first time and pretend like it was nothing. About lying in her bed and asking her to be my girlfriend, then taking pictures of her on my phone because she couldn't stop smiling and staring at me. About climbing on top of her in my bed and telling her I loved her. About driving her home from the *Emma* premiere, feeling dumb. About her moving in with me in March, when my bed became our bed. About eating avocado toast with her every morning, and watching *Alone* on our new orange velvet couch cover that we picked out together, and watching her learn how to pickle foods, and then driving pink jars of pickled onions to my parents' house, and sleeping with my cat between our chests. About everything that happened before Taylor Swift released her album and I became a werewolf; Emma holding me while I sobbed, when my body and mind were in agony, when my mental health was completely upheaved by fear of the virus, of the future, of living together, of growing together, of dying together, or dying apart.

I think about her playfully reprimanding me for walking out of our second-bedroom-turned-office every hour on the hour while I'm supposed to be writing my book but instead barge out seeking attention, and she says, "Go write your book!!!" for the thousandth time, and I think: *I don't want to write the book*—the book, which represents everything I've worked for in my life. Or not my "life" but my career, which I now realize are different things. My whole life, I thought I had to stand out, to work harder, to succeed, to immortalize myself, to sign the book deal, to sign two, to make movies, to accept awards, to purchase a house like Ellen's, to be special, to become dark matter. But nothing I've worked on in my career nor in my life has been as rewarding, as fulfilling, or has made me feel even a fraction as good as it feels to be in love with Emma. Maybe I love my stupid little life, and I just want a house and kids and a vegetable garden and pets named after fictional characters and to learn how to pickle and to crochet and to be loved. Maybe I don't need to be special anymore. Maybe I can let that go.

I catch a glimmer of my own reflection in the bucket that I piss in, and I stop. I stare at myself, and I'm disgusted, but I'm not the beast right now, I'm just . . . me. Am I the beast I never wanted to become? Was I ever the beast? Or, all this time, have I just been running from the beast, scared that she and I were one? I need to go home. I need to go back to Emma.

I turn the camcorder off.

The next day, I barge out of my office for the second time in an hour, hair studded with twigs, dirt smudged on my face, feet rotted and sour. I tug at my stained *Beavis and Butt-Head* shirt, remembering a time not long ago when I was in the woods, cold and naked and afraid. I look at my living room that I built with Emma, our orange couch cover, our sad Chinese money plant that we can barely keep alive, our evil lump of a cat that bites our feet at night but purrs on our chests during the day. Emma looks at me with her seafoam eyes and her peach-pink lips and her bouncy ponytail, tied up in my pink scrunchie that she says is ugly but always steals, and she waits to hear what I have to say for myself this time. She tilts her head, playfully judging me with her eyes—about being tipped into disarray by a Taylor Swift album, about procrastinating more than I work, about the unflattering white Crocs I've refused to take off since they shipped two weeks ago. She smirks, and I know that despite it all, she loves me.

"What if I don't want to be special?" I ask. "What if I just want to be out here with you?"

ACKNOWLEDGMENTS

I have to begin where *Girls Can Kiss Now* did: One day I received a Twitter DM from a fellow author saying their literary agent wanted to contact me. Soon after, I started conversations with Katelyn Dougherty. She asked if I'd ever thought about writing a book. I was shocked! I actually hadn't considered it--I didn't think I was capable. I didn't think that my voice was strong, unique, or coveted enough. Despite my insecurities, I slammed the gas pedal and said, "I want to write a novel about lesbian aliens." Katelyn replied gently, "What about a book of essays?"

Katelyn, thank you for helping me mold the shape and heart of this book from its very inception. Without you, there would be no book. I'm so grateful for your passion and dedication, for your friendship, and for every in-depth call we had about Taylor Swift, gay books, and *Killing Eve*. Thank you for championing me when no one else would.

Sean deLone, my partner in this. Your enthusiasm, support, and guidance made writing this book such a joy. Thank you for believing in me and my writing, for your honesty and trust, for nodding patiently while I explained the titles of Britney Spears's albums and what a "dykecon" is. Thank you for urging me to go to the places I was scared to go to, but also for encouraging me to rant about lesbian items. Writing a book during a pandemic felt like both an exorcism and catharsis. Our calls propelled me through it.

Cindy Uh, thank you for stepping in and kicking ass. I'm so thankful for your attentiveness and candor. Getting to know you and work with you has been so joyous. Ashley Silver, thank you for fighting for me when I needed a fighter.

Thank you to everyone at Atria for each read, note, and piece of helpful advice, including copy editor Laura Cherkas: Laura, thank you for your attention to detail and for correcting me on things like the location of Ashley Benson and Cara Delevingne's sex-bench-paparazzi photo; the nightclub Britney, Paris, and Lindsay were allegedly heading to; and the awards show Rihanna performed "Bitch Better Have My Money" on in the green Versace coat. I'm humbled.

Kelli McAdams, who designed my incredibly electric, pretty cover. My dream was to have a queer woman design the cover, and my jaw hit the floor when I saw your work on this. Thank you for creating the face of *Girls Can Kiss Now*. I'm eternally grateful.

Thanks to Elisa M. Rivlin for advising me on where to include a well-placed "allegedly." They probably weren't supposed to be, but our phone calls were a blast.

Mom and Dad, thank you for your unconditional, enduring support of me and my deluded aspirations, from wanting to be a famous actress to wanting to write a book about being gay. Your unbridled love and understanding made this book (and my entire career) possible. Thank you for growing with me, listening to me, embracing me, and for being such tender parents who never so much as flinched when I came out. I'm so lucky for that, for every sacrifice you made for me and Maddie, and for having grown up in such a warm household.

Maddie, every FaceTime call from you feels like an omen. Thank you for every piece of solicited (or unsolicited) advice you gave me while reading the book. I'm so proud of the woman you are, and I'm so thankful we've been able to grow alongside each other. You've come into your own strength, and it's been inspiring and powerful to watch. Thanks for being my best friend.

Grandma, thank you for being my biggest cheerleader. Your love is enduring and fervent. Lee McNeel, thank you for your blessing on *that* chapter. I'm so glad we got to grow up together.

Steph Stone, thank you for the generous amount of encouragement you offered through my most insecure moments in writing, editing, and agonizing over every minute decision. Your support bought me moments of ease and peace, and as you know, there's nothing more coveted than moments of ease or peace. Thank you for reading, for every gut-check, for each time you said "you deserve a prize" or "I can't wait to read this book," which made me feel so warm inside.

To all my friends who read early iterations of the book: Sam Lansky, Gabrielle Korn, Michelle Dean, Taylor DeLorenzo, Debby Ryan, Matt Bennett, Matthew Scott Montgomery, Nicole Linh Anderson, I value each of your unique and mighty voices so much. I'm so grateful for your friendship and advice. Thank you.

My therapist, Donna, sincerely, thank you for gracefully guiding me through the most painful moments of my life. I've learned so much from you.

Emma Nylander, I love you like a sea witch loves sea mist. As long as we've been together, you've encouraged me to believe in myself, to trust my instincts, empowered me to do so, and emboldened me to speak up for what I believe in. Thank you for every cup of coffee you made me, for every time I looked at you like the "mom I trew up" alien and you held me while I cried, for how much you opened my eyes to the world and to love, for making me laugh when I didn't want to. You've challenged me to be better, stronger, more emotionally intelligent, confident, open, and empathetic. You were a force of light for me for me through the writing process; the earliest versions of this book had far less soul and color. Somewhere along the way, I met you and my life changed, and, thus, so did the book. Thanks for sticking with me.